This book addresses the question of stability and change in our concepts of ourselves. The self is described as part of an ecological system, seen as a conjunction of other people, environments, and objects. These serve as the sources and settings, instruments and symbols of social experience. The external elements of the ecological system are reflected in self-related cognitions: so long as the ecology of the self is stable, the self-concept will likewise achieve stability. Self-concept change, therefore, can be studied from the point of view of change in the relationship between person and environment. Using a multi-method, multi-study approach, Stefan Hormuth takes relocation as his paradigm for assessing the meaning of the physical environment for the self-concept and everyday social behaviour.

This book presents results from an original and important research programme which is innovative both theoretically and methodologically. The author integrates social and psychological theorizing about identity and the self, and achieves an effective balance between the theoretical approach and his empirical investigations.

European Monographs in Social Psychology
The ecology of the self

European Monographs in Social Psychology

Executive Editors:
J. RICHARD EISER and KLAUS R. SCHERER
Sponsored by the European Association of Experimental Social Psychology

This series, first published by Academic Press (who will continue to distribute the numbered volumes), appeared under the joint imprint of Cambridge University Press and the Maison des Sciences de l'Homme in 1985 as an amalgamation of the Academic Press series and the European Studies in Social Psychology, published by Cambridge and the Maison in collaboration with the Laboratoire Européen de Psychologie Sociale of the Maison.

The original aims of the two series still very much apply today: to provide a forum for the best European research in different fields of social psychology and to foster the interchange of ideas between different developments and different traditions. The Executive Editors also expect that it will have an important role to play as a European forum for international work.

Other titles in this series:

Unemployment by Peter Kelvin and Joanna E. Jarrett
National characteristics by Dean Peabody
Experiencing emotion by Klaus R. Scherer, Harald G. Wallbott and Angela B. Summerfield
Levels of explanation in social psychology by Willem Doise
Understanding attitudes to the European Community: a social-psychological study in four member states by Miles Hewstone
Arguing and thinking: a rhetorical approach to social psychology by Michael Billig
Non-verbal communication in depression by Heiner Ellgring
Social representations of intelligence by Gabriel Mugny and Felice Carugati
Speech and reasoning in everyday life by Uli Windisch
Account episodes. The management or escalation of conflict by Peter Schönbach

The ecology of the self

Relocation and self-concept change

Stefan E. Hormuth
Institute of Psychology, University of Heidelberg

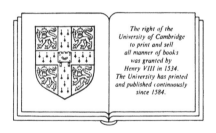

Cambridge University Press
Cambridge
New York   Port Chester
Melbourne   Sydney

Editions de la Maison des Sciences de l'Homme
Paris

CAMBRIDGE UNIVERSITY PRESS
Cambridge, New York, Melbourne, Madrid, Cape Town,
Singapore, São Paulo, Delhi, Tokyo, Mexico City

Cambridge University Press
The Edinburgh Building, Cambridge CB2 8RU, UK

Published in the United States of America by
Cambridge University Press, New York

www.cambridge.org
Information on this title: www.cambridge.org/9780521324014

© Maison des Sciences de l'Homme and Cambridge University Press 1990

This publication is in copyright. Subject to statutory exception
and to the provisions of relevant collective licensing agreements,
no reproduction of any part may take place without the written
permission of Cambridge University Press.

First published 1990
First paperback edition 2010

A catalogue record for this publication is available from the British Library

Library of Congress Cataloguing in Publication data

Hormuth, Stefan E.
The ecology of the self: relocation and self-concept change /
Stefan E. Hormuth.
  p. cm. – (European monographs in social psychology)
Includes bibliographical references.
ISBN 0-521-32401-71.
Self-perception. 2. Moving, Household – Psychological aspects.
3. Environmental psychology. I. Title. II. Series.
BF697.5.S43H67 1990
155.9´4 – dc20   89–77380   CIP

ISBN 978-0-521-32401-4 Hardback
ISBN 978-0-521-15496-3 Paperback

Cambridge University Press has no responsibility for the persistence or
accuracy of URLs for external or third-party internet websites referred to in
this publication, and does not guarantee that any content on such websites is,
or will remain, accurate or appropriate. Information regarding prices, travel
timetables, and other factual information given in this work is correct at
the time of first printing but Cambridge University Press does not guarantee
the accuracy of such information thereafter.

For Verena,
who has had her share of
experiences with relocation

Contents

List of tables	*page* xii
Preface	xv

1 Restructuring the ecology of the self: a framework for self-concept change   1
    The ecology of the self   1
    Stability and change   3
    Overview   6

2 Method considerations for an ecological approach   8
    Ecological validity   8
    Use of a naturalistic design: relocation as a research paradigm   9
    Combination of multiple methods   11
    Sampling procedures   12

3 Relocation and changes in commitment: a cross-sectional study over the first year   15
    The questionnaire   15
    Sampling   17
    Procedure   19
    Results of factor analyses   20
    Comparison of movers and non-movers   22
    Effects of national differences   24
    Effects of commitment and time   26
    Discussion   30

4 Implications of recent research in cognitive social psychology for self-concept change   32
    The self-concept as an organization of cognitions   32
    Self-concept as a mediator of cognitions and behaviour   37
    The orientation of the self-concept   44

Contents

5 Social psychological theories on maintenance and change — 54
- Self-concept maintenance and its failure — 54
- The emergence of knowledge about oneself — 61
- A summary of social psychological contributions to self-concept change — 67

6 Sociological approaches to the self-concept and change — 70
- The self-concept and social structure — 70
- Personal change in adult life — 73
- Identity theory — 76
- The conceptualization of commitment — 81
- Relating sociological and psychological notions of self-concept — 85
- Social and cognitive structure — 89

7 The development of self-concept-related measures — 92
- Problems in the measurement of the self-concept — 92
- The measurement of the self-concept through auto-photography — 94
- The measurement of satisfaction with self — 98

8 Functions of the physical environment for the self-concept — 107
- The function of things for the self-concept — 108
- The function of molar environments to the self-concept — 113
- A study on the meaning of urban environments for the self-concept — 118

9 Anticipation of transition from university — 124
- Perceptions of the environment at times of transition — 124
- Anticipation of the transition from university: into working life or unemployment? — 129

10 The experience sampling method — 133
- Data analysis, validity, and usefulness of ESM — 135

11 A quasi-experimental study of relocation and satisfaction with self — 139
- Procedure and design — 139
- Effects of social structure on satisfaction with self — 141
- Relocation status and satisfaction with self — 143

	Satisfaction with self and moving: results from ESM	145
	Results from autophotography	152
	Behavioural and perceptual predictors of satisfaction with self	154
12	**Relocation as transition and change in a physical and social context**	158
	Relocation as a subject of psychological research	158
	Relocation as a research paradigm for transitions	162
13	**A longitudinal questionnaire study over one year**	169
	Design of the study	170
	Changes over time	172
	Effects of self-monitoring and satisfaction with self	175
14	**A longitudinal study of students' transition to university**	180
	Overview of the design	181
	Effects of moving on the perception of interactional situations	185
	Effects of specific expectations	188
	Situational variance and satisfaction with self	190
	Results from autophotography	193
15	**Conclusion**	197
	References	203
	Author index	214
	Subject index	217

Tables

3.1	Factor analysis of importance of values	*page* 20
3.2	Factor analysis of activities	21
3.3	Factor analysis of valued objects	22
3.4	Mean comparisons between non-movers and movers	23
3.5	Effects of nationality and relocation	25
3.6	Effects of nationality, taking age into account	25
3.7	Distribution of subjects for time by commitment analyses	26
3.8	Effects of commitment	27
3.9	Effects of time since the relocation	27
3.10	Effects of commitment and time on solitary-social acts	28
3.11	Effects of commitment and time on 'entertainment' acts	29
3.12	Effects of commitment and time on activity objects	30
4.1	Correlation of the importance of aspects of self-concept with their location	51
6.1	Presentation of role relationships in commitment measure	84
7.1	Inter-rater reliabilities for autophotography	97
7.2	Reliabilities (alpha) for Satisfaction with Self Scale	101
7.3	Intercorrelations between SSS subscales	101
7.4	Principal component analysis of SSS Form N (N = 299)	102
7.5	Principal component analysis of SSS Form S (N = 299)	103
7.6	Correlations of SSS (Form S) with relevant scales (N = 200)	104
8.1	Occurrence and personal importance of photograph content	119
8.2	Ratings on functional dimensions for physical environment	120
9.1	Means of satisfaction with self and photograph ratings	128
9.2	Comparison of means of students anticipating graduation	131
9.3	Predictors of satisfaction with self across all groups	132
11.1	Interaction of type of relationship change by impact on SSS	143
11.2	Relocation status and satisfaction with self: overall effects and planned contrasts (F, df)	144

11.3	Mean values satisfaction with self by moving status	144
11.4	Effects of the covariate age on ESM data	145
11.5	Main effects of moving on ESM data	146
11.6	Effects of satisfaction with self on ESM data	146
11.7	Interactive effects of SSS and moving on ESM data	147
11.8	Main effects for SSS subscale Global on ESM data	148
11.9	Interaction effects for SSS–Global and moving group	149
11.10	Main effects for median split on SSS–Social on ESM	149
11.11	Interaction effects for SSS–Social and moving group on ESM	149
11.12	Main effects for median split on SSS–Family on ESM	150
11.13	Interaction effects for SSS–Family and moving group on ESM	151
11.14	Main effects for median split on SSS–Work on ESM	151
11.15	Main effects for median split on SSS–Object on ESM	151
11.16	Interaction effects for SSS–Object and moving group on ESM	152
11.17	Means of photograph ratings by moving status	153
11.18	Planned contrasts of photograph ratings by moving status	153
11.19	Means of photograph ratings for interaction SSS by moving status	154
13.1	Changes in the importance of things from T1 to T4	172
13.2	Changes in important values from T2 to T4	173
13.3	Changes in frequencies of home-centered activities T1 to T4	174
13.4	Changes in the frequency of social activities from T1 to T4	174
14.1	Factors of expectations for the new environment	183
14.2	ESM-items regarding the perception of social situations	184
14.3	Means and standard deviations of P19 to P25 over T1 to T3	186
14.4	Regression of SSS on P19 to P25 at T1 through T3 and differences between T1 and T2 resp. T3	187
14.5	Regression of 'Readiness for change' on social experiences	188
14.6	Regression of 'Expectation of continuity' on social experiences	189

14.7	Regression of 'New relationships' on social experiences	189
14.8	Situational variance over T1, T2, and T3	191
14.9	Regression of SSS on behavioural variance	193
14.10	Correlations of variance in conversational behaviour with SSS	193
14.11	Change in photograph content and functionality between T1 and T3	194
14.12	SSS and differences in meaning of photographs from T1 to T3	195

Preface

This book is about the relationship between humans and their environment. I have tried to look at this relationship from the perspective of the self-concept: what do the people around us, the places where we live, and the way we create our home contribute to our understanding of self?

As a social psychologist, I draw upon a tradition which the study of the self has had in this field. At the same time, the sources of modern self-concept research, like William James and George Herbert Mead, have been sources not only for a stream of social-psychological research, but also for other fields, notably sociological work on self and identity. Thus, the study of the self-concept cannot be restricted to one discipline alone: it not only allows but necessitates taking an interdisciplinary approach. Studying this in an ecological context leads one into other fields again, such as environmental psychology.

I have chosen a specific paradigm, namely relocation, to study changes in person–environment relationships. When one moves from one place to another, new friendships may form and others change, and a different life may be lived, but our home may allow us to build some continuity. I see relocation as an opportunity for self-concept change. Beyond the work described in this book, the choice of relocation as a research paradigm has led me to some further interesting work, both of a basic and applied nature, on relocation, the stress it can place on families, and the experiences people gain from it.

The work described here has had a long and personal history that makes it impossible to thank all people who have contributed in many ways, through ideas, discussion, and critique, as collaborators, research participants, and friends. I will name a few and will not forget the others. Robert A. Wicklund and Thomas D. Cook not only provided me with ideas, but taught me how to be a social psychologist. I was fortunate to be able to work in two environments that were supportive and gave me plenty of freedom for my work. When I was an NIMH Postdoctoral Fellow at Northwestern University, Tom Cook was responsible for my having two years to develop the bases for the later work that I did at the University of Heidelberg, where C. F. Graumann gave me the necessary independence. The empirical work in Heidelberg was supported by a grant from the Deutsche Forschungsgemeinschaft (DFG: the German Science Foundation). I thank Marco Lalli for the work he did with me at that time. An earlier version of the typescript was accepted as a *Habilitationsschrift* by the Faculty of Social and Behavioural Sciences of the University of Heidelberg.

The final typescript was read and commented on by several people, among them Mark Snyder, William Ickes, and Richard Lazarus. I am most grateful to Sheldon Stryker, who was supportive and encouraging from the outset. He read the whole typescript and wrote many pages of comments – I only hope I did justice to his efforts.

1 Restructuring the ecology of the self: a framework for self-concept change

Stability and change in a person's answer to the question 'Who am I?' vary throughout the life cycle. While at some points in life continuity may prevail, at others this question requires radically new answers. The loss of another person, a change in living conditions, or entrance into a new life stage can change the self-concept. The study of the processes of the self-concept undergoing change also provides information about the nature of the self-concept. I will present here the idea of the self-concept existing as part of an ecological system, and describe and study the processes of continuity and change under changing person–environment relationships.

A summary of the ideas and bases of the research programme will be given first. It should help evaluate the relevance of later, more detailed discussions of theories and findings from psychological and sociological social psychology and their implications for an ecological approach to self-concept change.

A person's understanding of self is acquired and developed through social experience. This basic idea has guided almost all theory and empirical research on the self-concept in modern psychology, beginning with William James's (1890) discussions of the self, and elaborated upon by Cooley's (1902) conception of the 'looking-glass self' and G. H. Mead's (1934) major work *Mind, self, and society*. Recently, more empirical tests (Shrauger & Schoeneman, 1979) and theoretical elaborations (Stryker & Statham, 1985) build on these foundations. From this common basis, psychologically orientated social psychologists are concentrating on the relationship between 'mind' and 'self', i.e. cognitive structure and self-concept, whereas sociological social psychologists are interested in 'self' and 'society', i.e. self-concept and social structure.

The ecology of the self

The present approach will make use of this basic idea and draw together several lines of thinking about the sources and symbols of social experiences and their meaning for the self-concept. The constituents of the self, namely others, environments, and things that provide, mediate, and perpetuate social experience, will be described as the *ecology of the self*. The self both shapes this ecological system and is a reflection of it. Development and change happen within the ecology of the self; therefore, to understand change, the stabilizing and changing forces have to be understood not only as existing within the person but as encompassing the surroundings of that person, too.

The constituents of the ecology of the self are *others*, as the sources of direct social experience, *objects*, as symbols and representations of social experiences, and *environments*, as the setting for social experiences. They are reflected in *self-related cognitions*.

The first function of *others* for the concept of self is the reflection of and reaction to one's actions, both verbal and non-verbal. These ideas are rooted in the writings of Cooley (1902) and Mead (1934). For Cooley, the reactions of others to one's own actions provide a mirror for the self. For Mead, the self develops by mirroring society. Both the self and societal rules, expectations, and reactions thus depend upon each other, and one is unthinkable without the other. Exchange with others is therefore the central process by which the self can be maintained as well as changed, as has also been shown by more recent research (for example Archer & Earle, 1983; Backman, 1985; Swann, 1983).

In a more abstract way, the self can be described as the internal organization of external roles of conduct, for instance, in the prescription of roles that can be used to form one's *own* course of action (Becker, 1968). Another function of social interaction is thus to provide the role models that may be incorporated into one's own concept of self. Continued development and change of the self needs exposure to alternative models of conduct or to the novel combination of existing ones. In all instances, the exposure to and interaction with others provides a person with the experiences necessary for development and change.

While social interactions are thought to be central to the dynamics of the self-concept, others do not necessarily have to be physically present to provide social experiences, nor do they have to exist as a concrete person. Social experiences are generalized and symbolized in various forms: in rules and expectations, for instance, but also in physical objects.

Objects may serve several functions for the self (Csikszentmihalyi & Rochberg-Halton, 1981). For many social experiences they are the necessary social tools, such as a record player for a dance, and can thus be prerequisites for acquiring a certain component of the self-concept, such as a dancer, a skier, or a music-lover. They can also function as the representation of past social experiences to stabilize and maintain those aspects of self that are related to the past. For instance, a photo album or memorabilia can serve this function. A third function of objects is that they can be symbolic of the self, such as the contents of one's bookshelf or china cabinet.

Such symbols of the self serve either to strive toward or maintain a certain status of self (Wicklund & Gollwitzer, 1982), or to present a desired image of oneself to others (Schlenker, 1980). Objects are thus able to provide or reflect social experiences and have to be considered as elements in the ecology of the self.

Environments or settings also have to be considered. They provide the place for a person's experiences or actions and can also be symbols of one's identity (Proshansky, 1978). Settings can inherently provide societal rules of conduct (Barker, 1965). Like certain objects, environments also provide prerequisites for self-concept-relevant behaviour, such as a mountain for a skier or a sea for a sailor. But it is not only natural and macro-environments which are relevant for the self-concept. Environments can also be arranged, for instance, when furnishing a flat. The arrangement and creation of environments can be a reflection of the self-concept and thus serve to stabilize it. Another stabilizing function of the environment can be in its use and arrangement to allow for the protection of privacy (Altman, 1976; Kruse, 1980).

While none of these aspects has been neglected by psychological theorizing and research on the nature and function of the self-concept, they have usually been considered separately. When they are taken together, however, the picture of an ecological system emerges. The self-concept exists in interdependence with its ecology of others, objects, and environments. As long as the ecology of the self is stable, the self-concept will be stable and strive toward maintenance. Self-concept change, on the other hand, results from an imbalance in the ecology of the self that leads toward restabilization under different ecological conditions, a restructuring of the ecology of the self.

Stability and change

What are some of the conditions for the stability of the ecology of the self, and under which circumstances do these change? In the area of social relationships, the interdependence between the stability of the self and the stability of one aspect of its ecology can be exemplified by extending the concept of commitment to an identity. For instance, Becker (1960) points out that a person's commitment to a social relationship is stabilized through a system of 'side bets': giving up a commitment to a social relationship impacts not only that one relationship but others that are linked to it. For instance, a commitment as 'husband' can be tied to a number of other relationships, such as 'son-in-law' or 'stepfather'. A social commitment thereby stabilizes a system of social relationships which in turn contribute to the person's concept of self.

Centrality of a social relationship to the self-concept can now be defined through the number of other social relationships that are influenced or tied into place by this one commitment. As long as the central social commitment stays in place, a larger network of social role-identities that define the self-concept is stable. The termination of one central social commitment destabilizes the social system, and opens the way for changing the self-concept. Of course, several commitments of this kind can exist with little linkage between their related systems, a fact that James (1890) early recognized. Social relationships are organized into several subsystems, the nodes of which are formed by social commitments.

The above constitutes an analysis on a more sociological level, but the entering or leaving of a social commitment can be shown to have implications for stability and change of the self-concept on a more psychological level of analysis as well. The beginning or end of a central social commitment is usually based on an evaluation of the self-concept, both by oneself and by a significant other. A social commitment is entered into after both partners have implicitly, or sometimes explicitly, evaluated each other's past performance in an attempt to project this past into the future. Therefore, the opportunity to enter a central social commitment constitutes a reinforcement for the self, based on a positive evaluation. On the other hand, the self is being questioned by an evaluation that can lead to the end of a commitment. Satisfaction or dissatisfaction with oneself will be the immediate consequence. Thus, satisfaction with self combines the effects of social structural stabilization and destabilization and of the concurrent psychological evaluation.

If social relationships are destabilized and the self-concept is questioned, the whole ecology of the self is affected. On the way to restructuring this ecology, the individual starts a search for new aspects that can be incorporated into the concept of self through exposure to new social contexts, social activities, and ultimately the possibility for new social commitments. Social experiences exposed to in that process are central to all self-concept-related processes.

The process of exposure to new aspects for the self can affect all dimensions of the ecology of the self. If some remain the same, self-concept change can only be limited. The more components of the ecology of the self are involved, the more complete the process of self-concept change can be.

Changes in the ecology of the self can either be self-related and direct, or externally imposed and indirect. A change in a central social commitment is an example of a self-related change in the ecological system of the self as it directly reinforces or questions a person's self-concept. A reinforcement of a person's self-concept will lead to self-concept maintenance and possibly enhancement processes. As these are related to the ecology of the self, the person tries either to preserve the ecological system or to resist changes in the environment that could lead to self-concept destabilization.

Changing environments are examples of externally imposed changes in the ecology of the self. If in the face of externally imposed change the self-concept is neither reinforced nor questioned, self-concept change through situational adjustment will take place. Situational adjustment was the only course of self-concept change described by Becker (1964). The current analysis adds another mode of self-concept change, namely the active restructuring of the ecology of the self. It emphasizes the agentic element in self-concept change.

An active pursuance of change consists of making use of the opportunities a new social and physical environment affords to structure a new ecology of the self and thereby change central aspects of the self-concept. Active pursuance of change can result from a destabilization of the ecological system concurrent to a questioning of the self, or from making selective use of those new elements that can enhance the existing concept of self.

In the face of changes in the social and physical environment another factor contributing to self-related evaluations and processes can be identified. Being a stranger in a new environment or generally being separated as a figure from a new ground focuses attention on oneself. A theory of self-awareness (Duval & Wicklund, 1972) identifies conditions and consequences of self-focused attention. In a new environment, the self-concept is made salient until the once-new environment becomes familiar. A familiar environment is one where the self-concept and its ecological system are stabilized. While this is not meant to imply that all conditions leading to self-focused attention are those eliciting self-concept change, it can be stated that changes in the ecology of the self-concept lead to self-focused attention and thus facilitate self-concept-related processes such as change or maintenance, whichever is required by the current evaluation of the self-concept.

The basic elements of the theoretical framework underlying the research reported in this book can now be summarized: The self-concept develops and exists in interaction with its social and physical environment to form an ecological system for the self. Certain factors serve to stabilize this ecology, above all social commitments. These are central to the self as they involve and bind together a number of social relationships. Changes in central social commitments either reinforce or question the self-concept.

A questioned self-concept can only lead to self-concept change if the ecological system of the self affords the opportunity. This can be facilitated by external changes in the environment of which the person can make use. Making use of such opportunities allows an *agentic* process of self-concept change to take place. External changes without self-related events lead to change through adjustment.

For persons satisfied with their concept of self changes in the ecology of the self that do not support the present self-concept may be resisted. In that case, the only changes which will be considered are those that connect the existing self-concept to new elements (Hayden, 1979). Then, only those new aspects from the environment that support and enhance the present self-concept may be incorporated.

An impediment to agentic self-concept change is the self-imposed restriction which usually accompanies low self-esteem. This poses the question whether a person who is dissatisfied with his or her self-concept will indeed make agentic use of his or her opportunities, or can only be an agent of his or her own fate from a position of strength. As low satisfaction with oneself, low self-esteem may initially inhibit an active search of the environment for new aspects of the self-concept, whereas if one has high self-esteem, one is more able to take advantage of new structures in one's social and physical environment to enhance one's present self-concept.

In general, a person dissatisfied with him- or herself may be slower in making use of new opportunities, and may then embark upon a more general search for new elements of the self-concept before they finally become incorporated. A person who is satisfied with his or her current concept of self may, when in a new environment, more selectively consider those elements of the ecological system that enhance the present self-concept by building on it. In one case, the direction of change is open, and change becomes increasingly agentic. In the other, the direction of change is predetermined. In both cases, self-concept change requires a rearrangement of the ecological system in which the self-concept exists.

Overview

The above presents a concise summary of the theoretical basis and approach that is taken in this book. In what follows, the bases for these assumptions will be reviewed in detail, always from the perspective of what the work reviewed means in the light of an ecological approach to self-concept change. As should have become evident, the roots of the above model can be found in diverse areas of psychological and sociological social psychology, personality psychology, and environmental psychology.

At the same time, empirical research related to such a theoretical approach has to meet certain criteria. These criteria are related to ecological validity, to the necessity to evaluate long-term processes, to the assessment of person−environment relationships in the face of changes, and to the concentration on social process rather than on changes in outcome. Since all these criteria cannot be met by employing one particular method, a multi-method approach has been chosen. A separate chapter will discuss the rationale of an ecological approach in method as it should complement an ecological approach in theory. Specific methods will be presented that are more likely to fulfil these requirements than other, perhaps more traditional, methods of self-concept research in social psychology.

A number of very diverse studies have been conducted in this research programme. All of them share the common theoretical assumptions as presented here and try to find empirical validation for the ecological approach to self-concept change. However, they do this using different designs and different methods, and studying different aspects of the change process. The multi-method approach also requires a multi-study approach. That way, no one study presented here should be considered by itself, but in the context of the whole research programme.

The methodological considerations and consequences will be discussed in Chapter 2. Chapter 3 describes an initial study conducted to show the appropriateness of 'relocation' as a paradigm for investigating changes in person–environment relationships, and the relevance of changes in commitment for the form this process takes. The next three chapters look at self-concept change from a social-psychological and a sociological viewpoint. This has consequences for the measures to be employed. An ecological approach has to take the functions of the physical environment for the self-concept seriously, as reviewed in Chapter 8.

In Chapters 9–11, relocation is investigated from the anticipation phase through the initial time spent in a new environment up to about one year after the move. Chapter 12 reviews the role of relocation as a subject of psychological research and as a research paradigm for transitions in the person–environment relationship. The studies discussed in Chapter 13 do this in cross-sectional and quasi-experimental designs; those in Chapter 14 employ longitudinal designs and a variety of methods. Putting together the information provided from the programme of research, the Conclusion assesses the status of the theory and the place of an ecological approach in psychological research.

2 Method considerations for an ecological approach

An ecological approach in theory should be complemented by an ecological approach in method. What does this entail? Various answers could be given. The current research programme attempted to incorporate several ideas into the design of the research. Taken together, these should present one possible, ecological methodological approach appropriate to this research question of stability and change in an ecological context.

Relevant ideas such as the enhancement of ecological validity or the assessment of subjective experience cannot be expected to be fulfilled equally by one single method, nor can they be followed to the same degree in different kinds of studies. A multi-method approach has therefore been chosen, guided by the assumption that while no single method and no single study is able to fulfil all requirements, the combination of different methods in different studies can help approximate such an ideal.

The following principles were taken into consideration in the research project:

> Enhancement of ecological validity.
> Use of a naturalistic research paradigm allowing quasi-experimental research.
> Combination of multiple methods.
> Sampling procedures allowing access to varied populations and experiences.

Ecological validity

'Ecological validity' is a term that has been used with various meanings of varying degrees of precision. According to Brunswik's (1949) definition, it refers to the occurrence and distribution of stimulus variables in the natural or customary habitat of an individual. A psychological method is ecologically valid to the extent that its stimulus variables are a representative sample of those in the individual's habitat. This principle was combined by Brunswik (1952) with the postulate that one should study functional organism–environment relationships. This requires that 'situational circumstances should be made to represent, by sampling or related devices, the general or specific conditions under which the organism studied has to function' (p. 30).

Brunswik's postulate extending the sampling requirements from persons to situations has methodological implications as far as the number of variables included in a research design is concerned. He conceived of representative designs as involving the selection or creation of stimulus conditions representative of the population of stimuli. However, the population of possible stimulus conditions and their configuration is rarely known. More recent methodological developments allow the sampling of experiences in natural situations. The random sampling of moments in individuals' lives *in situ* rather than sampling from situational stimuli to recreate the situation may be one of the best answers to the call for ecological validity. An appropriate method, experience sampling, will be described later in detail.

Use of a naturalistic design: relocation as a research paradigm

Self-concept change is a long-term process involving changes in the person–environment relationship. This basic statement underlies the theoretical approach of this work. It should therefore also be a starting point for the methodological approach that, if taken seriously, requires that change be studied in its *natural context*; and to understand the processes of change, *actual social experiences* have to be studied as they occur. If change has to be studied in a natural context, quasi-experimental use has to be made of naturally occurring changes in the person–environment relationship. A similar approach has, for instance, been taken by Wapner (1981; 1987) in his transitions-of-persons-in-environments paradigm. The rationale guiding this approach has been summarized by Hormuth (1984).

One of the main conditions for studying individual change in the face of change in the person–environment relationship is that the individual has the chance to influence and select from environmental opportunities, even create or recreate aspects of it. In the regular course of life, such opportunities are limited. Within a given social and geographical setting, a person's ecological system and the potential for social experiences within it are relatively fixed and can usually be changed only gradually.

The situation is different when the social and geographical setting changes, as is the case when persons move from one place to another, that is, in a relocation. A relocation usually constitutes a radical change from one social context and physical setting to another one, thereby providing the opportunity for change. In a new environment, the individual is exposed to new contacts and role models, acquires a new behavioural repertoire, and undergoes role transitions. The opportunity to seek out new and different aspects of the self-concept is given. On the other hand, the maintenance of previously existing social contacts requires more effort, too, after a relocation: continuity becomes an active process. To provide for continuity, the individual has to actively maintain contact with the previous social environment. If stability is desired in spite of environmental changes (i.e. situational adjustment is resisted), the importance of previously existing social contacts may be increased and actively enhanced (for example through telephone calls, letter writing, or visits). Absolute continuity in the person–environment relationship is impossible. However, continuity in selected aspects can be approximated by the way one's personal environment is created, for instance through furniture or other long-term personal possessions. For all these reasons, relocation is an appropriate paradigm for the naturalistic study of self-concept change because it offers opportunities for change and maintenance.

In addition, relocation frequently occurs in connection with changes in one's place in the social structure, that is, the beginning or termination of a commitment. People move because they get married, because they start a new job, as a result of a separation, because they finish their education, or for a variety of similar reasons. Not all, but many of these changes involve changes in central social commitments.

The study of relocation under natural conditions makes difficult any causal conclusions about resultant changes in interaction patterns, roles, and self-concept. If change occurs, is it due to the intentional activity of the individual or to the necessity for situational adjustment?

The study of naturally occurring changes, as they take place in relocation, precludes the random assignment of individuals to conditions. Use has to be made instead of other natural control conditions, either between persons through comparisons with non-movers, or within persons over time as the degree of novelty of the environment changes. Generally, the study of naturally occurring change requires the implementation of *quasi-experimental* designs (Cook & Campbell, 1979).

> Quasi-experimentation is a term referring to experimental designs that are not based on the random assignment of treatment and control groups. Rather, quasi-experimental designs rely on many methods, principally the use of nonequivalent control groups and multiple times of observation, in order to determine whether change occurred and to address the relative contribution of the treatment versus alternative explanations for the observed change.
> (Hormuth, Fitzgerald, & Cook, 1985, p. 210)

Quasi-experimentation does not just consist of specific research designs but of a variety of principles and techniques. They have in common that they are responses to threats to internal and external validity created by suboptimal research conditions (Cook, 1985; Hormuth, 1985).

Combination of multiple methods

Recent work by Cook and associates (Cook, 1985; Houts, Cook, & Shadish, 1986) has extended the thinking on quasi-experimentation and shown that it is much more than a specific design technique. It is an attempt to provide a post-positivistic framework for doing research in the social sciences. For that purpose, the term 'critical multiplism' has been chosen by Cook to refer to an approach to research that does not rely on any one specific method but takes advantage of the specific strengths of some existing and some new methods, by countering their specific weaknesses through combination with others that have different strengths and weaknesses. This approach is critical of all *individual* methods employed in social science research taken in isolation while recognizing that many of them allow specific access to relevant information.

> Since no perfect options (among methods) exist, the multiplist stance is to implement more than one option in a research study. *Critical* multiplism is concerned with how these options are selected. It assumes knowledge of the strengths and weaknesses of different justifiable options and advocates selecting those that complement each other's limitations; it further suggests that all proposed and actual selection concerning question formulation, research design, data manipulation, and substantive interpretation be openly scrutinized from a wide variety of theoretical perspectives, including overtly antagonistic ones.
> (Houts, Cook, & Shadish, 1986, pp. 53–4)

The present work takes the call for multiplism seriously. Multiplism refers not only to multiple methods, but to multiple studies, multiple samples, multiple operationalizations, multiple variables, and multiple approaches to data analysis. A short summary will illustrate how the present research tries to implement a multiplistic approach; later, the relevant methods will be described in detail. I have made more detailed critical evaluation of the methods used here elsewhere (Hormuth, 1986a; Hormuth & Brückner, 1985; Hormuth, Fitzgerald, & Cook, 1985).

The study of processes relating to self-concept change concentrates on using relocation as a research paradigm because it seems especially powerful. However, it will be supplemented with results from a few studies related to other relevant processes, such as the anticipation of change, or the importance of social relationships to the self-concept. Long-term change can rarely be studied from the anticipation phase through the actual change to adaptation in one single study. A number of studies therefore consider relocation in different research designs: a cross-sectional design studying changes in time after relocation on randomly selected heads of household, a longitudinal design doing the same within individuals,

12   *Method considerations*

and a quasi-experimental design comparing movers and non-movers. The design of each of these studies had to compromise in different ways. Other studies look at specific aspects of the person–environment relationship, namely behaviour in environments, and the subjective perception of the environment, each using a variety of operationalizations.

Several different methodological approaches to data collection have been selected, combining known and established methods of questionnaire construction and application and novel approaches to the study of actual behaviour in its natural setting. The experience sampling method (Hormuth, 1986; Larson & Csikszentmihalyi, 1983) allows access to personal experiences which have been virtually inaccessible before. Autophotography, another method chosen, provides a phenomenological, subjective approach to the perception of the relationship between self-concept and the actual social and physical environment. In autophotography, subjects take photographs of self-concept-relevant aspects of their environment (e.g., Ziller & Smith, 1977). Large-scale data collection on random samples was made possible through the implementation of telephone interviews (Hormuth & Brückner, 1985) that preceded and helped prepare the studies using the above-mentioned methods. In the course of this book, the methods will be presented in more detail; critical assessment of their uses and limits can be found in my work on this topic referred to above.

Sampling procedures

From the above, it becomes clear that the term 'sampling' as used here applies to the sampling of subjects and the sampling of situations. Both will be considered below.

The sampling of subjects

Social psychological research has frequently been criticized for its over-reliance on students as research subjects. This criticism, however, can often be countered with the argument that the processes studied, for instance those of a cognitive nature, can be presumed to be universal: only the content of the cognitions is thought to be subject to cultural or subcultural influences. Such an argument is more difficult to apply when the theoretical approach specifically takes an individual's relationship to his or her actual social and physical environment into account. Even if a degree of universality is assumed for the processes operating between the individual and the environment, the form the processes can take is much more context-specific in complex naturalistic settings than in the abstract setting of the social psychological laboratory. Hence it becomes necessary to make wide sampling a guiding

Sampling procedures

principle. However, this does not have to mean representative sampling, nor can the principle be applied equally in every study. Comparing groups in experimental or quasi-experimental research designs does not require a representative sample to detect differences in process. In addition, the specific requirements of a design may necessitate use of specific populations which fulfil those requirements better than others. This specific population may be very different from other populations. Therefore, the call for wide sampling of subjects cannot be meant to apply to individual studies, but only to research programmes.

The present research programme is concerned with relocation − a topic that has frequently been studied in psychology (see Chapter 12). However, researchers into relocation have usually been interested in specific questions, for instance the effects of involuntary relocation, that required or allowed the study of specific populations, such as the inhabitants of institutional settings. Such research connects the sampling procedure to the research question and tries to enhance the possibility of finding persons who undergo a specific form of relocation. One aim of the present research, on the other hand, is to make use of the wide variety of reasons and circumstances under which relocations take place. Therefore, whenever possible, the populations of subjects for the studies in the research programme have been defined as widely as possible, encompassing various groups of persons. Only when other requirements of a specific study made it more feasible to concentrate on subpopulations such as students was this done.

The sampling of situations

The quest for ecological validity, as defined by Brunswik (1949), has been answered here through the random sampling of moments in individuals' lives. In recent years, a number of investigators have developed methods that allow the study of the ongoing behaviour and the everyday experiences of people in their usual environment. One approach among these methods, the experience sampling method (ESM), allows the random sampling of a person's experiences in natural situations. For this purpose, research participants carry beeper devices that remind them at random times during the course of the day to report their experiences at the time of the signal. That way, a random sample can be taken of thoughts, experiences, moods, or self-reported behaviours. The method will be described in detail in connection with the first study reported here that made use of it (see Chapter 10). It has been critically evaluated by Hormuth (1986a).

Experience sampling makes use of *random* samples of everyday subjective experiences. The element of randomness is also introduced to minimize the chances of reactivity. Some similar approaches have persons report on their everyday experiences, either in a diary, or when a certain event happens, or at regular or preset intervals. All of these methods increase the risk of the research participant anticipating that a specific event has to be reported, or it is open to selective memory. Random sampling of experiences, on the other hand, reduces reactivity effects and increases the chance that the immediate impact of the experience can be researched.

In summary, the methodological approach of the research programme tries to do justice to the ecological perspective. It does not promote any one specific method, nor does it promote the approach taken here as a general paradigm for research in psychology or the social sciences. On the other hand, it suggests that each research programme needs its own specific combination of methods and studies. In the present case, these needs arise from the longitudinal nature of the problem under study, from the ecological nature of the theoretical approach taken, and from the subjective nature of the experiences that form a person's concept of self.

3 Relocation and changes in commitment: a cross-sectional study over the first year

Chapter 1 summarized the theoretical basis of the ecological approach to self-concept change and introduced a number of conditions and variables to be considered in such an approach. Chapter 2 considered the methodological approach chosen here, and introduced the rationale for using relocation as a research paradigm for the study of naturally occurring change in the person–environment relationship. To test the validity of some of the theoretical assumptions, and to assess the appropriateness of relocation as a research paradigm, a telephone survey was conducted. In particular, the survey was designed to study the social behaviours of persons in new environments, the relationship of persons to their physical environment and personal possessions, and the life events concomitant with relocation. Of theoretical interest was the variable 'commitment' and its relationship to social behaviours and changes after a relocation.

The study of the course of change and adaptation in a new environment poses a variety of problems, especially if a longitudinal design is chosen. Therefore, as a first step, a *cross-sectional* questionnaire study was designed to assess the course of behavioural change and adaptation after moving to a new environment in dependence from changes in commitment. Two telephone surveys served this purpose, one conducted in the summer of 1981 in Evanston, Illinois, United States, the other, a replication, in the winter of 1982 in Mannheim, Federal Republic of Germany (conducted with the support of ZUMA). For these surveys, a questionnaire was designed and a sampling method developed to identify and randomly sample persons who had recently relocated. Some results from a preliminary analysis of these data were included in Hormuth (1984).

The questionnaire

The questionnaire was designed to be answerable in a short telephone conversation of about twenty minutes. Its main parts addressed themes of change and stability in social interactions. It also asked about recent life events and their connections to transitions in commitments.

The first part of the questionnaire contained twenty items asking about the importance of different aspects of one's life. Items emphasizing stability were, for instance, 'keeping contact with friends and relatives even over long distances', or 'having memories of the important times in your life'. To assess their willingness to change, respondents were asked how much they liked to have 'challenges in their life' or to have 'chances to do new things and do things differently'. The importance of change in social relationships was addressed by items such as 'being able to make new friends' and 'having contact with many different kinds of people'. All statements were answered on a ten-point scale, indicating how important these issues were to the respondent at that time in his or her life.

The second set of questions asked about the importance of a series of specific personal possessions. It followed Csikszentmihalyi and Rochberg-Halton's (1981) research which basically identified three groups of personal possessions as relevant at different stages in life. Young people, that is, mainly adolescents, especially valued objects that served as tools for specific activities, for instance sports equipment or a stereo set. In middle age, value was attached to possessions that presented a certain picture of who one is, for instance antique furniture or display objects like china. For the elderly people in the Csikszentmihalyi and Rochberg-Halton sample, objects that were reminiscent of earlier times in their lives were most important, such as photograph albums and memorabilia. To assess whether objects play a role in the transition between environments and in self-concept change, thirteen different objects were listed and had to be rated for their personal importance to the respondent.

In the third part of the questionnaire respondents were asked for the actual frequency with which they engaged in particular activities. A list of twenty-two activities was given, and the frequency of an activity during the preceding four weeks was to be given as the answer. An example is: 'How many times approximately, during the past four weeks, did you actively participate in sports or athletic activities?'

The items were selected to cover different clusters of social activities. Those that were assumed to stand for continuity between environments were, for instance, 'played cards or games with family', or 'made a personal long-distance phone call', presumably to contact old friends or relatives. The first one indicates the company of familiar persons independent of the environmental transition; the second could be an indication of reaching out from the new environment, possibly to keep contact with familiar persons independent of the new environment one lives in. On the other hand, the seeking out of new social opportunities should be indicated in behaviours such as 'went out with friends for dinner', or 'were entertained by friends at their place'. Such activities have to involve friends living at the new and current place of residence. A more cautious seeking out of new social contacts may be expressed in behaviours such as 'went to community- or church-sponsored activities'.

At this point in the interview there followed a list of life events involving transitions (for example 'got promoted'), beginning new commitments (for example 'started a new job' or 'got married'), or ending old commitments (for example 'divorced or separated'). Respondents were asked whether this event happened in their lives within the last two years. Included among the twelve (in the German version thirteen) items was: '... moved to a new home ...'. If this item was answered in the affirmative, more specific questions were asked. These questions asked how long ago the move was, and the distances covered (i.e. within or from outside the region). The respondent was also asked the following question:

> The circumstances of some moves sometimes involve changes in relationships and commitments. Now, may I ask you, in very general terms, was this move the result of making a new commitment, for instance following a new job offer or getting married, or had it something to do with the end of an old commitment, such as getting divorced or losing a job?

The responses were recorded as 'starting new commitment', 'ending old commitment', or 'some of both'.

Sampling

Sampling is, as already discussed, a special problem when people who have just moved to a new residence have to be identified. Partly for that reason, most research on relocation makes use of special populations that are more easily identified, for instance of immigrants, or the residents of a whole retirement home moving to a new location, or those graduating from college (see Heller, 1982; Wapner, 1981). However, if relocation is to be used as a research paradigm for the study of transitions and self-concept change in general, then the selection of special populations related to specific occasions of relocation merely confounds the effect because the method of sampling is not independent of the variables to be studied. Such confounding should, if possible, be avoided by trying to find different methods of sampling for relocators. This can be attempted by defining neutral events usually concomitant with a move, but not related to the reason the person moved.

One method of sampling which fulfils the requirement of independence of the occasion from the reason for the move was found in the identification of people having a new telephone. Nowadays, getting a telephone is one of the first things most people do when moving to a new place, both in the Federal Republic of Germany and in the United States. Because both countries are practically saturated with telephones for private residences, most new numbers will be those of persons new to town rather than existing households that had no telephone previously.

A simple method of identifying new numbers was comparing the new edition of a telephone directory with the previous year's edition. Because directories are compiled with the assistance of computers, the information in a new directory is very recent – no more than four to six weeks old. Names and telephone numbers appearing in the new edition but not in the old one are extremely likely to be those of people who moved within approximately the last year (and a few months beyond) to the geographical area covered by that telephone directory.

The study was conducted in the United States (Evanston, Illinois) and the Federal Republic of Germany (Mannheim). Both sites chosen have a very high telephone density. Evanston is known to be among the places having the highest density of telephones in the United States, and Mannheim also was reported to be saturated by 1982 (Post Office, personal communication). In Evanston, the new directory was provided by the telephone company on the first day of issue. In Mannheim, the Post Office provided the page proofs of the new directory as early in the production process as possible.

Using random number tables, pages in the new directory were randomly chosen, and then, listing for listing, compared to the corresponding place in the old directory. For instance, if the page randomly chosen listed at the top 'Miller, George, 123456', the same name and number was located in the old directory. If Miller's was a new listing not in the old directory, the next listing on the same page occurring in both the old and new directory was identified. From there on down, for the whole page in the new directory, every name, address, and telephone number was compared. Listings obviously referring to a business were excluded.

All listings that appeared only in the new, but not in the old directory, were considered to be part of the sample. A new listing was defined as a previously unlisted name and address and a new telephone number. This should reduce the probability of including persons having moved within town. Doubtful cases were also not included. From the Evanston phonebook, only every second new listing was used to reduce the chance of sampling relatives. This precautionary measure turned out not to be really necessary and was therefore dropped when compiling the sample in Mannheim.

In addition, a group of listings that appeared unchanged both in the old and in the new telephone directories were sampled randomly as the control group. Name, address, and number had to agree. The control group sample was obtained by randomly drawing a quarter of the number of new listings obtained from a page among the unchanged listings on the same page. The final sample consisted of 80 per cent new listings and 20 per cent old listings.

Procedure

The old and new listings were randomly mixed in the list of telephone numbers which were actually used to conduct the survey. That way, and by including questions relevant to relocation only toward the end of the interview, interviewers were blind as to the relocation status of the person interviewed throughout most of the interview. The final list of telephone numbers obtained consisted of 571 in Evanston and 682 in Mannheim.

Procedure

Two hundred and fifty interviews were conducted over a period of several weeks in the summer of 1981 by one interviewer in Evanston. In Mannheim, where 251 interviews were conducted, the support of ZUMA (Centre for Surveys, Methods, and Analyses) allowed the use of five telephone lines and five interviewers working simultaneously, making it possible to conclude the interviews in nine days (two weekends and the weekdays in between) in January 1982. Interviews were conducted in the afternoon and evening hours during the weekend, and between 5.0 p.m. and 9.0 p.m. on weekdays. More procedural details can be found in a description of telephone interviewing procedures based on the present study by Brückner, Hormuth, & Sagawe (1982; see also Hormuth & Brückner, 1985).

Interviews were conducted with heads of household in order to reach persons who presumably responsibly participated in relocation decisions. 'Head of household' was defined in accordance with the 1980 US Census as being independent of the sex or income of the person. This meant, in essence, that the persons interviewed were adults who were not living as dependants in a household with other adults.

Of all telephone numbers obtained, several had to be excluded for reasons unrelated to the interview, either because they were never answered, or turned out to be business numbers, or were ineligible for other reasons (for instance, the subscribers were incapable of speaking English or German). This left 383 telephone numbers eligible in Evanston, and 493 in Mannheim. Of those, 70 per cent agreed to participate in the interview in Evanston, and 55 per cent in Mannheim (for a detailed analysis of response rates, see Brückner, Hormuth, & Sagawe, 1982). This represents a response rate within the normal range of social science surveys.

Altogether, 501 interviews were conducted, 251 in the U.S., and 250 in Germany. Of those responding, 350 (70 per cent) of the participants indicated they had moved sometime within the last two years, although some of the moves were within the city and took place in connection with the founding of a household.

Results of factor analyses

As a first step in the data analysis, individual items from the three main scales 'Importance of Values', 'Objects', and 'Activities' were subjected to factor analyses to obtain distinct factors of values, groups of valued objects, and related activities. The factor analysis used a varimax rotation, and only those items were included in the factors which had a loading of at least .40.

The scale 'Importance' yielded five factors. The first described the willingness to change and do things differently in a network of old and new friends. It was called 'Social change'. The second one was called 'Stability in the family'; it loaded negatively on challenge, positively on provision for old age, home decoration, and family life. The third factor described the importance given to 'Financial security' by way of property and provision for old age. The fourth factor, called 'Continuity', stressed ties in the community, the family, and through reminiscences. The final factor emphasized the person's independence. Individual items and factor loadings are presented in Table 3.1.

Table 3.1 *Factor analysis of importance of values*

Factor item	Factor loading
Social change	
Having challenges in your life	.46
Being able to make new friends	.78
Being close to old friends	.56
Having chances to do new things and do things differently	.55
Doing things with friends	.78
Being liked	.45
Having contact with many different kinds of people	.56
Stability in the family	
Having challenges in your life	−.40
Providing for old age	.52
Decorating your home well	.74
Doing things with the family	.67
Having a good family life	.71
Financial security	
Being financially secure	.68
Owning your home	.74
Providing for old age	.53
Being liked	.47
Having stability in your life	.52
Continuity	
Having memories of the important times in your life	.52
Keeping contact with friends and relatives even over long distances	.71
Being involved in community- or church-sponsored activities	.52
Having close relationships with relatives	.76
Independence	
Being independent	.61
Being able to be alone, to read, or to reflect	.74
Having contact with many different kinds of people	.41

Results of factor analyses

The factor analysis of the list of twenty-two different activities yielded seven factors. The first describes 'Outgoing' activities, like making telephone calls, going to new restaurants, and going out with friends. The second one describes involvement in the 'Church community', with church and charitable activities. 'Activities in the home', for instance, games and home improvements, form a third factor. The fourth factor includes 'Sports' activities, as participant and spectator, but also the political arena. The fifth factor includes what could be called 'Solitary-social' activities, because though the individual is alone, a social world is created through a medium: long-distance telephone calls, books, letters. Genuinely 'Solitary' activities form the sixth factor. Finally, the seventh factor combines activities of 'Entertainment' with and of others. The items and factor loadings are presented in Table 3.2.

Table 3.2 *Factor analysis of activities*

Factor item	Factor loading
Outgoing	
Made a personal long-distance phone call	.48
Went out by yourself or only with the immediate family	.51
Went to a restaurant that you didn't know before	.75
Went out with friends for dinner	.71
Went to a restaurant	.80
Church	
Went to community- or church-sponsored activities	.88
Did charitable volunteer work	.47
Went to church	.86
Activities in the home	
Played cards or games with family	.56
Made home improvements	.55
Played cards or games with friends	.66
Sports	
Did political volunteer work	.67
Engaged in sports with others	.58
Went to a sports event	.54
Engaged in sports by yourself	.43
Solitary-social	
Made a personal long-distance phone call	.40
Read a book	.77
Wrote a personal letter	.55
Solitary	
Went out by yourself or only with the immediate family	.46
Worked in the garden	.78
Entertainment	
Entertained friends at your place	.61
Went to see a live performance	.63
Were entertained by friends at their place	.67

Of the factors into which personally valued objects were classified, 'Household' items form the first group. The following three factors were: objects of a more 'Reflective' kind (arts and books), for an 'Active' person (stereo and sports), or having to do with 'Pictures' (camera, photographs, and television). The fifth factor showed the person's 'Home orientation', including pets, plants, and musical instruments. Table 3.3 shows the items and respective factor loadings.

Table 3.3 *Factor analysis of valued objects*

Factor item	Factor loading
Household	
Special appliances	.67
China, glass, or silverware	.82
Special furniture, e.g. antiques	.65
Television set	.45
Reflective	
Paintings or other art objects	.73
Books	.77
Activity	
Stereo equipment	.74
Sports equipment	.82
Pictures	
Camera equipment	.65
Photographs and photograph albums	.66
Television set	.48
Home orientation	
Pets	.67
Musical instrument	.43
Plants	.76

Comparison of movers and non-movers

Because the design precluded before–after comparisons to assess the effects of moving on values, activities, and importance of objects, the first set of analyses compared the group of movers (N = 350) with the non-movers (N = 151) on the factors obtained. As it became clear that movers were more likely to be young, and many of the items were frequently associated with age-specific values and activities, all analyses (employing the general linear model of the analysis of variance) took age into account as a covariate. Older persons were included in the group of movers, but in smaller numbers.

The differences between movers and non-movers are, it should be noted, not of immediate theoretical relevance. No theoretical variable has been introduced. In addition, great variance exists in the sample as to how long ago the move was. For some who were classified as movers, the relocation was more than one year ago. Hence the differences as I shall describe them are very conservative estimates of possible general effects of moving on the importance of certain values, the frequency of certain activities, and the value placed on certain possessions. Because of this, some marginally significant effects (p < .10) will be mentioned. The means are compared in Table 3.4.

After taking age into consideration, on the factors relating to the importance of personal values, relocation made no difference in 'Social change', but did in 'Stability in the family', $F (1, 492) = 9.01$, $p < .005$, such that non-movers value it more than movers (9.02 versus 7.58 on a ten-point scale). 'Financial security' is also valued more by non-movers, with age controlled, than by movers, $F (1, 497) = 4.46$, $p < .05$. The other values, referring to 'Continuity' and 'Independence', were not differentially important to movers and non-movers.

Personal possessions and things were not clearly differentially valued depending upon the moving status. Although 'Household' items were slightly more valued by non-movers than movers, this difference was not significant at the 5 per cent level when the covariate was taken into account, $F (1, 498) = 2.78$, $p < .10$. Active objects were only more valuable for movers before the covariate was entered, i.e. for the younger group, showing a similar age effect for stereo and sports as Csikszentmihalyi and Rochberg-Halton obtained, $F (1, 498) = 15.62$, $p < .0001$. Another slight effect before the covariate was found for 'Pictures', $F (1, 498) = 2.91$, $p < .10$, but age accounted for that. Finally, the covariate age did not account for a slight difference in the value of 'Home orientation' (pets, plants, musical instruments), which were valued more by non-movers, $F (1, 496) = 2.76$, $p < .10$.

Table 3.4 *Mean comparisons between non-movers and movers*

Scale/Factor	Non-movers	Movers
Values		
Stability in the family	5.42	4.54**
Financial security	9.63	8.77*
Objects		
Household	5.30	4.63+
Activity	4.85	5.65(**)
Pictures	5.43	5.10(+)
Home orientation	5.90	5.67+
Activities		
Outgoing	22.60	27.00*
Sports	7.80	11.05+

Note: Importance of values and objects is expressed on a ten-point scale, with 10 being most important. Activities show the actual frequency of the group of activities during the past four weeks.
** $p < .01$; * $p < .05$; + $p < .10$;
in parentheses: significance level before the covariate age.

Overall, having lived in the same household for a longer time period seems to create a very slightly greater attachment to items belonging to that household. The emerging pattern of the role of the covariate age suggests relationships similar to those found by Csikszentmihalyi and Rochberg-Halton (1981) with objects allowing activities belonging to younger age groups and special items furnishing a home being more important to older age groups. Thus, while the specific relevance of personal possessions at the occasion of environmental change could not yet be established, the short questionnaire version does seem to capture the essence of the Csikszentmihalyi and Rochberg-Halton findings.

'Outgoing activities' were more frequently undertaken by persons who had moved, $F(1, 495) = 4.43$, $p < .05$; though the covariate age almost reached significance, $F(cov)(1, 495) = 3.08$, $p < .10$. A clearly higher engagement in sports by movers was not quite significant after age was taken into account, $F(1, 497) = 2.90$, $p < .10$. Interpreted together very cautiously, these findings suggest that movers more than non-movers engage in activities that are outside the new home and involve other persons.

Effects of national differences

It should, of course, not be forgotten that the total sample of 501 persons consisted of two very different samples in two cities in two different countries, namely the United States of America and the Federal Republic of Germany. While actual national differences in attitudes and activities following a relocation are of little theoretical interest in the current context, one should be aware of possible interactions of nationality with those effects of relocation that are of interest in the present context. The variable nationality was not entered directly into the analysis of the theoretically interesting variables, commitment and time, because this would have further reduced the number of subjects per cell to in some cases unjustifiably small cell sizes. However, before conducting these analyses a possible interaction of nationality and relocation effects should be examined.

Of all analyses, using nationality and relocation as independent variables, and age as covariate in a general linear model approach to the analysis of variance, only two interactions yielded significance, namely sports activities, $F(1, 495) = 7.67$, $p < .01$, and the importance of social change, $F(1, 493) = 4.63$, $p < .05$. After a move, Americans engage considerably more in sports. On attitude toward social change, relocation has no effect on Americans, whereas Germans who have not moved value it less than those who have. The means are presented in Table 3.5. Of course, because Germans in general move less, in Germany it may be a segment of the population that is open to social change which is also more likely to move.

Effects of national differences

Table 3.5 *Effects of nationality and relocation*

Nationality	German		American	
Relocation	No	Yes	No	Yes
Sports activities	7.5	7.4	8.2	14.7
Importance of social change	6.8	7.4	7.8	7.9

Although the direct effect of nationality is of less interest, main effects of nationality, after taking age into account as a covariate, are presented in summary form in Table 3.6.

These results have to be treated very cautiously. Effects on the frequency of activities are confounded by time of year: the American interviews were conducted during the summer, the German ones during the winter. This could account totally for the higher frequency of outdoor activities, which includes solitary activities in the garden. Americans attach more value to social change and independence, but also financial security and continuity. Germans prefer the stability provided by the family. Objects of a reflective nature, those used for activities, and pictures are all valued more highly by Americans. However, none of the differences on objects interacts with relocation.

Table 3.6 *Effects of nationality, taking age into account*

	German	American	F (df)
Importance of values			
Social change	7.18	7.91	$F(1,493) = 38.01$
Stability in the family	5.40	4.22	$F(1,490) = 65.23$
Financial security	5.48	5.84	$F(1,495) = 12.86$
Continuity	6.28	7.38	$F(1,495) = 55.04$
Independence	7.50	8.06	$F(1,496) = 17.89$
Importance of objects			
Reflective	5.90	6.70	$F(1,496) = 21.10$
Activity	4.97	5.86	$F(1,496) = 13.27$
Picture	4.92	5.48	$F(1,496) = 14.45$
Activities[a]			
Outgoing	20.70	30.70	$F(1,493) = 15.62$
In the home	17.00	8.70	$F(1,493) = 37.09$
Sports	7.50	13.20	$F(1,495) = 11.99$
Solitary	4.90	10.40	$F(1,493) = 44.70$

[a] Confounded by seasonal influences.
All F-values significant at $p < .0001$.

Effects of commitment and time

The next analyses were only conducted on persons who had actually moved. That way, the time since the last move could be included in the cross-sectional comparison. In addition, the theoretically most interesting variable, namely changes in commitment concomitant with the move, could be entered as an independent variable in the analysis. Both variables were applicable to the movers but not to the non-movers.

Of the 347 subjects who had responded to the commitment question, 36.84 per cent had entered a new commitment, 11.70 per cent had ended an old commitment, 7.02 per cent said some of both had happened, and 44.44 per cent indicated that their move had to do with neither of those two events. For more than half of the persons, changes in commitment were concomitant with a relocation, demonstrating the appropriateness of relocation as a research paradigm in the present context. Since 'some of both' and 'neither one' were both unspecific, the groups of respondents were combined for the analyses.

Time since the move was divided into six stages. Because of the sampling procedure, only a few (5 per cent) subjects were included for whom the move took place within the immediately preceding month. The distribution of subjects by time since moving and commitment is presented in Table 3.7.

Table 3.7 *Distribution of subjects for time by commitment analyses*

Months since move	1	2–3	4–6	7–9	10–12	13+	Total	%
Entering a new commitment	3	8	18	42	27	26	124	36.8
Ending an old commitment	3	6	6	9	10	6	40	11.7
Neither or both	11	18	28	33	52	41	183	51.5
Total	17	32	52	84	89	73	347	
%	4.9	9.2	15.0	24.2	25.7	21.0		100

To be able to conduct analyses despite the quite uneven distribution of subjects in the conditions, again the general linear model approach to the analysis of variance was used, always entering age in the regression. This can be considered a cautious approach, because the fact of moving may be age-dependent, but not necessarily the course of adaptation over time or the concomitant change in commitment. However, some of the criteria serving as dependent variables may also be age-related.

Analyses were conducted using as the independent variables 'Commitment', with three levels, and 'Time', with six levels, and age as covariate.

On commitment, the first two levels were entering a new commitment and ending an old commitment, and the third level consisted of those with no clearly definable change in commitment, thus serving as a control group. That group's change over time should therefore demonstrate situational adjustment, rather than active maintenance or change.

On the factors measuring the importance of values, Factor 2, 'Stability in the family', showed significant main effects for commitment, F (2, 327) = 5.41, p < .005. Stability in the family was valued highest by the control group, and least by those ending a commitment. Also significant was the main effect for time, F (5,327) = 4.00, p < .002, such that persons whose move was two to six months ago valued family most. Age had a clear effect on this value, F (1,327) = 37.49, p < .001. No further factors of values showed significant effects.

To summarize the effects, the following tables present the means for the main effects of commitment (Table 3.8) and time since the relocation occurred (Table 3.9). For values and objects, scores refer to a ten-point scale; for activities, to the actual frequency of the acts during the past four weeks.

Table 3.8 *Effects of commitment*

Variable	Entering a new commitment	Ending an old commitment	Control group
Stability in the family	4.8	4.4	4.0**
Church and community	4.3	5.6	5.0*
Entertainment	7.8	11.2	7.7**
Activity objects	5.4	6.2	5.3+

** p < .01; * p < .05; + p < .10.

Table 3.9 *Effects of time since the relocation*

Time in months	1	2–3	4–6	7–9	10–12	13+
Variable						
Stability in the family	4.3	5.3	5.2	4.5	4.0	4.5**
Church and community	4.1	2.8	4.9	6.9	4.4	4.1**
Entertainment	7.1	12.1	7.5	8.3	8.1	6.9**

** p < .01.

The third factor of objects, 'Activity objects', showed a main effect for commitment, $F(2,328) = 2.87$, $p < .06$, such that persons entering a new commitment valued activity objects more (Table 3.8). Marginally significant was the interaction of commitment by time, $F(1,328) = 1.73$, $p < .075$. The course of time affected the control group only slightly; for subjects in the two commitment groups, activity objects were relatively important in the beginning and lost steadily in importance over the first six months, whereas subjects in the control group only showed somewhat greater variance during the first half-year. Age was also clearly related to the importance of activity objects, $F(1,328) = 45.97$, $p < .001$. No other groups of objects showed significant effects for either commitment, time, or their interaction.

The second activities factor, 'Church and community', yielded main effects for commitment, $F(2,326) = 3.48$, $p < 0.5$, and time, $F(5,326) = 3.70$, $p < 0.1$. Persons entering new commitments engaged most in church-related activities, the control group least. Those in the second and third months after the move were least involved in church activities, those in the fourth quartile of the year most. Interestingly, age was not significant in relation to church activities.

The fifth activities factor, 'Solitary-social' activities, yielded a significant interaction effect for commitment by time, $F(10,327) = 1.91$, $p < .05$, but no age effect. 'Solitary-social' consists of activities (long-distance phone call, reading a book, writing a personal letter) that create a social reality which is independent of the actual environment one is in, either by reaching out to others, or by interacting with phantasy figures. As can be seen from Table 3.10, the two commitment groups are largely parallel during the first six months, starting low with a sudden increase and then a decrease, whereas the control group shows a quick drop from a very high start. The curvilinear relationship for the commitment groups is obvious, with a slow beginning and a peak at two to three months after the move, whereas the control group appears to be adapting more linearly after a high frequency in the first months. On this variable, groups having any change in commitment differ from those moving unrelated to any changes in their lives that affect the social structure.

Table 3.10 *Effects of commitment and time on solitary-social acts*

Time in months	1	2–3	4–6	7–9	10–12	13+
Entering a new commitment	22.0	45.8	26.7	32.7	27.8	36.3
Ending an old commitment	23.0	40.3	27.0	25.4	33.3	30.1
Control group	45.5	28.8	27.6	25.2	31.4	19.8

Effects of commitment and time

The seventh factor, 'Entertainment', includes inviting friends for dinner, going to the theatre, and being invited by friends. Age showed a clear relationship with such activities, $F(1,326) = 16.4$, $p < .001$. But after taking age into account, both main effects (see Table 3.8 and 3.9) and the interaction effect were also clearly significant: for commitment, $F(2,326) = 6.06$, $p < .003$; for time $F(5,326) = 4.40$, $p < .001$, and for the interaction effect $F(10,326) = 2.39$, $p < .01$. Table 3.11 presents the means for this factor.

Table 3.11 *Effects of commitment and time on entertainment acts*

Time in months	1	2–3	4–6	7–9	10–12	13+
Entering a new commitment	4.7	9.6	7.6	7.9	7.4	8.0
Ending an old commitment	9.0	25.4	7.8	11.7	7.3	7.0
Control group	7.3	8.7	7.4	8.0	8.5	6.2

People who have ended an old commitment seek out entertainment very frequently after the initial adjustment to the new city has taken place, that is after the first month. The second and third month in a new environment are a very busy time for them; a similar effect is sometimes attributed to divorcees. People who have ended an old commitment take almost a year to seek out entertainment to the same extent as the other groups. Persons starting a new commitment are somewhat less likely to seek the company of other friends and the public during the first month, but later this group is largely indistinguishable from the control group. Although the number of persons in these groups is relatively small, the interaction effect is clearly significant. Whereas solitary-social activities differentiated all relocations concomitant with any type of change in commitment, entertainment separates those who left a commitment.

The effects on the importance of possessions are less clear. Here, only one factor, 'Activity objects', showed any effect (Table 3.11). However, only the covariate age was clearly significant, $F(1,328) = 45.97$, $p < .001$. After controlling for age, the main effect for commitment was marginally significant, $F(2,328) = 2.87$, $p < .06$, and so was the interaction effect, $F(10,328) = 1.73$, $p < .075$. Persons beginning a new commitment value stereo and sports more, with little difference between the other two. The course of time affected the control group only slightly; in both commitment groups there was a drop from an initial high to the level of the control group (reached after about three months). A generally higher level of activity was expected for these groups, which is reflected in the importance of these objects.

Table 3.12 *Effects of commitment and time on activity objects*

Time in months	1	2–3	4–6	7–9	10–12	13+
Entering a new commitment	8.5	7.3	5.2	6.7	6.1	5.7
Ending an old commitment	7.0	6.0	4.8	5.2	5.2	4.5
Control group	5.9	5.0	6.0	5.0	5.3	5.5

Discussion

The results of the present study, taken together, strongly show the appropriateness of the chosen approach. Relocation is indeed an occasion of many changes in commitment, and may well affect values, the perception of the environment, and social activities in that environment. The theoretical variable commitment, as defined by the respondents themselves, was able to differentiate in different ways on different dependent variables between control groups, whose relocation had nothing to do with a change in commitment, and groups who either entered a new commitment or left an old one in connection with the relocation. While different effects emerged on different variables, overall three separate behavioural patterns are distinguishable among these three groups. None of the variables showing these effects was affected by an interaction of nationality and relocation. Therefore, the effects of commitment and time shown are not likely to be due to an unknown underlying factor of nationality.

The operationalization of the variable of commitment in this study was very simple, leaving it to the respondent to classify his or her personal situation. It could therefore only indirectly assess the extent to which a person's social network was affected by these changes. The salience of the relationship left or begun makes it likely that it was also a central relationship connected to others. An additional analysis of the frequency of life events and their relationship to commitment showed that divorce is the most classical end of a commitment. However, when combining some life events that signify the end of a commitment, namely unemployment, end of education, divorce or separation, and end of a work relationship, a chi-square analysis with self-reported end or beginning of a commitment was not significant. On the other hand, life events that indicate a beginning, namely marriage, birth of a child, professional success, and start of a new job were much more frequently associated with self-reported beginning of a new commitment, chi-square (1) = 18.01, $p < .0001$.

Two possible explanations can be found for the clearer definition of beginnings than ends: one is the possibility that persons are less likely to admit

Discussion

to failure, and the end of a relationship can be considered to be to some degree a failure — hence its proposed relationship to the necessity of self-concept change. If that is the case, the current operationalization may be very conservative and a definition through objective life events may be more precise for future research. However, it could also be that persons are not willing to admit failure to themselves, as recent research on self-handicapping and attribute ambiguity suggests (see Hormuth, 1986, for a research example). If that were the case, it should not be a more objective measurement, but rather a more subjective measurement that may yield clearer effects on a person's behaviour. Self-esteem or satisfaction with oneself would be an approach to a subjective conceptualization.

Another other possible interpretation is that every end also carries with it a beginning. This is to some degree true of the end of education. While such a transition certainly means the end of a commitment and frequently entails leaving a social network related to the education, it can also imply the beginning of a new working life. Separation from a person may lead to an openness to new relationships. A time of more than one year was covered in the present cross-sectional study. Over such a time span, the impact of a separation may already have been cushioned by the establishment of new social relationships. Greater closeness of measurement to the actual event may help to focus on more in the rebuilding of self-identities.

The results of this first study have confirmed some of the basic assumptions of the present theoretical framework, and have established relocation as an appropriate paradigm for the study of self-concept change. Problems in the realization of studies on the special population of persons in new environments have become clearer. The present study justified the design of more elaborate and costly studies of relocation and pointed the way to more specific ways of identifying and operationalizing some of the important variables.

4 Implications of recent research in cognitive social psychology for self-concept change

Since the early seventies or so, experimental social psychology has been ever more interested in the self-concept's function in mediating cognitions and behaviour. Theories such as self-awareness (Duval & Wicklund, 1972) or self-monitoring (Snyder, 1974) studied the realization of self-related attitudes or implicit theories about the proper role of the self in social interaction. Other, existing theories incorporated the concept of self. For instance, dissonance theory (Festinger, 1957) was modified by specifying the self-concept's role in the dissonance reducing process (Aronson, 1968), or else an attempt was made to replace it with an explanation of the process through which people perceive themselves, that is, self-perception theory (Bem, 1967). With the exception of self-perception theory, which attempted to explain how impressions about oneself are formed, the theories did not question the stability inherent in the mediating concept they called the self. It was assumed instead that it is the self that provides *stable* standards, values, or attitudes.

Some of this research will be examined in this chapter to see whether despite a basic assumption of stability implications for self-concept change can be found. Considering the current breadth of self-concept research, such a review has to be selective; in this case, only theories, hypotheses, and findings of immediate relevance to the present theoretical model of self-concept change can be reviewed.

Recent research in experimental social psychology has basically taken two perspectives: some addresses the *structure* of the self-concept, its elements, their relation to each other, and the development of a complex self-concept from simple elements. Such research owes much to the social cognition paradigm that has emerged over the last decade. Other research emphasizes the *functions* of the self-concept as a mediator of cognitions and behaviour or as a motivator to maintain or strive toward identities.

The self-concept as an organization of cognitions

Kihlstrom and Cantor (1984) define the self-concept as 'one's mental representation of oneself ... not unlike other concepts, that is stored in memory as a knowledge structure' (p. 2). Similarly, Greenwald and Pratkanis

(1984) describe the self as a 'central cognitive structure, a self-concept with content that varies from person to person' (p. 166). The self is seen here both as the object of an attitude and as an 'active, functioning organization that both acquires and receives knowledge' (Greenwald & Pratkanis, p. 166), and is thus better described as a central attitudinal schema.

Kihlstrom and Cantor's (1984) conception of the self as a cognitive structure has two sets of implications for this work, namely its relation to the external environment, and its possibilities for change. Both are to some degree addressed by Kihlstrom and Cantor.

Their approach to personality and the self starts with the assumption that *social* cognitions are the most important mental processes, namely those involving mental representations of the self, of others, and of situations in which interactions with others take place. Social context has effects on human thought and action, and is at the same time the creator of that environment. However, the influence of a person's environment on thought and behaviour is not direct, but rather mediated through the mental representation of that situation. This, of course, is a position not unique to Kihlstrom and Cantor, but is the basis of all cognitive approaches in social psychology. Rarely, however, is the role of the environment as clearly stated as when they characterize the relation between cognition and environment as one of reciprocal determinism. They conclude, however, that 'although this implies mutual influence and a powerful role for the environment, in the final analysis, the balance of power favors cognitive control over environmental control' (p. 4).

Acknowledging, as Kihlstrom and Cantor do, the role of the social environment and of the situations in which interactions take place for the cognitive structure is an important step in accepting the necessity of studying not only one's social cognitions but also the actual environment. The self-concept is made up of cognitions about oneself. These cognitions result from constellations in the environment of that person. Most of the experiences a person has about him- or herself are of a social nature. This view is not only accepted by proponents of social cognition. It is also the basic assumption guiding self-concept research in sociological traditions in social psychology, such as symbolic interactionism, which will be discussed later in detail. Thus, the study of a person's social environment and the events therein is a central contribution to the study of a person's self-concept.

What kind of knowledge about oneself is represented in the self-concept? A distinction that has been shown to be useful (for example Hastie & Carlston, 1980) is that between declarative knowledge, that is, factual knowledge about the external world, and procedural knowledge, that is, operations that relate and transform declarative knowledge. The dynamic features of personality, of which self-concept change is one, may, according to Kihlstrom and Cantor (1984), be 'identified with the subset of the individual's procedural knowledge that guides the organization and transformation of social information and the transformation of social cognition into social behavior' (p. 16).

The description of declarative knowledge as including interactional skills, self-presentational skills, or scripts for social interaction is reminiscent of a definition of the self-concept as consisting 'of all the roles we are prepared to take in formulating our own line of action, both the roles of individuals and of generalized others' (Becker, 1968, p. 197). This definition from a symbolic interactionist viewpoint comes close to the identification of procedural knowledge with the dynamic features of the self-concept. While procedural knowledge from Kihlstrom and Cantor's point of view can be used to 'generate and test plans for responding to current and anticipated events', from Becker's point of view, knowledge of roles is used to formulate one's line of action.

By using self-presentation strategies as an example of consciously accessible procedural knowledge, one possible process of self-concept change is addressed at the same time. People trying to create a certain impression of their own personality on others may do this in a way either congruent or discordant with their own view of themselves. Congruency is an instance when people disclose intimate information about themselves to others. Self-disclosure research has studied the interactional and self-concept relevant consequences of such behaviour (Archer & Earle, 1983; Hormuth & Archer, 1986). Other kinds of behaviour are enacted independently of a person's view of him- or herself to create an impression in others, for instance, as being particularly skilful or as possessing a socially valued attribute. Such processes have been discussed by Jones and Pittman (1982), Schlenker (1980), and Baumeister (1982).

Both kinds of self-presentation, authentic and strategic, can be linked to the coming into existence of new cognitions about the self, that is, new elements of the self-concept, by making use of self-perception theory (Bem, 1967). Hormuth and Archer (1986) exemplified this for the authentic self-presentation taking place in self-disclosure, and Kihlstrom and Cantor (1984) for strategic self-presentation.

Self-perception theory is one of the most frequently cited theories about how people infer attributes of their own person. According to Bem (1972), 'individuals come to "know" their own attitudes, emotions and other internal states partially by inferring them from observations of their own overt behavior and/or the circumstances in which this behavior occurs' (p. 5). He also specifies what 'partially' can mean: 'to the extent that internal cues are weak, ambiguous or uninterpretable' (p. 5). In such a situation, a person uses a situational analysis of the circumstances under which a behaviour

Self-concept as an organization of cognitions

took place to decide whether this behaviour was caused by situational demands or was not under external constraints and therefore is an expression of a personal attribute.

In the case of authentic self-description, according to Hormuth and Archer, the content of self-disclosure consists frequently of a perception about oneself, the meaning of which is still not clear even to that person. Uncertainty may actually contribute to the perceived intimacy of some information about oneself. If that information is given under circumstances that are considered to be completely voluntary (Fishbein & Laird, 1979), the certainty of that cognition is enhanced by the perception of the circumstances of its communication. Thus, an uncertain cognition about oneself can become part of the factual though subjective knowledge about oneself.

Even strategic self-presentation may turn into authentic self-presentation, as suggested by Kihlstrom and Cantor, and thus, of course, create new cognitions about oneself. However, 'the conditions under which these transformations occur, if indeed they do, and those under which the changes are maintained are unknown at present' (p. 19), though dissonance reduction and self-perception are proposed as possible mechanisms. An example of a dissonance reduction mechanism would be a parallel to forced compliance, except that the person is not forced by another into certain behaviour but rather forces himself or herself into it for strategic self-presentational reasons. Because the perception of a strategic behaviour may be dissonant from other cognitions this person has about himself or herself, the strategic behaviour may come to be perceived as being authentic. Thereby, new cognitions about oneself have been added to the self-concept and may have altered central elements of it. Self-perception theory may account for processes where the original reason for displaying a behaviour may have become less salient, for instance, because the behaviour has been displayed repeatedly and thus become routinized so that its situational control cannot be easily established any more. If no situational control over behaviour is perceived, its causes can be attributed to oneself.

What kind of information is added to the self-concept? The kind of information consists, of course, of both declarative and procedural social knowledge. As information is added about oneself, the content and structure of the self-concept changes. New information may also change not only the content of the cognitions about oneself but also the way they are connected, which cognitions are central, and which ones are peripheral in a network of self-related cognitions. From a cognitive point of view, the self-concept is constantly changing, because it constantly acquires new information. However, at the same time it maintains stability because it is very conservative with respect to cognitions added to knowledge about oneself. Thereby, the self-concept 'provides for continuity amidst change, congruent with the individual's overall self-concept' (Kihlstrom & Cantor, 1984, p. 29).

Some evidence suggests that such cognitions are added to the self-concept that show the distinctiveness of that individual. For instance, McGuire and McGuire's work (for example 1981) on the spontaneous self-concept shows that features are encoded as part of the self-concept which point to the person's individuality. Also, Hastie (1981) has shown that information added to memory is more likely to be inconsistent with an already existing impression. Kihlstrom and Cantor use these findings to argue that people will encode those features of themselves that make them stand out in their social context.

Their interpretation is hardly surprising. The very process of gaining an identity consists of relating oneself to one's environment. The distinction between person and environment can only be undertaken by using those elements by which a differentiation between oneself and others is possible. However, this need not mean that elements common to oneself and to others cannot be part of the self-concept. For instance, if a person is asked to describe himself or herself in his or her home country, it is possible that the initial description will be in terms of occupation. This is an element of the self-concept that the person does not have in common with all of those around him or her and that describes his or her relationship to his or her social environment through a number of features unique to a given occupation. If, however, the same person is asked to identify himself or herself in a foreign country, his or her nationality may be the feature of self mentioned first. Self-awareness theory, which I shall discuss later, uses a similar figure–ground argument to describe situations that can focus attention on the self.

Kihlstrom and Cantor's (1984) discussion of the mental representations of the self has several implications for the study of the process of self-concept change. The self-concept is conceived as a complex set of interconnected cognitions to which new knowledge is constantly added. For several reasons, some of which will be exemplified later in the discussion of Swann's work on self-verification, the new information is not radically different from the old, but it may add support to the existing concept of self. This process favours maintenance of the self-concept rather than its change. The actual process of change is unknown in such a framework.

While Kihlstrom and Cantor started by relating the concept of self to the environment, their discussion of change in the self-concept assumes a constant environment and thereby neglects this environment. Attempts at explaining or predicting change in the self-concept only focus on changes in the cognitive representation. No account is taken of changes in the self-concept that are related to changes in the environment. Changes in a person's environment require a change in the cognitive representation of the self. As the relationship between oneself and one's environment changes, other features of self may become unique and thus identifying. Changes in the external environment add new and possibly unanticipated cognitions that have to be added to the existing knowledge. This, however, may also require a reorganization of the existing knowledge about oneself. Therefore, if change within the cognitive system is only gradual and tends to support maintenance, major change in the self-concept has to consist of a radical alteration of the self–environment relationship, frequently caused by changes in the environment, and cannot be accounted for by a purely cognitive analysis.

Self-concept as a mediator of cognitions and behaviour

One theory that has been concerned with the self-concept's role as a mediator between cognitions and behaviour was presented by Duval and Wicklund (1972). Self-awareness theory is concerned with the circumstances and consequences of self-focused attention. The attention of a person fluctuates between aspects of the environment and aspects of the self. The theory postulates that attention focused on the self actualizes personal standards, norms, or other self-concept relevant information. This information is compared to the actual state of the person, and an attempt is made to adhere behaviourally to these personal standards. A large body of research supports some conclusions of relevance to a study of self-concept change:

(a) If self-aware, persons act on the basis of standards, values, or attitudes related to their self-concept.
(b) If a person is not self-aware, the self-concept and self-related cognitions are not drawn upon.
(c) If a person is self-aware but does not have personal standards relevant to the actual situation, social or group standards are used.

Since at some point self-focused attention seems to be necessary for self-concept processes to take place, the conditions focusing attention on the self-concept are of interest. Because this is not an actual element of self-awareness theory, but only a precondition, little attempt has been made so far to summarize the conditions. However, research within and outside the theory has shown some of the classes of events that bring about self-focused attention, so that a somewhat more systematic summary shall be attempted here.

Environmental conditions for self-focus

Self-awareness theory, in its original statement (Duval & Wicklund, 1972), had little else to say about the conditions leading to self-focused attention other than that they are 'nothing more than stimuli that cause the person to focus attention on himself (or on the environment)' (p. 7). These stimuli can be impersonal, such as seeing oneself 'externalized' as in a mirror or a photograph, or becoming aware of a part of one's body; or other people can serve as a source of self-awareness if the person becomes aware that another's attention is focused on him or her.

Self-awareness can very easily be brought about in the social psychological laboratory, most frequently by use of a mirror. Of special interest in the current context are, however, naturally occurring events that are likely to turn attention either toward oneself or toward the environment. Carver and Scheier (1981) discuss some naturalistic variations in attentional focus. The degree of novelty of an environment is one feature of the environment that turns attention away from oneself and toward the environment. Another one is the pace of events. The faster paced an event, the more attention it requires, thus diminishing the attention available for oneself.

On the other hand, Carver and Scheier identify bodily activity, and the awareness of the attention of others focused on oneself through observation by others and eye-contact as naturalistic sources of self-focus. The first of these sources, bodily activity, is closely related to a finding reported by Hormuth (1979, 1982). There, in trying to compare self-awareness and drive theory, generalized drive was induced through running in place. It was unexpectedly found that, although several of the variables showed that arousal was successfully induced, results on other variables pointed to parallels with the self-awareness conditions. This finding can be interpreted by relating it to other studies indicating that the bodily concomitants of arousal, such as sweating and heartbeat, have self-focusing effects. Fenigstein and Carver (1978) found that the perception of one's heartbeat leads to effects related to self-focused attention; Wegner and Guiliano (1980) replicated my manipulation of arousal and found evidence of self-awareness.

The final naturalistic source of self-focus identified by Carver and Scheier is being observed and making eye-contact. Several studies (e.g. Carver & Scheier, 1978; Scheier, Fenigstein, & Buss, 1974; Fenigstein, 1979) demonstrated that the presence of an audience can enhance self-awareness if the person is aware of that presence, for instance by being reminded through eye-contact.

Additional naturalistic situations can be identified besides those described by Carver and Scheier. Those can be expected to enhance the proportion of attention focused on the self to the detriment of the attention focused on the environment. These are: personal novelty, membership of a group, standing out as an individual in a new environment, and the disruption of ongoing activities. With the exception of the last, these effects can be subsumed under a theoretical analysis of figure–ground relationships as a mechanism for arousing self-awareness (for an elaboration of ecological conditions for the occurrence of self-awareness, see Hormuth, in press).

Duval and Wicklund (1972) drew upon the Gestalt principle of figure and ground, as proposed by Koffka (1935). According to this principle, the focus of attention in the perception of the segregated portions of a figure is drawn to the 'stronger' part of a given field. The strong element is defined by the relationship of one element to the other and is the figure upon which attention is drawn; the weaker element is perceived as the ground against which the figure is perceived. Koffka's principle states that if the two segregated regions are of different sizes, the smaller one will be perceived as the figure. The smaller a segregated portion is compared to the other segregated portion, the stronger it is: the focus of attention is on the smaller unit. Duval and Wicklund applied this principle to self-awareness. The two segregated portions are the self and the environment. The smaller the self against a social environment, for instance a group, the more attention is focused on the self.

Mayer, Duval, Holtz, and Bowman (1985) have used this principle to manipulate self-awareness in an experimental context. They prepared 'astrological charts' for subjects in an experiment, and told them that their specific planetary alignment was either a very common one (50 out of 100) or a very uncommon one (1 out of 100). A standard manipulation check for self-awareness indicated that subjects who saw themselves as a much smaller element among all the elements focused more on themselves.

Following the same line of argumentation, Mullen (1983) has proposed that members of a group become more self-focused as the size of their subgroup decreases. In heterogeneous groups, subgroups can be defined on the basis of some perceived salient difference. Using the ratio of others to the total number of group members, Mullen made several predictions about the occurrence of self-awareness effects, in particular behaviour in adherence to one's standards. His predictions were generally borne out by the data (Mullen, 1983, 1984).

Wicklund and Frey (reported in Wicklund, 1982) used the same line of reasoning for a field study of tourists in different countries of Europe. They administered a questionnaire to tourists, assessing the degree of figure–ground differentiation, and the level of self-awareness. Figure–ground differentiation was measured by relating characteristics of the tourists to those of the place and country where the data were collected, for instance distance from home country, language spoken, family ties between home and host country, and the size of the travelling group. Their findings indicated that, generally, the amount of self-focused attention increased with greater strangeness of the environment, as defined by being in a new country for the first time and travelling alone.

The figure–ground analysis and the findings above seem to contradict Carver and Scheier (1981), who identified novelty of an environment as bringing about self-awareness. If one uses the more general figure–ground analysis, then only specific elements in the environment which become salient through their novelty, that is, because they present a novel figure on the generally familiar background, should be subject to their argument. If the environment as a whole is novel, then the individual is more likely to be the focus of attention.

In general, then, self-concept-related processes require an increased degree of self-focused attention. It is assumed here that processes of self-concept change are long-term processes because of the general stability of the network of self-related cognitions. Therefore, life-cycle instances have to be identified that possess qualities such as those described above to raise an individual's general level of self-focus. Such instances can be all those in an individual's life that separate or distinguish a person from his or her familiar surroundings, physically or psychologically. The present research makes use of one such instance: relocation. Relocation creates the experience of being a stranger in a novel environment. The novelty of environments, persons, and situations encountered emphasizes the status of the newcomer, thus creating self-focused attention. This generally higher level of self-awareness as it is brought about by life circumstances is comparable to chronically higher self-awareness (Fenigstein, Scheier, & Buss, 1975). Only after some time will aspects of this new environment acquire familiarity and thus slowly reduce the general level of self-focused attention again.

The acquisition of new standards

The effects of self-focused attention, however, are not necessarily those that inevitably bring about change: according to a self-awareness analysis, one can expect the course of resistance to change over time in a new environment to be curvilinear, starting low, increasing over time and only later decreasing again. Self-focused attention makes salient certain aspects of self relevant in the situation. In addition, according to self-awareness theory, those self-related cognitions are brought to the fore that indicate the standards an individual has in relation to those salient aspects of self. Standards can be attitudes, values, or ideals, for instance.

In a state of self-awareness, an individual experiences the discrepancy between his or her actual state and the relevant individual standards.

This discrepancy, according to the theory, creates a motivation either for avoidance of the self-focus or for reduction of this discrepancy through a change in behaviour. Ample research supports this notion, whether it is stated in the motivational terms of the original formulation of self-awareness theory (Duval & Wicklund, 1972; Wicklund, 1975) or the control theoretical terms of a more general reformulation of the theory (Carver & Scheier, 1981). Behaviour adhering to a standard has been found, for instance, in the areas of achievement motivation, honesty, sex guilt, originality, altruism, and avoidance of aggressiveness (see Hormuth, 1982). In all these instances, self-aware persons' behaviour was more in line with their self-concept-related standards as compared to other persons who were less self-aware. These results apply to the state of self-awareness as well as to the trait of self-consciousness.

What implications does this have for the process of self-concept change and adaptation to new environments? The self-relevant standards made salient through the self-awareness brought about by being in a new environment are likely to be (a) acquired in the old environment or life situation, and (b) those where most discrepancy with the actual state in the new environment is perceived. This should make the discrepancy between the old and the new even more evident, and create an initial resistance to adaptation to the new environment, its standards, expectations, and role behaviours. One consequence of such a state is, as is known from laboratory research, the avoidance of self-focus. When one is a stranger in a new environment, the reduction of the general level of self-awareness and avoidance of the self-awareness-creating function of the new environment can take the form of creating for oneself an environment consisting of familiar elements. This can apply to the social environment by increasing contacts with familiar others, as well as the physical environment by recreating parts of the old one. However, because the new environment is not usually completely avoided, over time more and more elements of the new will become familiar, and thus the general level of self-awareness will become reduced. Resistance to the new environment and its standards will also become less and the willingness to acquire information will increase.

How are self-concept-relevant standards acquired from the new environment? While a general answer is, of course, not limited to an analysis within the framework of self-awareness theory, some suggestions can be taken from there. In particular, Duval and Wicklund (1972) discussed conformity to socially prevalent standards in cases where an individual holds standards that are opposed to those of a majority. They define conformity as 'a change in the person's attitudes, beliefs, or behaviors in the direction of the differing attitudes, beliefs, or behaviors of other people who are present in the same situation' (p. 57).

Their analysis starts with the assumption that in a confrontation between individual standards and those of a majority group, an individual may come to perceive a discrepancy. If applied to moving to a new environment, a newcomer may perceive that accepted standards of social behaviour or moral judgment of the majority in the new locale differ from those that he or she holds. This may be an especially obvious experience when moving to a different country or culture. The person has to try to localize the contradiction between personally held beliefs and those of the social environment as being due either to his or her own incorrectness or to that of the environment. 'Once a person believes that any of his perceptions of the world or behaviors toward the world are incorrect, those self attributes will become unstable, that is, ready for change' (Duval & Wicklund, 1972, p.62). Under which conditions do people come to perceive their own beliefs as incorrect, and thus ready for self-concept change?

When confronted with a differing majority opinion, or a prevalent discrepant standard in a new environment, a person will become aware of the discrepancy because a state of self-awareness will make the personal standard salient. Duval and Wicklund contend that the awareness of contradiction leads to the perception of some error, because x and non-x cannot at the same time hold true. This perception is the first step in creating instability in aspects of the self-concept.

The next step is a question of the causal attribution of incorrectness, which, as a state of cognitive disturbance, needs an explanation. According to a variety of studies within the focus of attention–attribution of responsibility context, the causal attribution of an event follows the focus of attention (Duval & Hensley, 1976; Hormuth, 1986a). If one is in a state of self-awareness, and an event needs a causal explanation that can be either internal, that is, related to oneself, or external, that is, related to the social environment, then the source of the state in need of explanation will be seen within oneself.

This hypothesis has been supported in a great variety of studies, many of which have presented short vignettes describing to subjects events needing explanation, and have asked for the percentage of internal attribution. Self-aware subjects attributed more responsibility to themselves (Duval & Wicklund, 1973). Other studies have made use of this principle and explained social and cognitive phenomena through the higher attribution to self under self-awareness (e.g., Duval, Duval, & Neely, 1979, increased felt responsibility and helping behaviour; Hormuth, 1986, applied the principle to attributional ambiguity). Therefore, it can be concluded that a person is more likely to locate the source of error in him- or herself under conditions that create focus on the self. A person in a new environment is in such a situation.

Two forces as postulated by the theory should now lead to an adoption of the socially prevalent standard over the personally held one. One is avoidance, where the perception of discrepancy is avoided. Avoidance of self-awareness can take the form of making oneself part of the majority, thus altering the figure–ground relationship. Ingratiation to the new social environment can result from an attempt to avoid self-focus. One form that ingratiation can take is the adoption of the majority viewpoint. From another point of view this is also the most likely consequence, because the attribution of error to the self indicates that one's own view is incorrect and the majority standard is correct.

This analysis by Duval and Wicklund has received partial empirical support. Some elements of the analysis are clearly supported, in particular the focus of attention–localization of attribution hypothesis. In addition, a study by Duval (1972; cited in Duval & Wicklund, 1972, pp. 98–100), indicates that 'conformity is inversely related to the size of the area of the field with an individual, and that the relationship between conformity and subgroup size is mediated by the focus of attention' (p. 100). Those subjects in lowest agreement with others and under conditions of self-awareness showed the strongest intensity and frequency of conformity. This study and the others discussed above have demonstrated that the ratio of individual to group, or an outsider or newcomer status, does indeed raise self-focus.

Difficult to interpret in the framework presented here are some self-awareness studies that confront individual versus group standards. In these studies, subjects are typically made self-aware through some standard self-awareness manipulation, and are confronted with alternatives for reacting to a situation that create a conflict between personal and social standards. Thereby, they separate the source of self-awareness and the source of standards, so that the adoption of the socially prevalent standard does not at the same time reduce self-awareness, and other circumstantial factors determining the salience of either one of the opposed standards become more relevant. Froming, Walker, and Lopyan (1982) concluded from their study that manipulations focusing on private aspects of self lead to adherence to personal standards, while those that focus on public aspects of self lead to adherence to social standards.

Diener and Srull (1979) conducted two studies indicating that under self-awareness social standards are prevalent. However, the personal standards of their study were not long-held-ones that were confronted with new ones, but were created in the experiment. Gibbons and Wright (1983) criticized the Diener and Srull study on the basis that the personal standards were not very salient. They studied students holding sexually liberated or conservative attitudes. Majority attitudes were created by stating that the social norms of their peers were generally liberal. Self-awareness was created by way of a mirror. The results indicated a shift in the socially prevalent direction for the more conservative subjects, but at the same time higher correlations between pre-test and post-test responses for the self-awareness group, indicating that conservatives had not given up their personal standards.

Thus, although these studies seem to indicate the general predominance of public over personal standards, none of the studies addresses this in a context where self-focus itself is created by being in the minority. The stability of previously held personal standards is not taken into account, and circumstances serve to focus attention on salient and specific public or private aspects of the situation. One of the assumptions of my analysis is the initial resistance to change, resulting in the predominance of personally held standards acquired in a previous environment. Only over time, as aspects of the new environment become familiar, is the individual ready to consider the contradiction in standards as described by Duval and Wicklund (1972). The processes described in their analysis may then take place. Taken together, these analyses lead to the assumption of a curvilinear course of resistance and adaptation over time in new environments.

In summary, self-awareness theory suggests that transitions from familiar to unfamiliar environments may enhance the likelihood of self-concept-related processes because they focus attention on the self. Confrontation with values or standards held in the new social environment may destabilize previously held ones, and the new ones may eventually be adopted. This is explained by avoidance processes that require one to join the majority, and by attributional processes that locate the source of conflict and of incorrectness in the self. Assuming the initial stability of previously held standards that become actualized under self-awareness, a curvilinear adaptation process is assumed.

The orientation of the self-concept

Thus far, how cognitions about the self are organized and how they are acted upon if they are the focus of attention have been considered. Persons whose self-concept is stable have been characterized as being orientated toward themselves, whereas persons whose self-concept has become destabilized have emerged as having to rely on external information about standards, or roles, or behaviours, that may eventually be incorporated into the self-concept. What is known about the difference between an internal orientation and reliance on one's own self-concept and an external orientation toward the behaviours, values, norms, and cues of others in the guidance of one's own behaviour?

Self-monitoring

Work relevant to this question has mainly been done under the label of 'self-monitoring' (Snyder, 1974). Self-monitoring is described by Snyder as a reliance on external versus internal cues in the guidance of one's own behaviour. It has been conceptualized by Snyder as a trait, meaning that persons differ in the degree to which they rely on cues from their self-concept versus those from the social environment.[1]

A great deal of research has been conducted on the correlates of self-monitoring, its behavioural and cognitive consequences. I shall argue below (a) that high self-monitoring is an appropriate strategy for persons whose self-concept has become destabilized and who are attempting to acquire new information that may eventually become incorporated into their self-concept, and (b) that results obtained in the context of self-monitoring research are therefore relevant to understanding the process and strategies of persons attempting self-concept change. Linking that information can greatly enhance the understanding of transference of information about the social environment to information about oneself.

The construct of self-monitoring, as conceived by Snyder and taken into consideration in the development of the self-monitoring scale, tried to encompass the following hypothetical components: (a) concern for appropriateness of social behaviour, (b) attention to social comparison information, (c) the ability to control or modify self-presentation, (d) the use of this ability in particular situations, and (e) cross-situational variability of social behaviour (Snyder, 1974). On the basis of information obtained in research in the years since, Snyder and Campbell attempt to provide more information on the construct and develop further hypotheses. I will now describe the general picture of high and low self-monitors as it emerges from their presentation.

High self-monitors are persons whose behaviour is orientated to their social environment. They are described by Snyder and Campbell (1982) as persons who construe their identity in terms of the specific social situations and the interpersonal settings in their lives. Snyder calls their self-concept a 'pragmatic self'. Cognitively, their identities are more likely to be located externally, that is, they describe themselves in terms of their social relationships, group membership, and other external elements, such as specific social

---

1 Unfortunately, Snyder called those people relying on cues from themselves 'low self-monitors' and those relying on cues from the social environment 'high self-monitors', thus actually reversing the meaning. I consider a suggestion made by Stryker (personal communication, March 1985) very appropriate and would prefer the term 'self-monitors' for persons relying on information from their self-concept (Snyder's 'low self-monitors') and 'social monitors' for persons relying on information from their social environment (Snyder's 'high self-monitors'). However, because the terms 'high and low self-monitors' are commonly used, I will keep them.

situations and interpersonal settings (see Sampson, 1978). High self-monitors are more likely to make situational attributions. They pay attention to the behaviour of others in order to manage and regulate their own self-perception appropriately, that is, they define themselves in relation to others. The monitoring of others' behaviour should provide a high self-monitor with a large store of knowledge about varieties of behaviours in a large variety of situations. If one considers this in terms of Becker's earlier-mentioned symbolic interactionist definition of self-concept, high self-monitors should be more likely to acquire role behaviour that can be incorporated into the self.

Behaviourally, their actions are orientated to situational cues and therefore should display greater intersituational variance. Indeed, in a study by Snyder and Monson (1975), high self-monitors were, in accordance with situative cues, either conforming or non-conforming in different situations, whereas low-self-monitors' behaviour showed little reaction to such situational cues. A high self-monitor would tend to perceive the behaviour of others as dispositionally determined because such a perception would facilitate the predictability of and orientation toward others' behaviour. High self-monitoring would result in more accurate and detailed attention to others' behaviour and appearance, and the cognitive organization of such information into traits or dispositions. Snyder and Campbell cite empirical work by Berscheid, Graziano, Monson, and Dermer (1976) as supporting this hypothesis. It can also be expected that high self-monitors are more likely to search out clearly structured situations that provide interpretable cues about appropriate behaviour.

On the other hand, low self-monitors construe their identities in terms of their personal characteristics and psychological attributes. They define themselves on the basis of their attitudes, values, standards, and personal norms. Snyder calls their self-concept a 'principled self'. They are more likely to use dispositional attributions for their own behaviour. Low self-monitors locate their identity in themselves. In planning and guiding social behaviour, low self-monitors will pay attention to their own internal states, dispositions, and personal characteristics. Whereas high self-monitors draw upon a store of knowledge about the behaviour of others, low self-monitors will have more information about their own behaviour in different situations. Low self-monitors will display more behavioural consistency and thus more predictability in their actions and attitudes. If possible, low self-monitors will choose 'to spend time in social situations and interpersonal settings that provide information indicating that it will be appropriate to engage in behaviors that express and reflect whatever traits and dispositions low-self-monitoring individuals regard as relevant to those situations' (Snyder & Campbell, 1982, p. 199). That is, low-self monitors are more likely to be comfortable in situations that are less structured and do not necessarily provide clear cues about appropriate behaviour.

High and low self-monitors are described by Snyder and Campbell as having different strategies and tactics for structuring their social world. They describe these in terms of Goffman's (1959) analysis of 'audience segregation', 'selective interaction' and 'front' as concepts of self-presentation. Audience segregation refers to the attempt to present consistent self-images to others. Because high self-monitors present themselves differently in different situations, they will be more likely to avoid situations where different audiences may come together to whom they have presented themselves differently. Selective interaction for low self-monitors would lead them to seek out other persons who allowed them to act according to their own personal attitudes, standards, and preferences. Setting up a front refers to the arrangement of the external aspects of a situation, that is, the arrangement of the physical setting in which behaviour takes place, and the person's appearance. Snyder and Campbell speculate that the front of high self-monitors would be selected to portray a specific self-image to others, and may also be more heterogeneous. On the other hand, the front of low self-monitors — their selection of clothing, furniture, and interior decoration — will reflect their personal preferences.

This presentation of the characteristics, preferences, and interpersonal strategies of high self-monitors and low self-monitors is not intended as a review of research on self-monitoring. It is intended to present two different interpersonal orientations in regard to the self-concept. One is the style of a person who has a secure self-concept, relies on this self-concept, and actively tries to maintain it regardless of environmental influences. The other is that of a person who may be insecure in his or her own convictions, attitudes, beliefs, behavioural norms and standards, and tries to behave in such a way as to elicit maximum information from the environment to enrich his or her personal repertoire of behaviours and cognitions that can be drawn upon.

The parallels to the cognitive, behavioural, and interpersonal consequences of actively maintaining one's self-concept in a new and different environment on one hand, and the active use of new information to integrate into a questioned self-concept on the other, should be obvious. Accordingly, high self-monitoring seems to be a strategy appropriate for active change in one's self-concept, and low self-monitoring seems a strategy appropriate for active maintenance of one's self-concept.

This is a slightly different approach to the construct of self-monitoring, because it conceives of it not only as a lasting disposition but also as a strategy appropriate for certain times or situations in an individual's life. The different terminology has been chosen because thinking about self-monitoring this way is a departure from Snyder's conception. This is not to deny that individuals may dispositionally differ on self-monitoring. More recent research (Snyder & Gangestead, 1985; Gangestead & Snyder, 1985) provides ample evidence for that notion. The present reconceptualization does, however, also include the possibility that while undergoing processes such as self-concept change, individuals may chose different preferred behavioural strategies. The strategy of high self-monitors is particularly adaptive for an individual whose self-concept has been questioned and who is confronted with a new environment from which to extract new potential for a rebuilding of the self-concept. The strategy of low self-monitors is particularly adaptive for an individual whose self-concept is stable and is to be maintained.

Location of identity

Many conceptions of self, identity, intimacy, or personality share a dimension of externality–internality. James (1890) early referred to the different selves a person has: the material, the social, the spiritual self and the pure ego. Based on Lewin (1935), researchers in the area of self-disclosure frequently conceive of personality as consisting of different layers that can be arranged on a central–peripheral dimension of a concentric model (Altman & Taylor, 1973). Peripheral layers have to do with biographical and public information about the self; internal ones with fears and basic values. The central layers of the onion-skin model are less common and less visible. Definitions of the intimacy level of self-disclosure content rely on the internal–external dimension. Snyder's self-monitoring construct, as discussed above, assumes that individuals differ in defining their identities through personal values and beliefs or their interpersonal and situative relations and behaviours.

Prelinger (1959) conducted a study that was closely orientated to the conceptions of self and personality as developed by James (1890), Allport (1937), and McClelland (1951). He suggested a structured space for the self, including (a) intraorganismic processes, (b) body parts, (c) objects within the close physical environment, (d) distant physical environment, (e) identifying characteristics, (f) possessions and productions, (g) other people, and (h) abstract ideas. One hundred and sixty items from these groups had to be divided by subjects into those which were part of their own selves and those which were not. The task was easy for all subjects, with wide differences in their definition and the extension of their self-region.

The subjects were asked to dichotomize the items. Prelinger himself transformed their assignments to a four-point continuum, taking into consideration how certain the subjects were of the object's location. Below the midpoint of that scale, that is, defined generally as belonging to the self, are (from the core out): body parts, psychological and intraorganismic

The orientation of the self-concept

processes, personal identifying characteristics, and possessions and productions. Generally placed in the non-self-region were: abstract ideas, other people, and close physical and then distant physical environment. Prelinger suggests that those falling in the self-region can be defined socially only with reference to a person (for example belongings), whereas there is no such need for the items in the non-self-categories.

Prelinger goes on to hypothesize about the variables associated with whether an object will be included in the self. Ratings of judges were used to test the hypothesis 'Objects over which a subject has control or which he can manipulate, as well as objects by which he can be affected ... are more likely to be perceived as parts of the self' (p. 18). 'Control' and 'Affected-by' ratings on the item and the category level were equally included in the self-region, but the other, neutral items, highly significantly less. Another variable suggested as contributing to inclusion in the self-region was physical distance from the body. Other factors held equal, a correlation of $r = .79$ was found between physical distance as rated by judges and distance from the core of the self-region as rated by subjects. (The test of further hypotheses was judged by Prelinger himself as 'arbitrary'.)

Prelinger's investigation obtained a stable and meaningful relationship between categories and the self-region. It is suggested that definition of an object by reference to a social variable (i.e. an anchoring in the social structure) and interactions with the object that include affecting and being affected by it, as well as the pure physical distance between object and person, may be some determinants of the inclusion of an object in the self-space.

Along similar lines of reasoning, Sampson (1978) suggested that different ways of categorizing identity characteristics involve as a common dimension the *environmental location* of identity. 'Simply stated, location refers to whether a characteristic is said to be part of the person (internal location) or a part of the external environment (external location)' (Sampson, 1978, p. 553).

Sampson claims that this spatial dimension of psychological structure has several implications:

(a) Individuals differ in their general environmental orientation. This statement is very close to Snyder's self-monitoring construct, and to the dispositional conceptualization of self-consciousness.
(b) Sampson recognizes that such dimensionality has already been assessed by several personality measurement instruments.
(c) Identity characteristics tend to cluster by location for individuals. This means that the characteristics by which an individual describes him- or herself all tend to be in a similar location on the internal–external dimension.

(d) Clustering is a result of an individual's general environmental orientation. If a person is generally externally orientated, he or she will look for identity characteristics in that location.

The scales that Sampson identifies as measuring traits related to environmental location are Snyder's (1974) measure of self-monitoring, Rotter's (1966) locus of control, Laird and Berglas's (1975) locus of causal attribution, and his own measure of general internal orientation ('Sampson's IO'). (Other data as reported by Sampson are omitted here because they are not relevant to the present argument.)

Sampson's major hypothesis predicts that a correlation should exist between general environmental location as measured by these four personality scales and the location of identity characteristics used by an individual for him- or herself. To measure importance of an identity characteristic by location, a list of twenty-two characteristics was given to subjects (for example my popularity and attractiveness to other people; places where I live or where I was brought up; membership in various groups; my emotions and feelings). These characteristics had to be rated twice, once for importance and once to indicate the subjective location of each characteristic. An internal location was defined as feeling like a part of oneself, an external location as feeling like a part of one's environment or one's surroundings. The most internal characteristics were thought to be: 'emotions and feelings'; 'thoughts and ideas, the way my mind works'; 'the ways I cope with my fears and anxieties, with the stresses and strains of living'; 'my dreams and my imagination'; 'the ways I deal with my good and loving feelings'. The most external ones were thought to be: 'membership that I have of various groups'; 'my work'; 'things I own, my possessions'; 'places where I live or where I was brought up'; 'my race or ethnic background'.

These results demonstrate empirically that the definition of one's identity, one's self-concept, arises for many individuals through features of the spatial–physical environment and place in the social structure. Correlations between location of important identity characteristics and the various personality measures of internal–external location show that, with the exception of locus of control, all are related (between $r = .43$ for locus of attribution and $r = .71$ for Sampson's IO). These correlations are interpreted as telling how the orientation varies as a function of each characteristic's environmental location. Of the internal–external scales, self-monitoring and Sampson's IO also show significantly different correlations with importance of internal and external characteristics.

The orientation of the self-concept

Data on self-importance and location

In a study which I conducted, students of the University of Heidelberg were asked to rate the location in reference to their self-concept of items from the (translated) list of items from Sampson and also indicate how *important* these items were to their own self-concept. This essentially followed the procedure described by Sampson (1978). However, Sampson had evidently not related the importance and location ratings to each other, but had rather constructed lists of internally and externally located characteristics without taking importance into account. Of particular interest here, however, was the actual relationship between internal–external location and importance to the self-concept. The correlations of the ratings are shown in Table 4.1.

Table 4.1 *Correlation of the importance of aspects of self-concept with their location*

r	Content of self-concept
− .77	My religion
− .71	My background
− .70	My possessions
− .70	My sex, being male or female
− .68	Places where I live or where I was brought up
− .67	My role of being a student
− .61	My family
− .59	My studies or my work
− .57	My dreams and my imagination
− .57	My gestures and mannerisms, the way I express myself
− .56	My values and ethics
− .56	The ways I deal with my good and loving feelings
− .55	The ways I have of influencing and affecting others
− .54	Membership that I have of various groups
− .53	My intellectual abilities
− .53	My physical features (height, body shape, face, etc.)
− .50	The ways I cope with my fears and anxieties
− .47	My future goals and aspirations
− .46	My close friends
− .46	My popularity and attractiveness to other people
− .38	My emotions and feelings
− .37	My thoughts and ideas, the way my mind works

As was to be expected, all correlations obtained were negative. This indicates that, in general, a relationship exists such that more externally located aspects are considered to be less important and the internal ones more important to the self-concept. However, the strength of the negative correlation coefficient can be interpreted as an indication of the degree of a general, shared understanding that this relationship exists. If the correlation is high, a general consensus exists about the relationship between an aspect's importance and its location vis-à-vis the self-concept. For the list provided above, this is the case for those variables related to social structure, for instance age, sex, religion, and similar variables related to role-identities. On the other hand, the correlations between importance and location become smaller as the aspects of the self-concept are more related to very personal and idiosyncratic characteristics. In other words, social structural variables usually have an assigned generally shared importance in relation to the self-concept. Personal, psychological variables vary considerably on the relationship between the dimensions of location and importance. Stryker (personal communication) suggested that this, in connection with other data, argues that 'idiosyncratic' elements are important as definers of self to persons themselves, whereas social structural locations are important to others in defining the person.

Identity mastery

Sampson relates his approach to a process of *identity mastery* that has implications and similarities to the processes of self-concept change discussed here. He bases his analysis on the following assumptions:

> 1. Persons are motivated to accomplish a stability and a continuity to their identity, to accomplish a sense of self-sameness. This process is termed identity mastery.
> 2. The process of identity mastery involves attempts to manage and control one's internal and external environments.
> 3. Individuals differ in their orientation to a particular environment. Some are oriented more towards the internal and others more towards the external environment.
> 4. Individual's environmental location will affect both the location of the identity characteristics by which they define themselves and the particular characteristics that must be managed in order to accomplish identity mastery. Thus, externally oriented persons come to define their identity in terms of externally located characteristics (e.g., places, possessions, etc) and will attempt to manage these aspects of the external environment in order to maintain their sense of selfsameness. By contrast, internally oriented persons come to define their identity in terms of internally located characteristics and will seek to manage these aspects of the internal environment in order to maintain their sense of self-sameness. (Sampson, 1978, pp. 566–7)

Again, as Snyder's construct of self-monitoring, Sampson's construct of location of identity is formulated as a lasting personality disposition. As such, the construct makes some valuable contributions to the model of self-concept change as it is developed here: the process called identity mastery is an active process related to the continuity of the self-concept. Where Sampson refers only to stability, it may also be applied to change if the

The orientation of the self-concept

self-concept has been destabilized and is not reconstructed in its previous form. Further, Sampson states that identity mastery involves the management and control of the internal and external environment. This statement clearly relates management of the self-concept to the management over the external environment, consisting of elements such as membership of social structures, work, personal belongings, and places where one lives. This management is a process closely related to the concept of construction of the ecology of the self described in Chapter 1. For persons having an external location of identity, Sampson expects their sense of 'selfsameness', that is, continuity in the self-concept, to be more threatened by events in the external environment, for instance disaster, sudden illness, separation or divorce, retirement, or threats to property. Such events are those that are conceivable as events destabilizing the ecology of the self-concept, and thus leading to the necessity to restructure it. The main distinction of the present model of self-concept change from Sampson's conceptualization of identity location as a personality characteristic is the same as with self-monitoring: rather than thinking of it as a lasting disposition, it also appears to be an appropriate orientation if internal elements of the self-concept have been threatened, questioned, or invalidated. In that case, elements of the self-concept will be rebuilt from the outside in, and external location of identity and social monitoring are adaptive orientations for that stage in the process.

5 Social psychological theories on maintenance and change

Self-concept maintenance and its failure

Some prominent recent theories in social psychology perceive of the self mainly as a defender of the status quo: self-verification (Swann, 1983) and self-evaluation maintenance (Tesser & Campbell, 1983). Others conceive of the self as striving toward a goal (self-completion: Wicklund & Gollwitzer, 1982). Only some isolated attempts have been made within experimental social psychology to understand the processes of *change* (for example by Hayden, 1979). I will now consider these approaches in turn and, where maintenance rather than change is concerned, search for implications for the understanding of change processes.

Self-verification

Swann's notion of self-verification is based on the idea that people prefer evidence confirming their own views of themselves. This preference is seen to exist especially in those whose self-concept is well articulated. Based on his review of attempts at changing the self-concept in clinical settings, in field research, and even in prisoner-of-war camps (for another review of related evidence, see Shrauger & Schoeneman, 1979), Swann's treatment of self-verification processes relies on the assumption of the basic immutability of the self-concept.

To support their views of themselves, people engage in various social and cognitive processes that are supposed to verify their own view of themselves. Socially, they will build an 'opportunity structure' for the self, that is, a social situation supporting their self-concept. To this end, according to Swann, three strategies are available: (a) the acquisition of signs and symbols of who they are (see also Wicklund & Gollwitzer, 1982), (b) being selective in their choice of interaction partners, and (c) using certain interaction strategies ('interpersonal prompts'). The strategies described by Swann are similar to those described by Snyder in his discussion of low self-monitors' seeking out of certain social situations. Cognitively, according to Swann, people will tend to overestimate and pay more attention to self-concept

Self-concept maintenance and its failure

confirmatory information. They are motivated to encode and retrieve such feedback. Ambiguous information will be interpreted as supporting their own view of themselves.

Self-verification is described as a routine activity, but also discussed in its implications for crises in one's self-concept at choice points. A choice point in the self-concept is one where decisions have to be made that have significant implications for how one is going to be perceived by others in the future, such as in the choice of a profession or a spouse. A crisis may also occur if a person receives self-discrepant feedback that may threaten the confidence one has in one's self-concept. Self-discrepant feedback is especially potent if it comes from a competent source, is supported by several people, is directly relevant to an important dimension of the self-concept, and is sufficiently different from the individual's self-perception without being so outrageous so as to be dismissed. In a crisis, following Swann's analysis, attention will be focused on to the threatened dimension of the self-concept, and self-confirmatory information will be highly accessible and may be used to guide behaviour. If made uncertain of their self-conceptions, people will make use of their aspirations and goals to seek out information. This description is very similar to the analysis of parallel situations in the context of self-awareness theory. There, an interruption of a task or another event focusing attention on the self was said to lead to a behavioural adherence to personal standards.

Swann suggests two basic ways that may lead to self-concept change rather than to successful maintenance. One is mainly associated with maturation and aging. When the community recognizes a change in an individual, it correspondingly treats that person differently; for instance adolescents after puberty are increasingly treated as adults. Alternatively, Swann suggests that persons may bring about change in their existing opportunity structure when they notice a discrepancy between their self-view and their opportunity structure. Swann (1982) relates *inter*personal and *intra*personal processes leading to self-concept change:

> At the intrapersonal level, people must reorganize their self-view, they must decide that they are not the persons they once thought they were. This step in the process is critical, since if people harbor doubts about their 'true selves' they may behave in ways that will verify and confirm their old self-concept, thereby undermining the change process ... For the self-concept change to be lasting, the individuals around her must validate and legitimize her new self-view. Thus, changes in self-views will be lasting only when there is a corresponding shift in the individual's social environment. (Swann, 1982, p. 40)

In its recognition that change does not occur in the cognitive structure but rather in the interpersonal environment through building an appropriate social support structure, Swann is in agreement with a basic assumption of the ecological approach to self-concept change which I propose. The starting point for Swann's treatment of self-verification processes is assumptions from symbolic interactionism that stress the close relationship between one's social environment and one's view of oneself. In parallel to more current statements originating from symbolic interactionist thinking that see the self as a social product and a social force (Rosenberg, 1981; Stryker, 1980), he too emphasizes that self-conceptions are determinants, as well as social products, of social reality.

Swann realizes that self-verification may fail, and processes of self-concept change may take over. It is important, however, that he conceives of change as a maintenance failure. Arguments suggesting the malleability of the concept (see, for instance, Gergen, 1977; Tedeschi & Lindskold, 1976) are rejected by Swann because studies supporting this argument focus on very recent events when they elicit a person's self-view (see also Schwarz, 1987, on cognitive judgment processes and the discussion in Chapter 7 below of self-concept measurement).

Indeed, I agree with Swann that empirical evidence and theoretical perspectives on the self-concept support the notion of long-term stability. He is certainly correct in suggesting that laboratory-induced changes in self-ratings are not relevant to actual self-concept change. However, this must not imply that change does not occur or is not worth studying. The study of self-concept processes relevant to *change* can greatly contribute to the understanding of the nature of the self. If self-concept change, and the circumstances surrounding it are identified, a theoretical analysis based on the understanding of the processes solely as maintenance failure may be inadequate and concentrate only on some specific social and cognitive processes to the exclusion of others. In particular, I argue that agentic processes, that is, active choice processes, involved in the acquisition of new elements of the self-concept cannot be part of such a theoretical conception that focuses on failure.

Self-completion theory

'A theory of symbolic self-completion' has been presented by Wicklund and Gollwitzer (1982). The theory conceives of the human as striving toward self-defining goals. It describes the process of striving toward those goals by drawing on *motivational* psychological processes and on *social recognition* as processes relating to the social environment, and it includes a consideration of the handling of elements in the non-living environment as signs and indicators (called 'symbols' by the authors) of a certain state of the self-concept in relation to the self-defining goal. By recognizing the goal-striving nature of humans, Wicklund and Gollwitzer claim to have built on early

Lewinian theory (Lewin, 1926), and by emphasizing the role of social reality for the individual, they incorporated symbolic interactionist thinking from Cooley (1902) and Mead (1934).

The theory has as its starting point persons who have a commitment to a goal or aspiration, such as to become a successful doctor, musician or athlete. The commitment to the goal implies a striving toward that goal through appropriate behaviour and through the use of objects as indicators of striving toward the goal. For instance, if the goal is to become a musician, the possession of a valuable instrument can serve as such an indicator. Titles, uniforms, or certain behavioural acts can also be used as indicators. A person makes use of these indicators if the self-defining goal cannot be reached directly. Then, the display of an indicator implies progress toward the self-defining goal. In principle, Wicklund and Gollwitzer consider indicators to be substitutable for each other.

Within the framework of self-completion theory, the use of symbols as indicators of goal-striving activity requires that they are socially recognized, that a *social reality* exists of their meaning. However, it is not for self-presentational purposes that indicators are displayed: their psychological function is to reduce the goal-striving tension. The theory thus emphasizes the importance of the social environment for the individual under conditions that are unrelated to strategical self-presentation, but are used instead for a non-strategic approach to self-construction.

Self-completion theory can be summarized as follows: (1) A person must be committed to a self-defining goal. (2) Self-symbolizing becomes necessary if the direct way toward the self-defining goal is interrupted. (3) A self-symbolization that is recognized by others, that is, has acquired a social reality, is especially effective. A series of experiments has addressed several aspects of the theory, and has demonstrated the importance of the constructs of substitution and social reality in individual's striving toward goals.

Identities are in this theoretical approach thought of as *constructed* identities. An identity is defined by a goal-orientation. In order to reach that goal, the person has to make use of indicators, of which a great variety for each identity exist, and has to construct the way toward that identity. The social context provides recognition of indicators for an identity. To this point, the theory has parallels to approaches coming out of symbolic interactionism. However, the social environment is for Wicklund and Gollwitzer just that − a *context*, whereas sociological approaches (see Rosenberg, 1981) consider the actual interaction between social environment and self. This implies also that for Wicklund and Gollwitzer *social recognition* is at the core of the concept of social reality, rather than the *shared meaning* of the symbols that has been acquired in interaction.

While this implements ideas from Cooley and Mead, the elements of the theory fall short of interactionistic qualities.

Rather than self-*concepts*, self-*definitions* are at the core of this theory. A self-definition is defined as an orientation toward a goal that, when reached, implies readiness to behave in certain ways. Self-definitions are more specific and involve only some elements of a self-concept. Further, they require a personal commitment. In most studies by Wicklund and Gollwitzer, commitment in the context of self-completion theory has been operationalized behaviourally: whether a person regularly acts in a way indicating a striving toward the self-defining goal, for instance how frequently an aspiring musician practises. Commitment is not defined as a *social* construct — otherwise an overlap with the construct of social recognition might become evident.

To summarize, self-completion theory sees humans as actively constructing their identity through the manipulation of elements in their environments in a social context. It emphasizes the active element in the construction of identity, and allows for choice. Unlike in many other social psychological theories, the social environment is here seen as supporting one's self-concept rather than as a cue for the strategic self-presentation that distorts the self-concept.

What implications does the theory have for self-concept change? It seems to describe processes as they take place *after* a decision has been made for a certain self-definition. It does not address how or why such a definition has been made in the first place, or under which conditions the self-definition has to be abandoned. The need for active construction and social recognition implies the possibility of failure. One way a self-definition may fail, and thus need to be completely replaced, may be a lack of social reality.

The assumption that symbols, or indicators, are substitutable implies their identical meaning. This assumption may not always hold. Each symbol carries with it connotations that may reflect on the individual who is displaying it. For instance, for a university professor either a long list of publications or a large number of theses supervised may serve as symbols. According to Wicklund and Gollwitzer, these should be substitutable. However, they are only exchangeable on a very low level of identity construction. Both imply very different types of global identity. By using them interchangeably at an early point, choices of certain acts or symbols toward the goal are implied for the further career (i.e. teaching or research). Therefore, I would argue that symbols always carry with them surplus meanings that may have implications for further choice. The substitution of symbols would seem possibly to alter and influence the course a self-definition may take in its specific realization. The doctoral student committed to teaching may end up at a teaching-intensive college with many student contact hours, and the doctoral student committed to research and writing will go to a research institute. Starting out from the same self-defining goal, both have reached different identities by making use of symbols and activities that, according to self-completion theory, should have been substitutable. The use and meaning of symbols, as well as the acts and choices implied, can thus shed light on processes of change at least as far as adaptation is concerned.

Self-evaluation maintenance

Social reality is also at the core of another closely related theory: self-evaluation maintenance (SEM: Tesser & Campbell, 1983). According to this approach, people are motivated to maintain a positive self-evaluation. One's self-evaluation is strongly influenced by social circumstances. Social circumstances exert their influence through two complementary processes, a *reflection* process and a *comparison* process. Reflection is a process whereby an individual participates in the achievements of others by association. It depends on the psychological closeness, and the quality of another's performance. Reflection can thus raise one's self-evaluation via association. Comparison with another can also influence, that is, raise or lower self-evaluation, depending on the same factors as reflection, namely closeness and performance quality. Tesser and Campbell thereby emphasize the self-evaluation-enhancing properties of social closeness and others' performance.

The relative importance of these processes is determined by the relevance of the performance dimension of the other to one's own self-definition. A close relationship with someone who does well on some dimension can raise one's self-evaluation via the reflection process, if this dimension is not one in which to excel involves the individual's own self-definition. For instance, my friend's success as a piano player raises my own self-evaluation because being a piano player is not part of my own self-concept. On the other hand, his success as a soccer player may lower my own self-evaluation because this is a field in which I hope to make a fortune as a professional. That is, if being in close association with someone who performs well can make one's own performance look bad by comparison, self-evaluation on that dimension can be lowered and thus lead to a reduced importance of that dimension to the self-definition.

The comparison process, leading to potentially lower self-evaluation if the other excels, and the reflection process, leading to potentially higher self-evaluation if the other excels, depend on performance and closeness in the same way. Importance by implication depends on the extent to which the performance dimension is relevant to the individual's self-definition. If closeness and performance are held constant, the better another's relative performance on a particular dimension, the less self-definitional that dimension will become to the individual.

Speculating on the implications of their theoretical approach for self-concept change, Tesser and Campbell suggest a distinction between emotional and performance dimensions of the self-concept. They presume a higher stability of the self on emotional dimensions, since these are presumably less susceptible to persuasion attempts because of their affective quality, and since they are adopted early in life and should have developed a strong social support system. On the other hand, performance dimensions (for example faster, higher, better than) are derived more directly from social comparison processes implying cognitive operations that are acquired later in development than emotions. This statement addresses only the relative malleability of performance over emotion dimensions. Overall, investment in particular performances and public commitment serve to make performance dimensions also relatively stable.

Generally, Tesser and Campbell's SEM-model operates on the assumption that humans are motivated to stabilize and enhance their self-esteem. Their model is one of stability rather than change. Emotional aspects are assumed to be more stable, and only very specific performance aspects are assumed to be malleable, as long as not much investment in time and effort and no public commitment have been made. In turn, change is only implied when a particular dimension or aspect of the self-concept comes to be less self-definitional as a result of a comparison process because another person is better on that aspect. That way, some aspects may lose importance, and others may give rise to new importance by basking in reflected glory. As compared to, for instance, self-completion theory or most theories deriving from symbolic interactionism, identities are not considered by this theory to be actively constructed. Rather, the human in the SEM-model is subject to social forces without contributing anything actively to the construction of his or her own identity.

The preceding theories, self-verification, self-completion, and self-evaluation maintenance, share many elements. They all start with the assumption of a basically stable self-concept and a unidirectional drive toward further stabilization and maintenance of the self-concept. They are critical of short-term attempts to change self-descriptions in the laboratory, and observe under the same short-term conditions cognitive and behavioural attempts to stabilize. Campbell, Gollwitzer, Swann, Tesser, and Wicklund recognize the importance of the social environment for the self-concept, though they differ in the degree to which they assign active and passive roles to the individual and the social environment. Self-verification and self-completion theorists have a view of humans as actively constructing their identities once a goal is identified. Other ways in which individual elements of the self-concept can be conceived, constructed, and implemented in the whole self-concept will now be discussed.

The emergence of knowledge about oneself

The approach to self-concept change presented here tries to include both active change and passive adaptation, and to cover processes leading to the exclusion of former elements of the self-concept and processes of the acquisition of new knowledge about the self. The emergence of knowledge about oneself is a part of the processes through which new elements of the self-concept come to replace old ones.

Self-perception theory

One of the most widely recognized theories addressing the acquisition of knowledge about oneself is Bem's (1972) self-perception theory. Self-perception theory starts with the assumption that under certain conditions a person observing him- or herself is largely in the same situation as an outside observer when it comes to inferring internal states:

> Individuals come to 'know' their own attitudes, emotions, and other internal states partially by inferring them from observations of their own overt behavior and/or the circumstances in which this behavior occurs. To the extent that internal cues are weak, ambiguous, or uninterpretable, the individual is functionally in the same position as an outside observer, an observer who must necessarily rely upon those same external cues to infer the individual's internal states.
> (Bem, 1972, p. 5)

These two statements on inference and ambiguity contain the core of Bem's theory. When a person is ambiguous or insecure about an internal state, he or she will observe his or her own behaviour and the circumstances of that behaviour. If the behaviour seems to be situationally explainable, or '*mand*ed' by the environment, then it is uninformative about a temporary or lasting state of the person. A *mand* is a behavioural reaction under control of the environment. If, on the other hand, such control of the environment over a person's behaviour cannot be found, its origin has to be attributed to some inner state of that person. This is the position an outside observer is in when trying to determine the thoughts, attitudes, or feelings of another. According to Bem's self-perception theory, the same technique can be used to obtain information about oneself, namely through the observation of one's own behaviour and its contingencies.

The statements of the theory are straightforward, and were tested in various contexts. It has met with criticism mainly from those who presumed that a general principle was stated and who did not take seriously the restrictions expressed in the terms 'partially' and 'weak, ambiguous, or uninterpretable'. This wording, of course, leaves other ways of knowing about one's own state. However, many states about which persons have clear knowledge about themselves started out in ambiguity. In particular, a person whose self-concept has been questioned, or who finds him- or herself in unfamiliar environments, is particularly likely to have problems interpreting many new experiences. Such conditions are indeed likely to be the ones described by Bem.

Two implications for self-concept change should be considered, namely that new knowledge about the self is acquired by acting, and that it is acquired at times of uncertainty. Acquisition by acting means that *behaviour* precedes the *cognition* about the self. Knowledge about the self can be acquired by performing certain acts, or behaving in new ways, and deducing from that certain states of oneself that, if they occur repeatedly or are interpreted as lasting characteristics, become part of the self-concept. The theory of act-identification (Vallacher & Wegner, 1985), to be discussed in detail later, addresses these issues. Exposure to new environments, to new possibilities for activity, or to new role models provides plenty of opportunity for behavioural acts that have not been performed before and thus require interpretation.

Exposure to novel environments and behaviours is also likely to induce uncertainty about the conditions of the environment that elicit a certain behaviour, whereas many of the conditions discussed as promoting self-concept change, namely questioning of one's view of oneself, induce uncertainty about one's own internal states. While uncertainty about the *internal* state requires interpretation, as stated by Bem, uncertainty about the *external* conditions has not been addressed directly by the theory. However, different interpretations of the objectively identical contingencies of behaviour may determine whether a cognition is accepted as an element of the self-concept.

In a study by Fishbein and Laird (1979), subjects were uncertain about their internal state (i.e. the meaning of a score on a test) and ambiguous about the conditions under which they described that state to others: further cues made them seem to be either voluntary or else involuntary. Disclosure under voluntary conditions led to a more positive self-attitude on the dimension supposedly covered by the test ('If I tell it to others, it can't be that bad'), and under involuntary conditions, to a more negative self-perception ('If I'd rather keep it to myself, it must mean something bad').

Similarly, a new environment induces uncertainty about the conditions under which a behaviour is performed, so that it is not only the internal state which is uncertain. This may lead to an almost inadvertent acquisition of knowledge about oneself, and thus offer an explanation for processes of adaptation to new environments. For instance a person may behave in a certain way, but because of unfamiliarity with the environment he or she may not be able to judge the contingencies of the behaviour, therefore attributing an actually environmentally controlled behaviour to an internal state. In another process taking place in new environments, the performance of new behaviour may require a focus of attention on the environmental conditions enabling that behaviour. Over time, as certain behaviours become more familiar, they require less outside attention and may be interpreted as not being performed under environmental control. That way, as acts become routinized, they may be more likely to be used as descriptions of internal states. Both of the processes discussed, unfamiliarity and routinization, describe in terms of self-perception theory the adaptation to new environments and the acquisition of new and changing knowledge about oneself.

Action identification

Self-perception theory is applied to single instances of acts providing information about the acquisition of isolated elements of self-knowledge. Vallacher and Wegner (1985) address the ways in which individual acts are identified on increasingly higher levels of meaning and then incorporated into the self-concept. They start with the observation that any action can be identified in several different ways: 'hitting a key on the keyboard' is a very low level, 'writing a word' a higher level, and 'completing the book manuscript' a still higher level of identification of the same single act. The levels of identification are hierarchically ordered and can be related to each other through 'by'-implications: 'I complete a book *by* writing words. I write words *by* hitting keys.'

At any point in time, there is only one identity that is cognitively represented in an act. Three principles define the conditions under which identities are maintained and changed. These principles form the core of the theory: (1) An action is *maintained* in terms of its pre-potent identity. (2) When an action *can* be identified at both a higher and a lower level, there will be a tendency for the higher-level identity to become pre-potent. (3) When an action *cannot* be maintained in terms of its pre-potent identity, there will be a tendency for a lower-level identity to become pre-potent.

Vallacher and Wegner use action identification also as a means to explain how persons come to define themselves. Superordinate levels of action identification move from being merely descriptive ('doing') to being ascriptive ('being'). As persons move on to higher levels of action identification, common themes emerge that not only identify action but are also used to guide action. For instance, different low-level acts (watching television, taking a bath, going to class) may all be identified on a higher level as 'enjoying life', thus suggesting one general life theme that guides further action and is part of the person's self-concept.

Identities for actions can also be suggested by the social environment. Higher-level entities may emerge as a result of feedback from the social environment, thus changing the person's understanding of his or her own actions. This is particularly likely in situations where people have to perform novel or unfamiliar acts for which the person cannot initially provide high-level identifications. Identifications offered from the social environment are therefore likely to be at a higher level, and hence are likely to be accepted.

Several theoretical approaches consider the self-concept as implying a readiness for action. Vallacher and Wegner's action identification theory describes the complete cycle from individual acts that form self-themes which imply readiness for action: a self-concept is built from the identification of individual acts at constantly higher levels that suggest common themes which in turn imply the possibility of other acts serving that self-theme. Certain acts would not have been undertaken had previous acts not acquired a common self-defining action theme.

This cycle can be related to processes of self-concept change as I conceive them. The questioning of an existing identity, or the disruption of a social structure relating to a specific identity, implies in terms of action identification theory that the identification of one's actions through a given self-concept cannot be maintained. In other words, questioning or interruption means that a certain concept of self has to be given up. The person has to go down to a lower level of action identification that falls short of providing unifying self-themes. To build new elements to be incorporated into the self-concept, new self-themes in Vallacher and Wegner's language, means to start from action. Novel behaviours and acts rise in the action identification hierarchy with increasing familiarity, and thereby acquire meaning for the self-concept by sharing common themes at higher levels of action identification.

Vallacher and Wegner's action identification theory demonstrates how elements of the self-concept acquire meaning, and how the self-concept is an emergent entity. In addition, and unlike many other theoretical approaches, they consider in their third principle the possibility of interruption from the outside that leads to a central element of one's self-concept and to the necessity for changing the self-concept through rebuilding it. The authors themselves do not claim that their theory can address all qualities a self-concept may possess, but the theory provides a general framework for understanding the self-concept as maintaining and organizing coherent action.

Possibilities for self-concept change

The question of change in self-related cognitions has very rarely been addressed directly. As has been argued here in the context of several theories that discuss self-concept change, usually only failed maintenance is implied, whereas studies that claim to address self-concept change are usually only investigations of change in individual attitudes or cognitions or more superficial self-images rather than complex self-concepts. One exception is Hayden (1979).

Hayden, along with Kelly (1955), Vernon (1963), and Epstein (1973), defines the self as a set of hierarchically ordered constructs, that is, of evaluations, interpretations, hypotheses, or postulates, that serve to interpret and anticipate one's own behaviour. The constructs serve as conceptual anchors through which a person defines him- or herself. The activity of interpreting and anticipating meaning is conceived as taking place on constructs of bipolar dimension, for instance, good versus bad.

The constructs of the self-system are linked to each other through inferential links or implicative relationships. An individual construct, by being linked to other constructs, gains meaning because it implies at the same time other predictions or constructs. The more implications an individual construct possesses, the more meaning it acquires for the self-concept. Thus, the meaning of each construct depends on its *implicative capacity*.

The notion of implicative capacity can be related to other notions that stabilize cognitions, attitudes, self-concepts, or person impressions. In a sociological sense, commitment to an identity is defined by Becker (1964) through the number of implications a certain role-identity carries with it. In the perception of another person, implicit personality theory (Schneider, 1973) links perceived behaviours to traits and observed traits to other unobserved traits, thus very quickly stabilizing the perception of a person. In conceptions of the mental representation of the self, notions of cognitive networks define the stability of cognition through the number of relationships to other cognitions. Thus, the notion of implicative capacity is a familiar one, accounting for stability, and is used here to provide a definition of the 'meaning' of self-related constructs.

Hayden (1979) relates the meaning, or implicative capacity, directly to its capacity for change. The possibilities for self-originating, agentic self-construct change depend on the meaningfulness of the possible alternative: 'With regard to self-defined change, the individual would change only if the alternative view provided more meaning and greater opportunities to elaborate the conceptual system' (p. 547).

Hayden's notion of the self consists of a hierarchically ordered system of constructs, containing a *current* and an *ideal* view of self, that possesses a specific number of implications which operationalize their meaningfulness. To test the notion that change is only considered possible by an individual if the alternative provides more meaningfulness, Hayden used a Kelly-grid, consisting of the subject and the nine people most important to the subject. For sets of three persons each (subject and two others), a bipolar construct had to be named on which two members of the triplet were different from the third. Thus, ten bipolar constructs were generated. In a second session, subjects considered each of the twenty poles of their particular constructs, and 'decided whether or not, given this quality as true of a stranger, any of the other poles also would be applicable or true'. Finally, resistance to change was measured. Each construct was paired with every other construct, and subjects had to indicate which of the two they would be more willing to change. This allows, for each construct pole, an analysis of a subject's receptivity or resistance to change.

A greater number of subjects resisted constructs on which the shift to the alternative pole would have meant a shift to fewer rather than more implications relative to the current status of self. There was also a greater number of constructs on which the shift was to a pole carrying a larger rather than a smaller number of implications relative to the current status of self. This supports the notion that, if they change, people move to the pole possessing the greater number of implications: 'subjects in general sought to maintain or increase the view of self's implicative capacity either by shifting towards more implications or actively resisting a shift which would have reduced meaningfulness'' (p. 552). If the preferred pole was avoided, it was because shifting to it would have involved a greater number of potential changes among the inferential links between the discordant construct (i.e. real does not equal ideal) and the other constructs within the overall conceptual system. This may imply that the initiation of self-concept change requires 'the ability to imagine change along self-defined dimensions and then elaborate the conceptual system so as to ensure an increase in meaning may precede a behavioral change' (p. 555).

Hayden provides a clear operationalization of stability and resistance to change, namely the number of implications a construct possesses for other elements of the self-concept. A motivation may be implied to strive toward higher complexity, which carries with it more implications. This would mean that the self-concept is a system that continually strives toward greater stability. Even change is considered only if it increases the implicative capacity of personal constructs, so that the function of change, too, is an increase in stability. Planned change requires complex cognitive processes in assessing the implicative potential of the alternative routes. If a person does not possess the cognitive capacity for this cognitive anticipation, a status quo would be preferred where change affects a minimum of implications.

Summary

A model such as Hayden's looks at the self-concept as a closed cognitive system. Consequently, it has problems taking into account the possibility of outside interference with the system of cognitive representations of self which a person already possesses. Influences from the outside can reduce the number of implications a construct has, and thus the meaningfulness of the person's self-concept. For instance, changes in rules, morals, social expectations, or others occurring outside the individual can influence the implications a certain construct has. Meaning has been defined by Hayden as a *personal* concept. However, meaning should be defined as a *social* concept because implications are also derived from common social experiences and expectations. Meaning and implicative capacity cannot be seen as divorced from a social context, and as long as that is the case, changes in the social context can affect a personal construct and self-concept by changing the implications of individual constructs.

By pointing to the consequences that the complex structures of implicative links have for the self-concept, Hayden's approach makes clear that the study of change in isolated attitudes and superficial self-images has no place in self-concept research. Implicative capacity as operationalization of meaning is an important contribution to explaining the form that planned change can take. However, it neglects the social nature of the self-concept by defining change only as an internal cognitive process.

A summary of social psychological contributions to self-concept change

This chapter has discussed a wide variety of recent theoretical and empirical approaches to the self-concept that were chosen on the basis of their relevance to the framework for self-concept change presented here. These theoretical approaches have some basic themes and elements in common, whereas some others vary. I will first summarize what seems to be common to the current view of the self-concept, its development and change.

Social psychologists currently think of the self-concept as a cognitive structure that organizes experiences and guides action. It is a dynamic structure, constantly acquiring new cognitions that are related to existing cognitions about the self and are therefore more likely to add stability to that structure. Indeed, the acquisition of knowledge that stabilizes the self-concept is fostered, whereas knowledge inconsistent with a person's self-concept is likely to be rejected. This basis is common to almost all current treatments of the self-concept.

The self-concept is a social construct. It is an almost universal basis for self-concept research – though not always explicit – that cognitions about the self can only be socially acquired. Self-concept-related processes require a social context. For some theorists, the focus remains on the psychological processes within the individual; others conceptualize the social nature of the self-concept as being interactionistic, that is, they think of the self-concept as a social product and a social force.

For some theorists, self-definitions are goals that are set and then filled by action and symbols. For other theorists, self-definitions emerge out of single acts. The first approach has the conception of a human as constructing an identity; in the other, identity is emergent. Neither necessarily excludes the other, but both can be complementary ways of acquiring identities.

Most of what has been called self-concept change in empirical, experimental research, and referred to as suggesting the malleability of the self, is only change in superficial cognitive structure, for instance in isolated cognitions about oneself or temporary self-images. This research does not explain how larger cognitive structures, or elements of the self-concept, come to change. Because from one point of view, the self-concept is a complex system of interrelated cognitions, or of implicative constructs, from another point of view, studies involving isolated aspects of self have little to say about self-concept change.

Some of the work reported directly takes into account the relationship between internal and external elements of the self-concept. It is recognized that elements relevant to the self-concept can be located outside a person, and still considered to be part of the self. For other theorists, the social environment has the capability of providing guidance in a way similar to the self-concept, and it is suggested that the arrangement of the social and physical environment is used in constructing identities.

These are the elements most theorists would agree upon. However, theorists clearly differ in the emphasis they put on various parts of the common ground. For some, the social nature of the self-concept is an integral part of their theoretical conception; for others, it provides only a background. For some, the human is subject to basic forces toward maintenance of self-concept and self-esteem, acting principally in ways supporting these two goals. For others, humans are conceived of as making choices, as defining goals, as identifying and interpreting what they are doing, and as selecting future behaviours on the basis of their choices.

The present theories make some suggestions about the circumstances under which one is forced to change the self-concept: unfavourable comparison with another and blocking a self-relevant goal are examples. Self-concept change is addressed by almost all only as the failure of maintenance. Little attention is paid to why a self-concept may fail, perhaps because a cognitive approach pays little attention to external events that can, in turn, basically alter the structure of cognitions. Because

Summary

the failure of self-concepts is not addressed, even those theorists who recognize the agentic nature of humans do not identify the point at which such choices are made. Therefore, while all of the theories discussed address some points in processes that have to do with self-concept change, none take into account the social structure and at the same time addresses the whole cycle of a self-concept that becomes destabilized and then reconstructed.

6 Sociological approaches to the self-concept and change

Psychologists and sociologists, when citing the common roots of their conceptions of self, emphasize the role of G. H. Mead's (1934) conceptualization of the relationship between mind, self, and society. While psychologically orientated social psychologists, as could be seen in the preceding chapter, are more likely to focus on the relation between mind and self, sociologically orientated social psychologists are more likely to focus on the relation between self and society. This chapter will deal with some recent theoretical and empirical approaches from that perspective. Most of this work is in the tradition of symbolic interactionism, especially the social structural version, and role theory.

The self-concept and social structure

The sociological approach to self-concept research shares the basic assumption with the psychological approach, traceable back to James (1890), Cooley (1902), and Mead (1934), that

> the self-concept is conceptualized as an organization (structure) of various identities and attributes, and their evaluations, developed out of the individual's reflexive, social, and symbolic activities. As such, the self-concept is an experiential, mostly cognitive phenomenon accessible to scientific inquiry. (Gecas, 1982, p. 4)

Sociologists give special emphasis to the social nature of the person's sense of self. The human is conceived of as a product of the interaction between individual and society. Bryson (1945) points out that these ideas originated in the eighteenth century with the Scottish moral philosophers (David Hume, Adam Smith, Adam Ferguson, and Francis Hutcheson), who provided a basis for the empirical study of society and the individual. Through the concept of 'sympathy', that is, the ability to put oneself in the place of others, these philosophers were able to provide a link between individual and society.

The more immediate roots of linking the person to the social context begin with William James (1890). James started with a very wide definition of the self: 'In its widest possible sense ... a man's Self is the sum total of all

Self-concept and social structure

that he CAN call his' (p. 291). He goes on to distinguish the material self (for instance, body, clothes, family, home, and possessions), the social self (the recognition of others), and the spiritual self (psychic abilities and dispositions).

The social self consists of the recognition a person gets from others. While recognition by others is a prerequisite for a social self, James's notion makes clear that it is not mere recognition of the person as it exists independently of the other, but that the resulting self is a product of interaction, because 'a man has as many social selves as there are individuals who recognize him and carry an image of him in their mind' (p. 294). In order to be distinct and dependent upon the other, a social self has to be the product of an interaction. James also recognizes the structure of the social environment which provides a sense of self: 'as the individuals who recognize him fall naturally into classes ... he has as many different selves as there are distinct *groups* of persons about whose opinion he cares' (p. 294). These short remarks by James about the social self carry in them the later fully developed notions of social structure, role, and role-identity.

How does a sense of self develop? Cooley (1902) provided a powerful metaphor that is still dominant in discussions of the development of the self: the looking-glass self. The self is reflected in the reactions of others to oneself, just as one is reflected in a mirror. One's own reaction to oneself is therefore the anticipated reaction of others to oneself. In Cooley's metaphor, the reflexive nature of the self becomes obvious. Reflection is a three-part process. It consists of the imagination of the perception through another, the imagination of being evaluated by the other, and an emotion aroused by this evaluation. Reflection is thus a prerequisite of the self-evaluative processes.

It was Mead (1934) who provided the most comprehensive theoretical system that brought the assumptions about the nature of the self and society together, and thus laid the common foundation for those groups of theories and approaches that have become known as 'symbolic interactionism'. Central to it is his thought that the person is a product of society. Society is based on a common set of symbols or meanings which originates from communication. The meaning of objects and symbols is acquired in ongoing social action; without that, objects do not have any meaning. The social and physical environment is constructed through a social process that assigns meaning to objects and others. An object or a gesture acquires meaning by being relevant to an act: activity is the basis from which meaning is derived. Because meaning results from social process, it is shared among the participants of social action. Persons anticipate the behaviour of others in interaction based on the shared meaning of significant symbols. The shared use of significant symbols thereby gives a common basis and order to social action.

The 'self', according to Mead, develops in the same way: it is an object that acquires meaning in social interaction. At the same time, however, it is the subject of social interaction. The reflexive nature of the human allows the duality of object and subject, and becomes a 'self': 'The self, as that which can be an object to itself, is essentially a social structure, and it arises in social experience' (p. 140). The self, being the product of social *inter*action, is therefore also a force on society.

The self as a process and the self-concept as its product are thereby linked to the individual social situation as well as the larger social structure. The social situation is the 'context in which identities are established and maintained through the process of social negotiation' (Gecas, 1982, p. 10). The larger social structure provides socially shared meanings for specific identities, that is, specific contents of the self-concept. Identities are frequently also referred to as internalized roles, making the connection between self-concept and social structure obvious.

These are the very basic assumptions of symbolic interactionism. A systematic, succinct summary of symbolic interactionism is provided by, for instance, Rose (1962). More recent summaries are provided by Clagett (1988), who describes the integration of social structure into symbolic interactionism, by Joas (1988), who emphasizes the contribution of symbolic interactionism to sociological theories of action, and by Stryker (1987b), who summarizes recent developments.

Different emphases on the importance of the social situation as a fluid *process* of interaction, and of the social *structure* as stable and organized, have historically led to the identification of two 'schools' of symbolic interactionism, the processual (or 'Chicago' school) and structural (or 'Iowa' school) interactionists. The former have commonly been associated with the attempt to capture the subjective and fluid element of social situations, the latter with the empirical investigation of the objective influence of social structure on the person. For many, these differentiations have carried with them different associations about the proper conduct of a science of human behaviour. In their extreme forms, they may be identified as humanistic, subjective, and interpretistic on one hand, and positivistic, nomothetic, and empirical on the other hand. However, there are recent attempts at disassociating schools, methods, and theories (e.g., Layder, 1982; McPhail, 1979). There seems to be no need, given the current variety of approaches within the wide framework symbolic interactionism offers, to assume any ideological stance that ties the theoretical framework to any particular position. Stryker (1980) makes the point eloquently but forcefully:

> There are certain views which serve as 'flags' in identifying those who take a dogmatic view of the ideas of symbolic interactionism, persons

> who tend to take stands not unlike members of a social movement. These include seeing humans as qualitatively different from other, nonhuman, animals, the focus being on symbolic interaction – and in particular language – as the differentiating feature; an insistence that internal communication made possible by symbolic capabilities removes humans from the deterministic world that nonhumans inhabit; the urging of the distinctive character of social science based on a view of determinism as an essential of conventional science; a consequent rejection of so-called hypothetical–deductive procedures and an insistence on a totally inductive stance: the assertion that 'meaning' cannot be captured in numerical terms and the rejection of quantitative work for that reason; the reliance on direct observation or on sympathetic introspection (à la Cooley); and the denial of the validity, under any circumstances, of the experiment or the survey as a source of sociological data. (Stryker, 1980, pp. 13–14)

Obviously, ideological and metatheoretical positions in symbolic interactionism are capable of raising tempers among those who are closely associated with it. I myself view the framework of symbolic interactionism from a greater distance, although as basic to the understanding of human nature and the self-concept, and therefore as subject to the same possibilities and problems associated with specific theoretical and methodological approaches as are other areas of investigation in the human and social sciences. The discussion of methods in the current context has therefore been taken up separately, disassociated from the theoretical assumptions of symbolic interactionism.

Some current approaches to the self-concept within the theoretical framework of symbolic interactionism will be discussed below, especially as they are relevant to self-concept change. Some key terms will emerge, such as 'identity', 'role', and 'commitment', and commonalities of these concepts across different approaches will be discussed.

Personal change in adult life

Symbolic interactionism has been used as a framework for analysing social *situations* and *processes* of socialization, or, in Rose's (1962) terms, it can be presented in analytic or in genetic form. If it can be used to explain the socialization of the child, as it is by Rose, it can also be applied to processes of socialization in adult life. Such an attempt has been undertaken by Becker (1964; 1968). Becker (1968) presents a definition of self that links individual changes to changes in social relationships through the role concept:

> The self consists, from one point of view, of all the roles we are prepared to take in formulating our own line of action, both the roles of individuals and of generalized others. From another and complementary

> view, the self is best conceived of as a process in which the roles of
> others are taken and made use of in organizing our own activities.
>
> (Becker, 1968, p. 197)

After presenting this definition, Becker goes on to state:

> The processual view has the virtue of reminding us that the self is not
> static, but rather changes as those we interact with change, either by
> being replaced with others or by themselves acting differently,
> presumably in response to still other changes in those they interact with.
>
> (Becker, 1968, p. 197)

In his definition and through its justification, Becker actually links a structural and a processual analysis. The process the individual undergoes in changing is directly related to changes in the social structure. In these definitions of the self, role transitions and changes in the self-concept are necessarily linked. Taking on a new role adds new dimensions to the self-concept. On the other hand, a change in the self requires the *readiness* to take on new and different roles. Becoming familiar with new roles, both by interacting with others and by taking over new roles, are therefore necessary prerequisites for self-concept change. A study of changes in the self-concept must be a study of the interactions a person has, the continuity and change in these interactions, and the relationships with the roles of the interaction partner.

Now that the process related to self-concept change has been defined, the conditions conducive to change need to be identified. Becker (1964) emphasizes two concepts as relevant to change and maintenance of the self-concept: situational *adjustment* as a condition for change and *commitment* to a role as a condition for stability. He presents the concept of situational adjustment as one that is similar to, but broader than, the concept of adult role learning:

> The person, as he moves in and out of a variety of social situations,
> learns the requirements of continuing in each situation and of success in
> it. If he has a strong desire to continue, the ability to assess accurately
> what is required, and can deliver the required performance, the indivi-
> dual turns himself into the kind of person the situation demands.
>
> (Becker, 1964, p. 44)

The individual learns certain behaviours as part of situational requirements. Becker's language can be translated into the psychological terminology of the preceding chapter: the acquisition of new behaviours requires a monitoring of the social situation (see Snyder, 1974), a commitment to a goal (see Wicklund & Gollwitzer, 1982), and an ability to anticipate implications (see Hayden, 1979). These are the social psychological components of the acquisition of a new role with which the individual identifies. Becker's interrelated definitions allow us to move from sociological structure to psychological process.

The condition fostering stability of the self-concept is commitment. The appearance of commitment is defined by Becker (1960) as a line of activity consistent over situations and time. A person can be committed to an activity, a set of activities, or a role. The crucial element achieving consistency is that a commitment creates a system of 'side bets': 'The committed person has acted in such a way as to involve other interests of his, originally extraneous to the action he is engaged in, directly in that action' (p. 35). The stabilizing function of a commitment is the result of its centrality in a pattern of social behaviours or roles. As long as a person has not yet entered a relevant commitment, these social acts or roles are not connected. Before entering into the commitment of taking a position in a business, a person's behaviour toward Ms A., or toward Mr B., or in the community may be completely unrelated. When someone enters a commitment, for instance as sales clerk in a local business, other behaviours and roles are locked into place. Ms A. is the boss, Mr B. is a customer, and the community looks upon the role-taker as a representative of his company. If one aspect of the system of roles is endangered other aspects are threatened too. Thus, it is the system of side-bets that provides continuity. The more a person's roles or behaviours are locked into place through such a system, the more the person has to lose by giving up a role or role-identity, and the more difficult change becomes.

Becker's analysis allows us, as has been stated before, to move from social structure to social process to psychological process. In some respects, it sees the human as active. Roles are not something into which a person is cast, but rather provide material for 'formulating one's own line of action'; roles are made 'use of in organizing our own activities'. In other respects, Becker does not assign the individual much choice in the change process. The process of situational adjustment is still a reaction to external changes rather than an action initiated by the individual. The individual's self-concept is changing, but the situation the person has to adjust to is described as an external condition. Although an analysis of situational adjustment alone provides information on the process of taking roles and changing the self, it does not necessarily provide information on self-initiated change and its conditions. However, Becker implicitly refers to the possibility of choice among a variety of social situations, leading to a commitment to a specific one. Commitment, in turn, is in Becker's analysis a decision by a person to forgo active choice. This should imply, then, that in order to be an agent of one's own change, commitment has to be forgone.

Identity theory

Stryker's identity theory has gone through a number of developments and extensions (Stryker, 1968, 1980, 1984). It rests on a synoptic statement of symbolic interactionism:

> 1. Behavior is dependent upon a named or classified world. The names or class terms attached to aspects of the environment, both physical and social, carry meaning in the form of shared behavioral expectations that grow out of social interaction. From interaction with others, one learns how to classify objects one comes in contact with and in that process also learns how one is expected to behave with reference to those objects.
>
> 2. Among the class terms learned in interaction are the symbols that are used to designate 'positions', which are the relatively stable, morphological components of social structure. These positions carry the shared behavioral expectations that are conventionally labeled 'roles'.
>
> 3. Persons who act in the context of organized patterns of behavior, i.e. in the context of social structure, name one another in the sense of recognizing one another as occupants of positions. When they name one another they invoke expectations with regard to each other's behavior.
>
> 4. Persons acting in the context of organized behavior apply names to themselves as well. These reflexively applied positional designations, which become part of the 'self', create internalized expectations with regard to their own behavior.
>
> 5. When entering interactive situations, persons define the situation by applying names to it, to the other participants in the interaction, to themselves, and to particular features within the situation, and use the resulting definition to organize their own behavior accordingly.
>
> 6. Social behavior is not, however, determined by these definitions, though early definitions may constrain the possibilities for alternative definitions to emerge from interaction. Behavior is the product of a role-making process, initiated by expectations invoked in the process of defining situations, but developing through a tentative, sometimes extremely subtle, probing interchange among actors that can reshape the form and the content of the interaction.
>
> 7. The degree to which roles are 'made' rather than simply 'played', as well as the constituent elements entering the construction of roles, will depend on the larger social structures in which interactive situations are embedded. Some structures are 'open', others relatively 'closed' with respect to novelty in roles and in role enactments or performances. All structures impose some limits on the kinds of definitions that may be called into play and thus limit the possibilities for interaction.
>
> 8. To the degree roles are made rather than only played as given, changes can occur in the character of definitions, in the names and class terms those definitions use, and in the possibilities for interaction; and such changes can in turn lead to changes in the larger social structures within which interactions take place. (Stryker, 1980, pp. 53–5)

Identity theory has been developed within this larger theoretical framework. It is concerned with the relationships between commitment to an identity and behaviour. It is assumed that the self-concept of a person consists of a *hierarchically organized set of multiple identities*. An identity is a specific content of the self-concept, and is usually conceptualized as an internalized role: role-identities. However, it has to be noted that roles are actively made rather than passively played.

The organized nature of multiple identities is reminiscent of James's (1890) notion of multiple social selves. The hierarchical order is defined through *identity salience*, operationalized as the probability of the performance of the role associated with the identity in a given situation. An identity has assumed its place in the hierarchy based on the person's *commitment* to that identity. Stryker (1968) initially defined commitment as the degree 'to which an individual's relationship to particular others depends upon his or her being a given kind of person'. This definition is very reminiscent of Becker's (1960) definition of commitment as a social structural variable. However, the initial statement had already assumed two dimensions of commitment: *extensivity* (number of relationships tied to an identity) and *intensivity* (depth of relationships). Later work suggested the multiplicity of linkages across networks created through specific identities as a third dimension, called *overlap*. In a reconceptualization (Stryker, 1984), the differentiation between more sociological components and more psychological components of commitment became clearer by referring to *interactive commitment* (related to extensivity and overlap) as the number of relationships affected by giving up a role, and *affective commitment* (related to intensivity) as the emotional cost attached to giving up a role.

Central to identity theory is the concept of *choice*: identities are chosen, commitments are entered by choice, and the specific realization, that is, the making of a role, also involves choice. Identity theory does not apply to all social situations, because some do not imply choices. Choice is used as a concept to connect the constraint implied by social structure on one hand and role-related options on the other hand. Identity theory, therefore, is a theory addressing minded activity.

The central statement of identity theory is that '*commitment impacts identity salience impacts role performance*' (Stryker, 1987, p. 89). This statement proposes a line from the social structure to individual behaviour mediated through the importance that a certain identity (i.e. an aspect of the self-concept) holds for a person. The definition of commitment specifies that the important aspect of social structure in relation to the self-concept consists of interactional networks related to given identities. Identities, their social representation, and their behavioural consequences are stabilized through the implications they carry with them in terms of social relationships and through the cost of giving those up.

Hoelter (1983) tested two hypotheses related to identity salience, namely that identity salience is positively affected by '(1) the degree of commitment to its respective role, and (2) the degree to which its respective role is positively evaluated with regard to one's performance' (p. 142). Empirically, students were presented with seven different roles (student, friend, son/daughter, etc.) that had to be rated on the *evaluative* dimensions (good/bad, successful/unsuccessful, important/unimportant), on *commitment* ('How important are those relationships which depend on your being a particular type of person?'), and on *identity salience* (central to who I am; important for self-definition; describes myself). A LISREL-model indicated a reasonable fit of the theoretical model to the data.

Most of the commitment measures related uniquely to the salience of their related identities, thereby supporting the first hypothesis. Further, the data showed that role evaluations did indeed positively relate to identity salience. Thus, two central propositions of identity theory received empirical support, emphasizing the importance of roles to one's self-concept. This, of course, is in complete contradiction to a more conventional view of roles that sees self and role as opposed, and even defines the self as a non-role, one being 'true' and the other being imposed, as for instance proposed by Sader (1969).

Identities are defined in behavioural terms as the making of roles related to a place in the social structure. While roles can be related to social class, positions of power, sex, and other structural variables, they are not defined as such by Stryker. Rather, social structure and its differentiation are meant to imply different degrees of probability with which persons may come into contact. For instance, persons of the same social class have a higher probability of getting together. That way, stable elements of social structure can be identified that carry with them specific roles and thus identities.

Stryker and Serpe (1982) provide a research example focusing on social behaviour in the context of the religious role a person has. Religious role performance fulfilled one condition of identity theory, namely that of choice. In contemporary Western societies, religious activities are usually performed from choice. The three major theoretical variables, derived from identity theory, were 'religious commitment' measured through a six-item scale as the extensiveness and intensity of relations with others in everyday life which are a function of participation in religious life. The second variable, 'location of religious role identity in the identity salience hierarchy', was operationalized as items asking for presentation of identities to others and choice of different activities. As an additional variable, satisfaction with the religious role was included. Age, income, and the presence of other roles (such as parent, spouse, and worker) were controlled for in the analysis. The

Identity theory

dependent variable was the 'time spent in the religious role', that is, actual role performance.

A path model of the variables was strongly supported, over half the variance being accounted for by the variables included. More specific hypotheses were also supported. In particular, a strong relationship between commitment and identity salience emerged, and role performance was strongly affected by both commitment and identity salience. The presence of other roles weakened the salience of the religious identity. Thus, using the example of one particular role, the basic propositions of identity theory were tested and received empirical support. However, while the measure of commitment took into account several aspects of this concept, the actual behavioural variable, namely role performance, was only very undifferentiatedly assessed. From a psychologist's perspective, an inclusion of more specific behavioural and cognitive variables seems desirable.

Callero (1985) studied the effect of the salience of a certain role-identity within a hierarchy using the example of the blood donor role-identity. He found clear influences of this role-identity on social relationships and their perception and, more directly, on behaviour. While not directly influenced by Stryker's identity theory, Callero relates his findings to this framework.

Again within the framework of identity theory, Serpe (1985, 1987) has conducted a longitudinal study addressing self-concept change. The study began with the assumption derived from identity theory that, although the structure of self is relatively stable over time, if changes occur, they are directly related to movement of a person within the social structure, either by choice or through normal life-course changes. In addition, the study was designed to address the causal order of commitment on identity salience, and identity salience on role performance, or, in other words, the causal sequence of social structure on cognitions and then on behaviour. Theoretically, the postulated sequence is based on the presumption that cognitions are more readily alterable than social structure, so that possible reverse effects of identity salience (a cognitive variable) on commitment (a social structural variable) should be less pronounced. This issue is also of interest in view of various possible conceptualizations of commitment, emphasizing differentially social structural versus psychological components of commitment. A later section will discuss the issue in detail.

Serpe's study addresses 'the causal order of stability of the structure of self by utilizing measures of commitment and identity salience at three points in time' (1985, p. 14). Specifically, interactional commitment, affective commitment, and identity salience of new students entering college were measured at three points in time, covering a period of approximately the first four months in college. Entering college was viewed as providing 'multiple opportunities to break old ties and establish new ones' (p. 20).

Unlike the study of Stryker and Serpe (1982) that concentrated on one identity, Serpe (1985, 1987) chose to investigate the *relative* importance of and changes among five different identities relevant to American college students: (1) academic, (2) athletic/recreational, (3) organized, extracurricular activities, (4) non-organizational friendship, and (5) dating. Serpe proposed that the five identities differ in the degree of choice they offer, with the academic identity offering the least choice, and friendship the most. Measures of affective commitment and of the relative salience of these identities were obtained at all three measurement points. Interactional commitment, that is, the number of people the student became involved with as a result of a specific identity, was assessed at the second and third measurement point.

The analysis suggested to Serpe a causal ordering of interactional and affective commitment, such that the social structural variable may have direct effects on the affective variable and on identity salience. Thus, the empirical model postulated the impact of affective commitment and identity salience at Time 1 on interactional commitment, affective commitment, and identity salience at Time 2, and again on the same three variables at Time 3. Generally, the model fits relatively well over all identities. Most importantly for the topic of change, the stability indicated by the model was very high for all variables across identities and over time. However, some differentiation in stability could be found. For men, stability was high in course-work, extracurricular, and personal involvement activities; for women, in course-work and extra-curricular activities. According to Serpe's analysis, course-work and organized extra-curricular activities offer the least amount of choice, and are therefore least open to change. These results support the theoretical model9 however, no explanation for the equal stability of the personal involvement identity for men can be offered. The lesser degree of stability for athletic/recreational and dating identities, where choice is presumed to be highest, offers support for the theory, implying that the rigidity and openness social structure affords different identities has in turn an effect on their stability and possibility for change.

Serpe's contribution has given us some tentative answers concerning stability and change in the self-concept, but leaves other questions open. Identity theory can account for differential change based on the amount of choice different identities carry with them. Identity theory can account for change in the self-structure as a product of normal daily activities, not only as a product of major life events (Thoits, 1983). These tentative answers were made possible by the implementation of a longitudinal design. However, Serpe poses the question of what the proper time frame for the assessment of change in the self-structure should be. This, of course, may not depend on chronological time only but also on social time, that is, the relationship of time to structural changes. In so far as the question of an appropriate time frame for the study of self-concept change in daily life cannot be answered in absolute terms, it should be related to the choice involved in the identity under study, to the probability of related events that add, change, or take away identities, and their related interactional networks. In addition, while Serpe's research hints at the relationship between different identities, it could not present a direct test. The interrelation of different identities is more directly addressed in an analysis by Thoits (1983) which also presents important considerations for the social structural versus psychological, subjective conceptualization of commitment.

The conceptualization of commitment

At this point, the conceptualization of commitment needs to be discussed in some detail. 'Commitment' is a term used with very different meanings within psychology and sociology. Of course, commitment to a certain activity, to a course of action, or to a cognition may be conceptualized very differently from commitment to an aspect of self-concept or an identity. These are frequently very different concepts sharing the same term. The following discussion will be restricted to commitment as a concept indicating stability in the self-concept, thus excluding conceptualizations such as Kiesler's (1971) in the framework of cognitive consistency, or Moreland and Levine's (1982) conceptualization of commitment to a group as a result of compared rewardingness of group membership, or Klinger's (1975) concept of commitment to incentives. While all these conceptualizations also have some relevance to the stability of the self-concept, it is either indirect or is conceptualized in a theoretical framework quite removed from the current social psychological one.

The major point of disagreement about the conceptualization of commitment lies in whether it either implies a subjective decision and can be localized within the individual, or whether it is a statement about the relationship of an individual to his or her environment. The theoretical emphasis has implications for the operationalization and measurement of commitment. Although the danger of doing so is obvious, I will refer to the former as personal commitment, and the latter as structural commitment.

Personal commitment is based on a decision by an individual that an aspect of identity is important to him or her. Subjective importance means that the individual will give up other identities or not pursue them in favour of the one he or she is committed to, and will invest more in that identity as well as spending more time on activities related to it than on others.

The operationalization of the concept has been discussed by, for instance, Wicklund and Gollwitzer (1982): (a) A person could be asked for an aspect of self that is important, and that he or she would not readily abandon. (b) The person's behaviour could be observed to ensure that he or she still pursues activities related to the specific commitment, or self-defining goal, in Wicklund and Gollwitzer's terms. (c) The accumulation of symbols relevant to the self-defining goals could be assessed. (d) A relevant activity could be interrupted, and the substitution of self-defining symbols be observed. All four operationalizations are focused exclusively on the individual, and assess only self-reported importance and observable engagement in relevant activities. In further studies (see Gollwitzer, 1986), commitment was measured through subjects' attaching a label ('dancer') to themselves, indicating that they were still actively pursuing a certain identity, and that they would be very distressed if they had to give up this identity. The effects of such commitment are described as an apparent force 'that propels people toward attainment of that identity'.

Some sociologists, too, prefer a personal approach to the concept of commitment. For instance, Rosenberg (1979) and Marks (1977) consider that the degree of commitment to a role is a function of the subjective importance given to it. Commitment is a statement about psychological centrality of an identity. Personal commitment as a variable has some clear explanatory value, and as a psychological concept takes into account the degree of choice and possibility of decision an individual has. Apparently it is a more agentic and less deterministic concept than structural commitment.

Structural commitment, on the other hand, has been exemplified in the definitions by Becker (1960) and Stryker (1980). A person's commitment is operationally defined as the links between a certain identity or aspect of self-concept and others. Commitment to one identity implies specific social relationships. Disengagement from a commitment involves giving up these links as well. Stability is therefore less a result of a decision than a necessity because of the high cost of disengagement from a commitment caused by structural disturbance. Whereas Becker and Stryker define its social structural implications, Hayden's (1979) approach to self-concept change considers the number of cognitive implications, that is, offers a cognitive structural approach. Although Hayden does not talk about commitment, he too conceptualizes stability as a function of cognitive structural differentiation. On the other hand, Jackson (n.d.) directly relates social structure to cognitive structure: 'The structural organization of one's commitments forms a schema, which directs activity and can be modified by experience' (p. 2).

Thoits (1983) has tried to point out and test empirically some opposing implications of the personal and structural approach to commitment to an identity. Her approach is based on the assumption that personal commitment implies an additive conceptualization, whereas structural commitment implies a multiplicative one. Personal commitment, as was exemplified through the measurement approach of Wicklund and Gollwitzer, is reflected in the amount of time and energy invested in identity-related behaviours. This in turn means assuming a limited amount of time and energy is available, that as the number of commitments to self-defining goals increases, the commitment to each individual identity has to decrease. On the other hand, as the number of self-defining goals or identities decreases, energy should become available to increase the commitment to other remaining identities. While many theorists do not discuss the question, because they implicitly assume that commitments are exclusive, a structural version should predict the opposite. Because commitments are defined as nodes in a network, identities are to some degree interrelated. Investment in one identity affects other identities as well: 'To the degree that relationships are multiplex in nature, limited time and energy may be invested in several roles simultaneously' (Thoits, 1983, p.178). The more identities a person is committed to, the greater the probability of overlap.

From these assumptions, Thoits derives hypotheses about the psychological impact of identity loss. If identities are considered separately and exclusively, loss of any one identity should not influence other identities. This is the additive conceptualization of personal identities. Otherwise, if identities are interrelated, loss of one identity affects others as well. Therefore, the personal conceptualization of commitment predicts a lesser degree of psychological distress from loss of an identity for persons holding several social positions ('integrated actors'), whereas the structural model predicts a greater psychological impact.

These hypotheses were tested using data from a panel study of over 700 men and women interviewed in two subsequent years. The following variables were used to test competing hypotheses: *identity accumulation*, that is, the sum of social positions held by an individual, and *psychological distress*, measured through a list of twenty psychological and psychosomatic symptoms. Results supported the structural conceptualization of commitment. For each loss of identity over the two-year period, initially integrated actors indicated significantly more psychological distress than actors who were initially isolated. In addition, it was shown that persons holding several identities showed less psychological distress, the opposite of what a personal, exclusive approach to commitment would expect, namely role strain or role conflict as the number of identities increases (Sarbin & Allen, 1968). Overall, Thoits concluded, 'the integrated actor has both more to lose and more to gain through change', a conclusion supporting the predictive utility of the structural notion of commitment, as, for instance, proposed by Stryker (1980), because it explicitly addresses the interdependence among identities.

However, this does not necessarily refute the utility of a personal, subjective approach to the measurement of commitment as long as it

84   *Sociological approaches*

implicitly acknowledges an underlying structural conceptualization allowing for interconnected identities. Marks's (1977) notion of subjective commitment cites four factors increasing commitment: spontaneous enjoyment of role performance, spontaneous loyalty to a role partner, anticipation of rewards from role enactment, and avoidance of punishment through role enactment. Thoits points out that all these factors are positively influenced when roles are non-segregated. Finally, Jackson's (n.d.) interpretation of structural commitment as a cognitive representation shows that it is not the psychological importance notion, but rather the exclusivity notion of personal commitment that is questionable. Thoits summarizes the advantages of the structural notion of commitment as follows:

> First, consistent with the thesis that identities are claimed and sustained in relationships with others, it points to straightforward indicators of key concepts using the structure of network ties. Second, it neatly subsumes the time and energy expenditure and subjective importance conceptions of commitment. Finally, it points to conditions which help specify when multiplicative effects of identity accumulation might be expected. (Thoits, 1983, p. 185)

The measurement of commitment

For the research described in this book, a way of measuring commitment was developed that relied closely on the notion that a social relationship is central to the self-concept as defined through the number of other role relationships that are influenced or tied into place through this commitment. A measurement instrument was developed that took into account the implications of changes in one particular role relationship for a number of other role relationships.

The measurement provided a list of fourteen common role relationships (see Table 6.1).

In the first step of the measurement process, subjects had to indicate which of the role relationships listed had most significantly changed, either during

Table 6.1 *Presentation of role relationships in commitment measure*

Parents	○	○	Spouse/partner
Children	○	○	Close relatives
In-laws	○	○	Distant relatives
Colleagues	○	○	Boss/supervisor
Employees	○	○	Customers, etc.
Close friends	○	○	Acquaintances
Neighbours	○	○	Other friends

Note: For specific populations, e.g. students, the list can be altered.

the past year or, if used in an investigation of relocation, immediately preceding a move. Subjects also had to indicate on the form whether this change in relationship consisted of a greater distancing or termination of that relationship, or a getting close or beginning phase in relationship formation.

In the next step, all other role relationships affected by this change had to be indicated. The instructions explained that frequently changes in one relationship involve changes in others as well. To indicate that, arrows had to be drawn from the primary affected relationship to all secondary affected relationships. This allowed a distinction between changes in social relationships that were either isolated from other relationships or else involved others.

That way, a measure could be obtained of the degree to which the entering or leaving of a social relationship affected larger areas of the social structure and therefore constituted a change in a commitment central to self. In particular, studies to be reported here later related such changes in the social structure to psychological variables such as satisfaction with self.

Relating sociological and psychological notions of self-concept

While there are numerous other examples of research in the sociological tradition of symbolic interactionism, and a complete review of that research would have to address a variety of questions, the following discussion concentrates on the relationship between sociological conceptualizations and psychological conceptualizations of self-concept. First, I shall be considering the question whether the symbolic interactionist concept of 'reflected appraisal' is acceptable from a psychological, cognitive viewpoint. Secondly, the relationship between the notion of social structure and identity on one hand and cognitive structure and self-concept on the other hand will be discussed.

One of the most basic assumptions of symbolic interactionism is that we come to see ourselves as others see us. In other words, one's concept of self is a function of the reflection of oneself in others' appraisals. Gecas (1982) goes as far as to call the principle of reflected appraisals the 'cornerstone of the symbolic interactionist perspective on self-concept formation' (p. 5). Any attempt to take symbolic interactionism seriously and relate it to notions of cognitive social psychology therefore has to consider the empirical status of reflected appraisals.

The notion of reflected appraisals is one of the most tested notions of symbolic interactionism, both in naturalistic and in experimental laboratory studies. The empirical evidence is given very different emphasis by different authors. For instance, Rosenberg (1981) states that empirical results consistently support the notion of reflected appraisal. Others (for example

Felson, 1985) do not consider the process to be convincingly demonstrated. Both sides cite a review by Shrauger and Schoeneman (1979) as one piece of evidence among others.

Rosenberg (1981) summarizes the evidence along these lines: (1) Individuals' ratings of themselves are likely to agree with ratings of others. (2) There are consistent and strong associations between what a person thinks others think of him or her, and that person's self-concept. (3) There is some relationship between what others actually think of a person and the reflected self, though people may misread the attitude of others toward oneself. (4) The reflected self, what one *believes* others think of him or her, is closer to the actual self-concept than the social self, what others *actually think* of him or her.

In the light of the empirical evidence he obtained, Felson (1985) reviews three postulates (derived from Kinch's, 1963, formalized theory of the self-concept) (a) on the effect of reflected appraisals on self-appraisals, (b) on the effect of actual appraisals on reflected appraisals, and (c) on the effect of actual appraisals on self-appraisals. In his studies, *projection*, that is, the tendency to attribute one's own opinion to others, accounted for most of the effect of reflected appraisals on self-appraisals. The effect of actual appraisals on self-appraisals was unrelated to reflected appraisals through lack of direct communication of appraisal to others and, where it occurred, their common irrelevance to global appraisals. The effect of actual appraisals on self-appraisals, when it occurs, is most likely short-lived or occurs on new dimensions of the person and therefore does not influence that person. Felson obtained only modest support in his own research. He considers the review of his own research to be in line with Shrauger and Schoeneman's review of the relevant research.

Shrauger and Schoeneman (1979) reviewed over sixty studies testing these basic assumptions of symbolic interactionism. Overall, they indicate that in naturalistic studies, little evidence could be obtained that self-evaluations are influenced by feedback received from others. However, these naturalistic studies generally showed relationships between people's perceptions of themselves and their *assumptions* about how others perceive them. Shrauger and Schoeneman conclude, 'currently, there is little evidence that in their ongoing social interactions people's views of themselves are shaped by the opinion of others' (p. 559), but rather by how they think others see them.

This evidence, as was mentioned, is cited by both sides as either supporting or damning the symbolic interactionist concept of reflected appraisals. However, what Shrauger and Schoeneman actually suggest is the importance of mediating social and cognitive processes in appraising others and oneself. Distortion of discrepant feedback, reactance to evaluation, and selective exposure to evaluators are some ways in which discrepant feedback may not lead to self-concept change. Frequently, discrepant feedback may not even be obtained, because of social restrictions on the communication of negative appraisals. Along similar lines are Felson's interpretations of how reflected appraisal has to be reconceptualized as mediated by social and cognitive processes. By restricting the relevance of non-mediated reflected appraisal on change and maintenance of the self-concept, he suggests factors reminiscent of Festinger's (1954) social comparison theory. When objective or institutionalized indicators of performance (which one could consider to be social judgments) are available, they tend to be used. Reflected appraisals, on the other hand, should be more relevant on dimensions for which social evaluation is critical, such as attractiveness.

In general, then, one of the basic principles of symbolic interactionism turns out to be subject to processes of social cognition. To understand the impact of social structural processes on the individual's self-concept, use has to be made of psychological principles known (or not yet known) to be working in making social judgments. A sociological notion of the self-concept is not possible without the consideration of psychological principles. At the same time, the stability of cognitive structures referring to oneself is based just as much on the stability of the social structure.

A study of the effect of reflected appraisals

In a thesis conducted under my supervision, Bossong (1983) studied the effect of the congruency between self-concept and perceived evaluation through one's spouse on social behaviour. Reflected appraisal vis-à-vis one's spouse is especially relevant to the self-concept because for most people marriage will be the one central social relationship that is most tied to the social structure. A discrepancy between how one sees oneself and how one thinks the partner perceives one constitutes a questioning of the self-concept because it may ultimately imply the failure of a central social relationship and dissolve the present social structure. Therefore, perceived lack of congruency in the spouse-relationship may lead to a seeking out of social interaction with other persons as far as they have the potential to supply congruent information.

Using information from the marriage register in a small city in southwest Germany, Bossong identified a group of forty-three women who had been married for four years, and a group of eleven women who had been married less than six months. It was assumed that the probability of a lack of congruency between self-concept and reflected appraisal from the spouse was higher among those married for several years, whereas for recently married women a higher congruency was considered to be more likely. Because this assumption was not borne out by the data, the following results are based on the total sample.

Congruency was measured by asking the wives to what degree they thought that their husbands saw them as they saw themselves. This global measure was complemented by a list of twenty-four self-concept-related statements that had to be filled out dealing with (a) how the wives saw themselves, and (b) how they thought their husbands saw them on each dimension. The difference between (a) and (b) correlated with the global measure of congruency $r = .53$. This is highly significant and can be considered one validation of the global measure. Measures of social strategies to affirm one's self-concept consisted of social activities in regard to old friends and relatives, other social activities (going to clubs, taking classes, etc.), and activities that are socially highly regarded, such as athletic or artistic activities.

The findings indicated no relationship between perceived lack of congruency and the frequency with which contacts with old friends and relatives were reported. However, there was a highly significant relationship between perceived lack of congruency and the wish to meet other and new people with whom to talk about oneself. This was not supported by actual activities. The only social activity in which subjects with low congruency engaged more frequently were organized social events in clubs or in church. As far as personal possessions were concerned, subjects were asked to indicate whether they were part of their *own* life sphere or belonged in the *common* life sphere as shared by husband and wife. Bossong found that a significantly greater ratio of personal possessions was seen as belonging to the common life sphere when the congruency was high.

For a number of reasons, especially the approach to statistical analysis chosen by Bossong and the limited number of variables relating to the stability of the social structure, the results have to be taken cautiously. Keeping that in mind, they do not seem to support a notion that congruent information is looked for where it seems most predictable, namely among old friends and relatives whom the wives knew longer than they were married. What is expressed is the desire to meet new people, but their present stable social structure does not allow the wives to realize this desire. The only outlet is that of organized social activities. Even with personal possessions, the things around them, wives with low perceived congruency have separated their own sphere much more clearly from that of their husbands. Overall, a tendency can be seen in the data suggesting that lack of congruency leads to a distancing along with a desired new orientation. Actual change, however, does not seem to be possible within the existing social structure that is created through the central commitment to the marriage.

The results indicate that reflected appraisals in a relationship central to the self-concept can have an effect on cognitions. Effects on behaviour are much less pronounced because behaviour is determined, not only by these cognitions but also by the opportunities the social structure does or does not afford.

Social and cognitive structure

How do social structure and cognitive structure relate to each other? The previous discussion has repeatedly hinted at parallels between psychological conceptions of self-related cognitions and sociological conceptualizations of social structure. Both use network models to account for the interrelatedness of individual elements in the self-concept, for the general stability of the system, and the impact of disturbances at nodes in the network. On the psychological side, Bower and Gilligan (1979) or Markus and Sentis (1982) have made use of such conceptualizations. Kihlstrom and Cantor (1984) point out that such a conceptualization of the self-concept, as the richest node in the cognitive network, also implies that it may be the best-organized one. Hayden's (1979) notion of an implicative network originated from a different theoretical framework but is nevertheless clearly a case in point. The notion of implicative meanings may also account for rapid access to the richness of self-related information.

On the sociological side, the notion of commitment and its structural interpretation by Becker (1960), Stryker (1980), Jackson (1981), Thoits (1983), and others shares many elements with the psychological notion. Stability is accounted for by the number of implications a given identity has for others. Thoits demonstrated that a higher degree of interrelatedness also implies a higher degree of disturbance of the whole system if single elements of the network are affected. Thoits (1983) related social structure to affective psychological processes, and Jackson (n.d.) tried to relate social structure to cognitive processes. Interestingly, Jackson's test of the function of information relating to the identities one is committed to shows strong mediating effects for affective commitment. This supports Stryker's (1984) reconceptualization of commitment as being *interactional* and *affective*, thereby relating structural and emotional components in one conceptualization.

The common elements in these conceptualizations are the relevance of the implications individual identities and their mental representations carry with them. Empirically, the relevance of affective processes has been demonstrated. Social structure directly impacts affective processes, and affective processes mediate the cognitive representation of social structure.

The review of psychological theories on the development of self also included the identification of acts as leading to self-themes (Vallacher & Wegner, 1985). Based on the discussion of symbolic interactionist theory to this point, one could construe the emphasis on social experience as not including processes such as action identification, thus leading to different processes of self-concept development and change from a psychological or a sociological perspective. However, Gecas and Schwalbe (1983) argue strongly from a symbolic interactionist standpoint that self-conceptions are also based upon one's *actions*, de-emphasizing the centrality of reflected appraisals as the 'cornerstone' of symbolic interactionism.

Their argument is traced back to Cooley, for whom the act of *possession*, associated with words such as 'my', and effective *action* constituted self-experiences along with reflected appraisals. Gecas and Schwalbe argue that 'beyond the looking-glass self is a self that develops out of the autonomous and efficacious actions of the individual' (p. 79), that is, the sense of self is also developed out of action attributed to a consistent characteristic of oneself. The argument can now be linked to a variety of psychological conceptualizations of the sense of control or agency. This approach is of interest to an ecological conceptualization of the self-concept because the opportunities for action an individual has are located within a particular social and physical environment. Social structures and environments provide constraints on and afford opportunities for individual actions. They provide contextual resources, both material and symbolic, which are necessary for action based on the individual's capacities. In addition, the context of action is used for the evaluation of that action in relation to the self-concept, that is, self-esteem. Gecas and Schwalbe's argument emphasizes an active, creative conceptualization of self and links through it the social and physical environment of an individual to psychological processes such as control, attribution, and action identification.

The importance of sociological approaches to the self-concept lies in their emphasis on the embeddedness of the individual in his or her environment. A concept of self arises out of social and efficacious action in an environment that provides stability through implicational links. To change oneself requires changes in the relationship between individual and environment. As Mead early recognized, to change oneself meant actively to change one's relationship to others (Ritsert, 1980).

Active change in relationships with others is difficult as long as the existing ecological system of the self stays in place, as for instance Bossong's data indicate. It is made easier, and especially better subject to research, if it happens in a situation where the whole person–environment relationship creates opportunities for change.

Another implication arises from the statement that to change the self-concept means to change one's relationship to others, namely that the study of social interactions is at the core of the study of processes related to self-concept change. Rather than assuming changes in social relationships between a pre-measure and a post-measure of the self-concept, we need to study actual social behaviour under conditions conducive to change. The next chapter will review some of the problems in measuring the self-concept and will describe those measures that have been developed here to relate self-concept to the actual social situation.

7 The development of self-concept-related measures

The research programme described in this book employed some novel methods to assess aspects of the ecology of the self and the evaluative component in order to overcome some problems that are unique to the measurement of the self-concept. Two very different methodological approaches were developed that seemed particularly appropriate in the theoretical context of an ecological approach. One of them, autophotography, is a method that should allow the assessment of the self-concept-relevant environment of a person via the rating of photographs on theoretically relevant dimensions. The other consists of the development and employment of a new questionnaire: a measure of satisfaction with the self-concept that covers different spheres of life and thus also takes into account some aspects of the ecology of the self.

Problems in the measurement of the self-concept

A discussion of the measurement of the self should start by distinguishing three different approaches: (a) An assessment of the *contents* of a person's self-concept. One person may consider himself to be a cook, another person may consider herself to be a ski-racer. Of course, every person has many different aspects with different degrees of centrality that constitute that person's self. (b) An assessment of a certain *function* or *process* of the self-concept, for instance to guide behaviour, or to compare real and ideal self. Usually, these functions of the self-concept are theoretically postulated as specific traits or states in which a person's self-concept is engaged, and appropriate measurement instruments have been devised. Prominent examples are measures of self-monitoring (Snyder, 1974), or of self-consciousness (Fenigstein, Scheier, & Buss, 1975). (c) An assessment of the *affect* associated with a person's self-concept. These are measures of self-worth, satisfaction with self, or self-esteem, of which there are many. Most of these measures obtain more global measurements of self-esteem.

The measurement of the content of a person's self-concept provides two very basic problems, having to do with uniqueness and salience (see also Wiechardt, 1977). Uniqueness refers to the fact that the possible contents, for instance, roles, abilities, idiosyncrasies, and whatever else can enter one's self-concept, are practically limitless. Objective measures cannot take this into account. They have to prestructure the possible dimensions of self and presumably include those that seem to be the most dominant ones in the population under investigation. In Western societies, these include dimensions referring to one's family situation, work and leisure activities, and roles. However, this solution cannot take care of any idiosyncratic elements of the self-concept. That means that an objective measure of the self-concept would not be able to assess the very nature of the self-concept. Therefore, objective measures are only appropriate if very global dimensions of the self-concept are necessary for research purposes, such as in studies involving large samples where scales only have to assess modal dimensions of the self-concept. However, the restriction to a few dimensions may underestimate self-concept change as measured by such instruments because they cannot take into account the addition of new elements to the self-concept that are not represented in the prestructured questionnaire.

For this reason, researchers in the self-concept area have also employed subjective measures, such as the 'Who am I?' measure of twenty open statements (TST: Kuhn & McPartland, 1954), or the 'spontaneous self-concept' (McGuire & Padawer-Singer, 1976). There, subjects typically provide a number of statements that all begin with 'I am ...', or they give open-ended answers to a question like 'Tell us about yourself.' Such measures can be very useful and can give information about the great variety of dimensions and contents that can possibly be represented in the self-concept. Because of their open-ended answering form, on the other hand, they present measurement problems. Wylie (1974) criticizes the TST as being of unknown validity and reliability.

Burke (1980) and Hoelter (1985) suggest measurement approaches from a symbolic interactionist, structural model of self-conception. Both provide a sophisticated discussion and research examples for the measurement of specific identities on several dimensions, theoretically justifying the use of semantic differential measures for this purpose. In both approaches, the ways the specific identities or contents of the self-concept are to be assessed are not specified. For instance, Hoelter (1985) has little to suggest but the use of the TST. Therefore, the problems of the TST are not avoided. On the other hand, Jackson (1981) has developed a social identity questionnaire that guides subjects in determining their most important identities which are later to be assessed in regard to commitment. It could be that such a form would be more useful in providing the identities on which Burke's and Hoelter's measurement requirements and models could be applied. The measurement of the self-concept would then be restricted to social identities, which are very important but according to an ecological approach not the only possible elements of the self-concept.

However, the measurement of the self-concept is supposed to provide the measurement of a theoretically relatively stable entity. Research on the self-concept as well as recent research in social cognition has demonstrated how easily cognitions and therefore statements about a stable state of oneself can be influenced by temporary, situation-specific circumstances that can make very different dimensions and contents of the self-concept salient. Wiechardt (1977) names several influence factors that can endanger objective ratings of the self-concept. They may influence subjective, spontaneous self-descriptions even more. Different elements in a situation, such as success or failure, can produce a selective attention to the self as well as some dispositional determinants (Mischel, Ebbesen, & Zeiss, 1973). Concentration on different specific dimensions can create different general conceptions of self (Filipp & Brandstädter, 1975). Research in the area of self-awareness (Duval & Wicklund, 1972) also points out that different aspects of the self are made salient in different situations. In the area of social cognition, Schwarz (1987) has presented a model of the cognitive process underlying judgments of the quality of life which emphasizes the different possibilities for error due to heuristic reference points. Therefore, the ease with which such judgments can be influenced seems to be an even greater problem with subjective, spontaneous measures. While it has been argued before that objective, prestructured measures of the self-concept may, from one point of view, artificially inflate the impression of stability of the self-concept, the present argument implies that subjective, spontaneous measures may inflate the impression of the malleability of the self-concept, especially if taken in different life situations.

For the measurement of the contents of the self-concept, it follows that no one approach seems to be able to capture the unique nature of the self-concept. Different approaches seem to be able to create artifactual assessments of the stability or malleability of an individual's self-concept. Taken to the extreme, these arguments suggest that the measurement of self-concept *content* and their changes may contribute little to the understanding of self-concept *processes*, such as processes involved in stability and change.

The measurement of the self-concept through autophotography

From the above considerations, common measures of self-concept were deemed inappropriate for present purposes. These purposes were (a) the consideration of an ecological approach to self-concept change that takes into account the individual's relationship to his or her social and spatial-physical environment; and (b) an assessment not only of content but also of the function of the elements of the self-concept for stability and change.

One method chosen was the use of photographs which were then rated by independent raters for content and function. Similar approaches are known as autophotography from the work of Ziller and his associates (for instance, Ziller & Smith, 1977; Ziller & Lewis, 1981). However, his approach differs from the one described here in procedure and especially in the ways in which the content was analysed and interpreted.

Subjects were given a camera to take photographs of people, things, and environments which they considered to be part of or expressive of their self-concept. In the present adaptation of the method, Polaroid cameras were used. Participants received a film with ten pictures, and were asked to return seven. This allows immediate control of the pictures, and allows retakes, if necessary. The content of each photograph was commented on by the participant in one line. Contents of the self-concept could then be freely chosen by the subject as long as they were open to pictorial presentation. The camera may have served to avoid the spontaneity of short verbal description and enhance the importance of the task. Research participants had use of the camera for one week and were given the option of eliminating some unsatisfactory pictures.

The pictures were then rated by two or three independent raters. First the *content* was rated as belonging to any of these categories: persons, things, and environments. All three can be represented within one photograph. In that case the relative percentage of the area covered by objects belonging to one of the three was estimated. The next step was more specific and, for instance, described the kind of persons depicted (adults, children, etc.), or the kinds of environments (nature, urban, etc.). So far, the entire content of the picture was the object of the rating.

The next step assessed the *function* of meaning of the items shown for stability and change in the self-concept, which could be considered the meaning of the picture. The rater had to decide which of the three categories was dominant in the picture. This decision was aided by the one-line description of the content of the picture given by the research participant him- or herself. This main content was then rated on seven dimensions, based on an analysis of the function and meaning of persons, things, and environments for a person's self-concept. Some of these categories were suggested from past research, especially Csikszentmihalyi and Rochberg-Halton's (1981) interviews on the meaning of domestic things for the self, and the work of Wapner and his associates (for instance Wapner, 1981, 1987) on the changing relationship between individual and environment during transitions. Other categories were less rooted in the present theory or past research and were more exploratory in character.

The first category is the *perspective* taken, that is, a close-up versus very distant approach to the object depicted. Research by Wofsey, Rierden, and Wapner (1979) has suggested this category as an indicator of psychological closeness or involvement.

Then, the *integration* of the object in the context of the picture was rated. Was the object presented in an isolated way, or was it integrated in a context? This could provide clues about the adaptation into the new environment of the person's self-concept-relevant items.

The next dimension tries to assess *self-presentational* aspects of the object photographed: objects that give a clear message about what kind of a person one is. Possessions may, for instance, be displayed to convey the image of an 'intellectual' or an 'athlete'.

Also assessed was the instrumental, *activity*-encouraging aspect of the content of the picture. Is it, for instance, a tool for certain sports activities, like a tennis racquet, or an environment, like a mountain for a skier? Instrumental aspects could be relevant for the acquisition of new activities or skills that later become an element of the self-concept. In addition, many activities carry with them social structures (such as a tennis club) and support systems that can stabilize the self-concept.

Some objects have value mainly for the memories that they revive: they are links to the past and can thus be used to create stability for oneself. For this aspect a *memory* value was scored. Its importance for self-concept change lies in the presentation of continuity with the past and the possibility of projecting this into the future.

If the picture and the related commentary indicated that the person had used the content as an opportunity to reflect on some greater issue, for instance, petrol pumps standing for the energy crisis, a high *reflection* score was given. Usually, this can be considered a social message, an invitation for the viewer to share in the thoughts and reflections of the person who took the picture. Thus, the picture presents part of the individual's self and reveals it to another.

Finally, the next rating considered the *symbolic* value of the picture: did the picture stand for something other than what it actually depicted, for instance a computer for unemployment? This category is different from the category 'reflection' because symbols are presented that are socially shared and generally used. Whereas 'reflection' reveals an aspect of the individual's self-concept to the viewer, 'symbol' shows the individual's participation in generally shared areas. The individual's self-concept is connected to items of societal discourse.

There were three independent raters in the first study and two in the second. In the first step, picture content was rated without taking the subject's own description into account; the second step considered the function dimensions by taking this information into account. Content was rated according to content categories (environments, persons, objects), and the percentage of the picture covered by these was estimated. The ratings of function dimensions employed seven-point scales. This allowed a statistical analysis of agreement between raters according to different categories. Each category was assessed through one single item. Stability of ratings is therefore a function of inter-rater reliability.

The first study that employed the method (see also Chapter 9) obtained 698 photographs from 101 persons. For these pictures, based on three raters, inter-rater reliabilities for content ranged between alpha = .77 and alpha = .94, and for the functional dimensions between alpha = .36 for self-presentation, and alpha = .83 for symbolism. A summary of the inter-rater reliabilities of the first study and their comparison with ratings obtained in a later study (Chapter 15) are presented in Table 7.1.

Table 7.1 *Inter-rater reliabilities for autophotography*

Category or dimension	Study 1: alpha	Study 2: r
Content		
Environments	.77	.76
Persons	.94	.91
Objects	.82	.78
Function		
Self-presentation	.36	.50
Activity	.58	.71
Reflection	.56	.61
Memory	.44	.68
Symbolism	.83	.47
Perspective	.70	.56
Integration	.58	.49

Note: Study 1 employed three raters; Study 2, two raters.

The inter-rater reliabilities are quite satisfactory for the objective content categories. As expected, they were lower and more varied for the dimensions that were supposed to evaluate the content's function for the self-concept. Particularly low was 'self-presentation'; in later studies the definition given to the raters was more precise and the reliability of these ratings rose to more acceptable levels.

Overall, although the average ratings for both studies were about the same (with one rater fewer), the variance in ratings on the function dimensions was smaller after changes in the raters' instructions had been implemented. Because of financial restrictions, a third rater could not be employed to increase reliability in the latter studies.

Autophotography is a new instrument; and the present rating categories are new not only to autophotography, but to the assessment of the self-concept in general. Therefore, in the present context an interpretation of results based on these ratings, which are almost all around or above .50, is quite justifiable, as long as it is used as one research instrument among others.

The measurement of satisfaction with self

Active attempts to stabilize or change the self are also thought to be influenced by the satisfaction with one's self-concept, or by self-esteem. Low satisfaction with an aspect of the self-concept is thought to lower resistance to change in the face of different environments, and to increase the willingness to consider new elements to incorporate into the self-concept. High satisfaction with an aspect of the self-concept, on the other hand, should be related to active attempts to maintain stability as well as a projection of the current status into the future, even in view of a different environment that may not directly support this aspect of one's self-concept. Elliott (1986) argues along similar lines that high self-esteem is related to the motivation for self-consistency.

Alternatively, however, it has been thought that low self-esteem frequently goes along with self-imposed restrictions, especially as far as social opportunities are concerned. These self-imposed restrictions may actually hinder a person low on satisfaction with self to make use of the opportunity for self-concept change a new environment may afford. On the other hand, persons with high self-esteem are willing to seek out new experiences, even if they ultimately incorporate into their self-concept only those that directly build on existing elements of the self-concept.

Because of the alternative hypotheses possible, a measure of satisfaction with self that is relevant to the ecological approach is an important instrument in the present research programme to help determine the paths adaptation and change take. In line with the theoretical approach taken in this book, a global measure of self-esteem does not seem to be able to capture satisfaction with one's self-concept in an ecological system which includes several spheres of social relationships, or different roles, as well as aspects of the physical-spatial environment. On the other hand, the differentiation of a measure of satisfaction with self does not necessarily present the same problems as a measure of self-concept content would. Satisfaction is indeed a more global concept and not tied to a very specific content of the self-concept, so that it seems appropriate to select some life spheres shared by most members in the culture that most influence satisfaction with oneself. Since such a scale could not be found, a new German language scale for

Satisfaction with self

the assessment of satisfaction with self was constructed (Hormuth & Lalli, 1988). Because the present studies made use of varied populations, and thus different subcultures, two versions were constructed, one for a general adult population (Form N) and one for a student population (Form S).

My theoretical approach considers the self-concept as a product of and force in an ecological system encompassing the social environment and aspects of the physical environment. Satisfaction with self results to some degree from being able to be both, product and force. In particular, its moderator function in the process of self-concept change depends on being able to influence actively the aspect of the environment in which dissatisfaction is expressed. Therefore, for the present purposes subscales were selected that were considered representative for the life spaces or roles usually taken by members of the population studied here. Furthermore, their nature should be such that an individual can, under certain circumstances, actively influence the relationship between himself or herself and those aspects of the environment. For the purposes of the construction of this particular scale, therefore, the meaning of place of residence and other molar environmental aspects (see Chapter 9) were not included among the subscales of the instrument to be developed. This aspect of the ecological system of the self, although a major contributor to a person's self-concept, allows a person much less individual active influence on it than do, for instance, one's personal possessions or close personal relationships.

The areas selected began with those where social relations are closest, namely 'family and intimate relationships'. The construction of a social network relies on 'social relationships and friendships' and 'work'. The aspects of the physical environment most open to influence by an individual are 'personal possessions and interior decoration'. These constituted the different subscales of the Satisfaction with Self Scale (from here on also referred to as SSS). In applying the scale to different populations, it was found that student populations and general adult populations differed in that family relationships for a student include parents and siblings, whereas intimate relationships and spouses belong to another sphere of life. Therefore, for the student form of the scale two separate subscales addressing these life spheres were constructed. In addition, items on the 'Work' subscale were altered to refer to 'Studies'. In addition to the subscales referring to life spheres, the scale also includes one subscale for the assessment of a 'global' value of self-satisfaction. The final scale includes five subscales of four to six items each for Form N: 'Global', 'Family', 'Social', 'Work', and 'Object'. Form S contains six subscales with four to five items each: 'Global', 'Family', 'Partner', 'Social', 'Studies', and 'Object'. The scale, in its original German version, is found in Hormuth and Lalli (1988).

The scale had to be constructed so that it could be employed in a variety of different modes as is necessary when using a multi-method approach: personally, via telephone interview, and by mail. Brevity of items and of the total scale was as important as a response scale that did not necessarily require visual presentation. All items were constructed as short statements that could be answered on a five-point rating scale anchored by 'Very true of me' and 'Not at all true of me'. In oral presentation, as on the telephone, the extremes were verbally defined and the respondent was asked to assign a score between 1 and 5. The negative and positive pole of the items varied, and items from different subscales were randomly alternated.

The items were constructed by first creating a larger pool of statements that were reduced and improved through a series of expert ratings and pretests. Some items expressed satisfaction with self; others, willingness to change. Larger tests of the scale allowed factor analyses that led to further improvement of the item pool and the subscales. The final scale contained 24 items for the general population form, and 26 items for the student form of the scale. The examples I give here are from an English-language version which I translated with the cooperation of McCuster (1985), who employed it in a study of Americans in Germany. (For the original, German version of the scale, see Hormuth & Lalli, 1988.)

The subscale Global assesses general satisfaction with self. It contains items such as 'I can be satisfied with myself' or 'There is a lot wrong with me.' The subscale Family has statements such as 'I could do just as well without my relatives' and 'One could characterize my family life as being harmonious.' The subscale Partner included statements such as 'Actually, I feel pretty lonely' and 'I am satisfied as far as intimate relationships are concerned.' For the general population, these two subscales of the student form were combined in one single subscale, Family. Separate factor analyses for student and general adult populations showed that the different factor structures also have respectively one and two factors for the life spheres in the different populations.

The subscale Social includes items like 'My friends support me fully' and 'The company of my friends really is fulfilling for me.' Work and Study are two parallel subscales on the two forms with items which also differ only slightly: 'A change of job/field of study would do me good', and 'My work/study satisfies me.' Satisfaction with personal possessions and surroundings was the topic of the subscale Object, including statements such as 'Many things that I possess don't mean anything to me any more', 'One can tell who I am by the way my flat is furnished', or 'At home I am surrounded by nice personal possessions.'

These scales were empirically assessed in their final form. Form N (normal adult population) was given in an identical version to 299 persons in three different studies that will be described in detail later. Of these, 47 per cent were male. Their average age was 29.6 (SD = 10.9), with a range of 18 to 91. The occupational diversity of this sample was high. Form S (Students) was administered to 264 students at the University of Heidelberg, of whom 45 per cent were male. Their mean age was 22.3 (SD = 2.98); they had attended the university for between one and twenty semesters (M = 4.4; SD = 3.8). Reliability and validity information as it will now be presented is based on these two samples.

Reliabilities are shown in Table 7.2 for the individual subscales as well as for the total scales. The item analyses show satisfactory values for the item difficulty between .48 and .66 for Form N and between .52 and .32 for the student version (Form S). Reliabilities according to Cronbach's alpha are between .71 and .87 (bias corrected between .86 and .94) for Form N, and between .73 and .87 (bias corrected between .88 and .94) for Form S. This demonstrates the comparable reliabilities among the subscales and between the two forms of the SSS. Reliabilities for the total scales are .90 (N) and .91 (S), corrected according to Spearman-Brown .95 and .96 respectively.

Table 7.2 *Reliabilities (alpha) for Satisfaction with Self Scale*

Subscale	Form N	Form S
Global	.75	.77
Family	.86	.79
Partner		.81
Social	.76	.73
Work	.87	.87
Object	.71	.76
Total	**.90**	**.91**

Intercorrelations (Table 7.3) between the subscales show the relative independence of the different subscales. The correlations between the different areas do not differ from their correlations with the subscale 'Global'. The greatest differences between the student form and the adult form are in the relevance of the family for global satisfaction.

Table 7.3 *Intercorrelations between SSS subscales*

Subscale	*r* Form N (Form S)				
	Family	Partner	Social	Work	Object
Global	.48(.17)	−(.32)	.37(.24)	.20(.29)	.26(.24)
Family		−(.33)	.36(.38)	.31(.20)	.28(.20)
Partner			−(.36)	−(.19)	−(.18)
Social				.26(.18)	.18(.24)
Work (study)					.20(.24)

102 Self-concept-related measures

Construct validity can be demonstrated through the empirically obtained factors and their comparison with the theoretically postulated subscales. Principal component analyses were conducted on both forms, using varimax rotation and setting as the extraction criterion an Eigen value of greater than 1. Table 7.4 for Form N and Table 7.5 for Form S present the results of these analyses and the factor loadings of the individual items. The results show a very good agreement of the subscales with the empirically obtained factors. All subscales can be clearly reproduced in factors.

Table 7.4 *Principal component analysis of SSS Form N (N = 299)*

Scale/item		F1	F2	F3	F4	F5	h-square
Family	2	**.62**	.09	.20	.15	.35	.58
	8	**.63**	.06	.19	.16	.14	.58
	18	**.82**	.07	.05	.02	07	.68
	19	**.68**	.25	.23	.08	.22	.63
	24	**.70**	.19	.09	.17	.07	.56
	26	**.81**	.05	.05	.08	.11	.69
Work	3	.13	**.79**	.17	.06	.01	.68
	11	.11	**.86**	.15	.07	.04	.79
	14	.08	**.81**	.09	.05	.09	.68
	17	.17	**.78**	.07	.17	−.03	.67
	21	.07	**.69**	.06	.08	.16	.52
Social	5	.08	.03	**.65**	.12	.19	.47
	9	.10	.19	**.69**	.08	.02	.52
	25	.24	.13	**.77**	.09	.16	.70
	28	.13	.12	**.77**	.04	.12	.64
Object	1	.14	.04	.15	**.73**	.03	.58
	7	.08	.05	−.03	**.75**	.00	.57
	13	.10	.13	.05	**.59**	.07	.38
	15	.20	.02	.17	**.67**	.18	.55
	27	−.04	.12	.06	**.62**	.12	.42
Global	10	.19	.06	.01	.12	**.75**	.62
	16	.28	.18	.38	.09	**.57**	.59
	23	.03	.00	.21	.18	**.72**	.59
	30	.36	.11	.14	.03	**.71**	.66
Variance explained		15%	14%	11%	10%	10%	Total 60%

On their respective factors, all items have loadings clearly above .50; on all other factors, items always load less than .40. This is true for both versions of the scale. The two independent samples and factor analyses, yielding comparable results on two different versions of the scale, can be considered quasi-replications of the construct validity, and are thus very satisfactory.

Concurrent validity information is presented for Form S. This information was obtained in a specific questionnaire study that was conducted mainly to obtain validity information on the scale. The scales that were

Table 7.5 *Principal component analysis of SSS Form S (N = 299)*

Scale/item		F1	F2	F3	F4	F5	F6	h-square
Studies	3	**.80**	.04	.14	.11	.20	−.04	.71
	11	**.81**	−.03	.13	.18	.15	.02	.73
	14	**.79**	.13	.09	−.02	.06	−.00	.65
	17	**.78**	.06	.10	.04	−.13	.15	.66
	21	**.75**	.09	−.00	.05	−.02	.13	.59
Partner	2	.18	**.71**	.08	.09	.08	.08	.56
	18	.03	**.76**	.10	.16	.17	.12	.69
	19	.07	**.67**	.08	.18	.11	.26	.57
	26	−.01	**.82**	.02	.05	.09	.07	.68
Object	1	.01	−.02	**.78**	.12	.06	.03	.63
	7	.15	.16	**.71**	.01	.02	.03	.55
	13	.14	.14	**.62**	.02	−.02	.04	.43
	15	.23	.11	**.61**	.11	.01	.28	.53
	27	−.07	−.12	**.73**	.05	.28	.06	.63
Family	4	.04	.18	.16	**.79**	−.03	.10	.69
	8	.07	.22	.12	**.83**	.08	.08	.77
	22	.04	−.11	−.01	**.60**	.11	.20	.43
	24	.17	.21	.03	**.75**	−.01	.16	.66
Global	10	.13	.39	.10	.00	**.56**	.03	.49
	16	.13	.19	.05	.12	**.77**	.09	.66
	23	.12	−.12	.08	.02	**.79**	.11	.67
	30	.10	.22	.05	.00	**.75**	.03	.62
Social	5	.12	.16	.12	.07	.07	**.64**	.47
	9	.07	.12	−.02	.19	−.10	**.76**	.64
	25	.12	.05	.07	.15	.12	**.82**	.74
	28	−.12	.16	.17	.14	.22	**.57**	.46
Variance explained		13%	11%	10%	10%	9%	9%	Total 62%

administered along with the SSS were selected based on some of the theoretical considerations discussed in earlier chapters and will be summarized briefly:

(a) The Self-Monitoring Scale (SM) (Snyder, 1974) was administered, using a slightly amended German translation from Amelang and Borkenau (1982). This instrument measures whether a person orientates his or her behaviour on social cues (called high self-monitor by Snyder) or on internal, self-concept-related cues (called low self-monitor by Snyder). It was hypothesized in Chapter 4 that readiness for self-concept change, and hence satisfaction with self, may lead to a higher orientation to the social environment.

(b) A scale to assess future-orientated achievement motivation (ZBL) (Modick, 1977) was included to capture a possible relationship between satisfaction with self and stability for the future expressed as expectations for future achievements.

(c) The Self-Consciousness Scale (SCS), developed by Scheier, Fenigstein, and Buss (1974), was used in a German translation by Filipp (n.d.). It is one of the assumptions of my work that in order for self-concept-related processes to take place, attention has to focus on the self. Without that, dissatisfaction may not turn into agentic change. Of particular interest are the spheres of life, that is, which subscales, activate private or public self-consciousness.

(d) A German translation of Crowne and Marlowe's (1960) Social Desirability Scale (SD) by Lück and Timaeus (1969) was used to detect a possible influence of social desirability on answers on the SSS.

(e) The Rosenberg scale to measure subjective stability of self (Rosenberg, 1965) was included, that is, the perceived stability of one's own self. This should relate satisfaction with self to self-perceived stability of self.

The correlations of these scales with the subscales and with the total SSS are displayed in Table 7.6, as far as they reach statistical significance of at least .10.

Table 7.6 *Correlations of SSS (Form S) with relevant scales (N = 200)*

	Self-monitoring	Future orientation	Private self-consciousness	Public self-consciousness	Social desirability	Rosenberg stability
Global	–	.24***	–	–	–	.37***
Family	–	.23**	–	–	–	.25***
Partner	–.16*	–	.29***	.36***	–	.31***
Social	–.16*	–	–	–	–	.27***
Studies	–	.23**	–	–	–.15*	.34***
Object	–.19**	–	–	.15*	–	.18*
Total	–.21**	.24***	–	.23**	–	.47***

*** $p < .001$; ** $p < .01$; * $p < .05$.

Of greatest interest is the highly significant relationship between the total SSS score and the Rosenberg Stability-of-Self Scale. As could be expected, persons that were dissatisfied with themselves are also more likely to consider their self-concept to be unstable. However, the relationship with the Self-Esteem Scale is quite low. In another study, using an English-language version of the SSS, McCuster (1985) found a highly positive relationship ($r = .55$) between the Rosenberg Self-Esteem Scale (Rosenberg, 1965; also in Robinson & Shaver, 1969) and the total score of the satisfaction with self.

The correlation between satisfaction with self and self-monitoring is also significant, indicating that satisfaction with oneself indeed goes together

Satisfaction with self

with an internal orientation, and dissatisfaction with oneself is related to an orientation to the outside world, and its social cues. This relation could be obtained for the total score and in the subscales Partner, Social, and Object. This could possibly indicate that for the population investigated in this study, partner relationships, friendships, and personal possessions are of particular relevance for defining the relationship between the individual's self-concept and the outside, social, and physical environment.

Future orientation in regard to achievement motivation was thought to be related to a positive self-image that one wishes to project into the future. Indeed, there is a positive significant correlation between the Future Orientation Scale and satisfaction with self on the subscales Global, Family, and Study, the latter two being the two life spheres where achievement-related issues are most likely to be salient in a student's life.

Public and private self-consciousness are highly positively correlated with satisfaction with intimate relationships (Partner). This could indicate that attention is focused on those aspects of self that one is satisfied with, if no other factors influence the focus of attention. Public self-consciousness is also positively correlated with the total SSS score and with Object. Personal possessions are likely to play a role in public self-consciousness because of the possibility of using them for self-presentational purposes.

There were no relationships to the Social Desirability Scale that would have indicated any serious problems with the SSS. Only the subscale Study has a relatively small negative correlation ($r = -.15$) with social desirability. Perhaps, within a university context, when data are collected by fellow students, German students think it is appropriate to indicate dissatisfaction with work and studies.

These data on the relationships between the Satisfaction with Self Scale and other scales which were selected on the basis of theoretical considerations are very satisfactory. The relationships obtained are interpretable within the present theoretical framework, and are differentiated according to different self-concept-relevant life spheres. The findings support some ideas about the relationship between satisfaction with and the self-perceived stability of the self. This can turn into readiness for change which requires an outside orientation in order to acquire new information and experiences which could at some point be incorporated into the self-concept.

With the autophotographical method and the Satisfaction with Self Scale, tools are now available for the specific purposes of the present research project. The first measures the way the environment is subjectively perceived as being relevant to a person's self-concept. The rating procedure tries to determine which function these aspects of the environment may have for the achievement of stability or change in the self-concept. The Satisfaction with Self Scale is based on an approach that sees the self-concept as anchored within a person's social and physical environment and concentrates on those life spheres where the influence between self-concept and environment is likely to be mutual.

8 Functions of the physical environment for the self-concept

The recognition of the social character of the physical world and hence its social meaning for the development of self can be traced back to Mead. Curiously, and perhaps significantly for the later treatment of the inanimate world by Mead's direct and indirect followers, he only dealt with objects in a footnote:

> It is possible for inanimate objects ... to form parts of the generalized and organized – the completely socialized – other for any given human individual, in so far as he responds to such objects socially or in a social fashion ... Any thing – any object or set of objects, whether animate or inanimate, human or animal, or merely physical, toward which he acts, or to which he responds, socially, is an element in what for him is the generalized other. (Mead, 1934, p. 154)

In the early seventies, Graumann (1974) still had reason to lament the neglect of things in psychology. Though he was able to point to a variety of authors who had considered the meaning and function of things for the human condition, things were left out of psychological theorizing because human activity, the subject matter of psychology, was studied separately from its physical context.

Since then, environmental psychology has emerged as a field of psychology in its own right to put human activity in its context. The emergence of environmental psychology was closely tied to dissatisfaction with social psychology in the early seventies (see Darroch & Miller, 1981), and several of its leading proponents broke away from social psychology (Proshansky, 1976). The psychological consideration of things and physical environments took place, to a large degree, independently of the theoretical developments within social psychology. Therefore, the emergence of interest in things and environments happened parallel to, but independently of the re-emergence of interest in the self.

By now, the physical environment has received much attention in regard to its role for a person's understanding of self. This applies to the molar environment, for instance the place where one lives, and to a lesser degree to elements of the molecular environment, for instance personal possessions, or, more generally, things. However, theory and research on the role of the physical environment have been curiously separated from other areas of self-concept research. Most of it has taken place in the context of environmental psychology and has not taken into account recent developments in self-concept research in social psychology. Social psychologists, on the other hand, have treated environmental psychology more as an applied offshoot and have rarely considered its theoretical notions as relevant to their central theoretical concepts.

I shall argue that physical aspects of the world surrounding a person can have several functions for the self-concept of that person. First, they can enable one to engage in self-relevant behaviours, either as a setting or as a tool. A skier needs a mountain, and a tennis player a racquet. Secondly, they can stimulate self-concept-relevant cognitions, for instance memories or projections of future goals for oneself. Instances would be places from one's childhood, or a picture of oneself. Thirdly, they can present the self to others. For some, this is done through the style of the house one lives in, or even the neighbourhood, or the books that are displayed on one's shelf. Fourthly, they can carry with them rules of social conduct, and thus have similar functions for the self-concept to role prescriptions. Examples would be a court of law or a church. The meaning of things and settings for the self-concept will be considered in turn.

The function of things for the self-concept

Csikszentmihalyi and Rochberg-Halton (1981) undertook a major study surveying the things that people cherish most. They interviewed over 300 women, men, and children from three generations in their homes and simply asked them to describe their homes and the objects in them. Special objects, that is, cherished possessions, were the main subjects of the interviews: why were they special, what would it mean to be without them, and how were they acquired? The answers to such questions provide suggestions about the functions of things for the self-concept.

Their data provided lists of the different kinds of objects mentioned most frequently. Of particular interest were generational differences in the kinds of objects mentioned most frquently as special. For the children, stereos were mentioned most frequently by far (46 per cent), followed by television (37 per cent), furniture (33 per cent) and musical instruments (32 per cent). For their grandparents' generation, photographs (37 per cent), furniture (34 per cent), and books (26 per cent) were most special. The parents' generation cherished furniture (38 per cent), visual art (37 per cent), and sculpture (27 per cent). The interpretation of these generational differences becomes more obvious through the results of

The function of things

the second rating step, which assigned meaning categories to the special objects (Csikszentmihalyi & Rochberg-Halton, 1981, Table 4.2).

The youngest generation were different from their parents and grandparents in that for them, special objects had less meaning for memories and fewer intrinsic qualities and referred less to the past and less to the immediate family or kin, but much more to themselves. For young people, obviously, objects gain their meaning not because they provide continuity in a temporal and social sense, but because they allow them to experience themselves and to gain experience by dealing with those objects: stereos, television sets, and musical instruments. Each object only becomes meaningful when dealt with as an instrument with a potentially constantly changing meaning depending on how it is used. For instance, a stereo set changes its meaning depending on which type of music is being played. These objects acquire meaning by being tools for action through which the young people experience themselves.

The parents' generation are different from the other two in that for them special objects hold more 'intrinsic qualities'. Intrinsic qualities are, for instance, defined through their uniqueness, as being hand made, or through the way their physical properties are described. The members of the other two generations ascribed fewer intrinsic qualities to their special objects. The parents' generation's objects (visual art, sculpture, and furniture) had a meaning that stands by itself.

One can speculate whether an object with 'intrinsic' qualities, as defined by Csikszentmihalyi and Rochberg-Halton, can communicate these qualities to other parties just as well as to the person to whom it is special. If the intrinsic quality is also a shared quality of an object on display, it may be likely to communicate information about its owner to others and thus acquire self-presentational qualities which were not included in Csikszentmihalyi's and Rochberg-Halton's meaning categories. The objects mentioned, furniture and art, are indeed most likely to communicate immediately to a visitor in someone's home what kind of person lives there. On the other hand, objects that acquire meaning through handling, or those that carry with them connotations only accessible through the knowledge of one's personal and family history, cannot communicate easily to others and therefore have less self-presentational value.

The oldest generation do not value objects so much for their intrinsic qualities or as something only relating to themselves; photographs, furniture, and books are valued for the memories they carry with them, the experiences attached to them, the relationship to the immediate family they hold, and their links to the past (all meanings above 80 per cent). In that, they do not differ very much from the parent generation's meaning, but the additional qualities ascribed there (intrinsic and self) are absent in the older generation. These objects and meanings relate the individuals to their social and temporal context. This analysis suggests a third dimension to an ecology of the self-concept, namely a temporal one, linking past and present in a social and environmental context. In similar vein, Graumann (1985) discussed the meaning of things for an ecology of memory.

The interpretation of these results offered by Csikszentmihalyi and Rochberg-Halton (1981) and Rochberg-Halton (1984) is similar when they suggest a shift over the life span from *action* in youth to *contemplation* in older age. The only element not considered by these authors is the possible self-presentational value of an object – its ability to communicate to others. In addition, it is particularly interesting to see the different ways in which objects relate an individual's self to that person's *social environment* through associations with family and others, to that person's *temporal context* by linking past, present, and future (the most frequent meaning category in all three generations), and to the *physical environment* by being a special element in the home environment.

While Csikszentmihalyi and Rochberg-Halton offer a primarily descriptive, though very rich analysis of the meaning of things, a study by Vinsel, Brown, Altman, and Foss (1980) examines the consequences that differential relationships between thing and self can have. They considered the function of things in the context of an analysis of privacy (Altman, 1975, 1976). 'Privacy' is for Altman a unifying concept relating to the control of boundaries between self and others through verbal and non-verbal means. In particular, he attempts to subsume concepts of spatial behaviour and territorial control as specific mechanisms of privacy regulation. Within the concept of privacy, territorial behaviour in particular aims at '(a) the communication of one's personal identity, whereby people display their personalities, values, and beliefs on the physical environment and (b) regulation of social interaction, which is achieved by control of spatial areas and objects' (Vinsel et al., 1980, p. 1104).

Vinsel et al. (1980) conducted a study that related mechanisms of privacy regulation to the effectiveness of the individual functioning of new students. Two mechanisms of privacy regulation were included: personal displays within one's territory, that is, wall coverings in students' rooms, and mechanisms of contact seeking and avoiding, that is, behaviours that enhance or diminish the chance of personal encounters with others. Examples range from opening one's door or using the bathroom at a busy time on one hand, to shutting one's door and going for a walk alone on the other hand. Generally, it was found that students who made more use of such social contact-regulating behaviours were more likely to stay in the university, whereas drop-outs made less use of most of these behaviours. The differences between stay-ins and drop-outs, however, are in the present context especially interesting when their personal decorations are considered. There was a tendency for later drop-outs to decorate more of their rooms with objects relating to personal relations (for instance pictures of friends and family) and idiosyncratic items (for example handmade items), and to music/theatre. Stay-ins used more decorations referring to entertainment/equipment (bicycle, skis, etc.). In addition, the decorations of later drop-outs were less diverse. Finally, an index of commitment to the new university environment was computed, and another index of commitment to the home town. These indices took into account displays relating to either the home or the university environment. Differences between drop-outs and stay-ins were significant in the anticipated directions.

The study demonstrates the relationships between effective functioning in a new environment (if drop-out versus stay-in is accepted as an operationalization of effective functioning) and the use of behaviours and displays referring to social interaction. The displays of the stay-in students belong in the 'active' category prevalent in Csikszentmihalyi and Rochberg-Halton's younger generation, whereas the displays of drop-outs belong in the 'self' and 'family' categories, more prevalent in the older generations. Their commitment to the previous home environment hinders their adaptation to the new environment. On the other hand, the self-presentational message of these items may be a lack of interest in the new environment and therefore demonstrate lack of interest in the people who belong to it.

The results of the above-cited studies can tentatively be related to a model of self-concept change. Socialization of the self in a novel context requires the acquisition of new experiences so as to provide meaning to the relationship between self and the new context. The acquisition of experience with objects occurs literally by handling them, that is, possessing objects that are tools to provide experience: the 'active' meaning category in one study, or the 'entertainment/equipment' category in the other. Adolescents as well as persons in a new environment are high in these categories. It can be speculated that any process of acquiring information about oneself, independently of age and status, may be facilitated through objects of this nature. Maintenance of the self-concept works rather through objects indicating stability and embeddedness of the individual in a social and temporal context. Such objects were in one study associated with the older generation, who presumably have a more stable self-concept, and with drop-outs, that is, those unwilling or unable to adapt themselves to a new environment.

Such an interpretation would relate the generations in Csikszentmihalyi and Rochberg-Halton's study to different stages in a process of acquisition or change of the self-concept, and would use the Vinsel et al. study to illustrate two different processes, namely facilitation of change and resistance to change in a new self–environment relationship. While on the basis of the data presented, such links are merely speculative, they provide important suggestions for an ecological approach to self-concept change.

A tentative, three-stage model of the role of things in self-concept change can now be offered. The three stages are (a) the acquisition of new knowledge about the self, (b) the stabilization of that knowledge as part of the self-concept, and (c) the maintenance of these elements of the self-concept, even in the face of challenges.

(a) New knowledge about oneself is acquired through action and interaction. At this stage, an important function of things is the facilitation of action. Such objects carry no meaning by themselves, but they are used to produce and mediate experiences about oneself. For instance, a stereo set can be used to produce the type of music that allows an adolescent to experience himself or herself. This experience may link him or her through social implications to his or her peers. A tennis racquet can be a tool allowing a certain activity that will provide a test of one's physical capabilities through social comparison as well as access to a social group.

Objects at this stage are tools which allow certain activities. The self-concept relevance of these activities comes from their embeddedness in a social context, and it is the activity and its context that provide meaning, not the physical object by itself. By being handled in a social context, the object itself may, at some point, acquire meaning of its own.

(b) Once new information about oneself is acquired and is becoming part of the self-concept, it has to be stabilized. Stabilization means establishing links to other elements of the self-concept. One way of doing this is to provide social reality for the new element of the self. Social reality, as elaborated by Wicklund and Gollwitzer (1982) and Gollwitzer (1986), can be established through the display of symbols of an element of the self-concept. Objects can thereby function in a self-presentational way by announcing an attribute of the person to others. This way, a public commitment has been established, and the new element of self-concept is recognized as part of the self. Giving it up would now incur a cost of some kind to the individual. The role of objects in this process is self-presentational and already provides links between the new element of self and its social and temporal context. Objects used as symbols *sensu* Wicklund and Gollwitzer can serve as indicators on the way to a self-concept-relevant goal. The social function of objects at this stage implies that they are more likely to have a meaning that can be shared with others.

(c) Once an element of the self-concept has been acquired and established, it has to maintain its stability even in the face of challenges. Stability in such a situation is created through links to other elements of the self-concept.

Therefore, objects are especially relevant in so far as they signify the relationship to the social, spatial, and temporal context of a person's self-concept. Objects that are reminders of persons, places, or events serve such a function. Their meaning does not necessarily have to be communicable to others, but it must be clearly understood by the person him- or herself.

In the course of adult life, new information about the self is constantly acquired, other information becomes established, and still other information about oneself is successfully or unsuccessfully being challenged. Therefore, different kinds of objects are meaningful to one person at the same time, and one object may have more than one function for that person's self-concept. Empirically, only a relative predominance of different kinds and meanings of objects may be establishable at times in one's life when one of the stages is likely to be predominant.

The studies cited above serve as illustrations. The different generations in Csikszentmihalyi and Rochberg-Halton's study are in a very general sense likely to be associated with the different stages in self-concept change: adolescents are constantly attempting to acquire information about themselves, persons in mid-life are more likely to stabilize their self-concept, and persons in later life have to sustain their self-concept in view of diminishing social reality for it. The study by Vinsel et al. concentrates on people who experience seemingly similar transitions in life, and who deal with them in ways that are associated with different stages of the above three-stage model. One group, the stay-ins, are willing to change the self-concept to that of a college student and acquire the necessary knowledge; the other group are maintaining their former self-concept and because of the strength of the new ecology that counters that self-concept, they are more likely to return to an ecology supporting their old self-concept.

The function of molar environments to the self-concept

The function of molar environments for the self-concept will be discussed here on the basis of two approaches in psychology: the concept of *behaviour setting* (Barker, 1968), and the concept of *place identity* (Proshansky, 1978).

The behaviour setting

'Behaviour setting' is a central concept of Barker's ecological psychology (1968) and was developed as an attempt by Barker to operationalize Lewin's (1943) concept of psychological ecology. Through the detailed, close observation of behaviour in natural settings over long periods Barker came to believe that behavioural variance is frequently due to the particular physical setting in which a behaviour takes place. Certain settings allow certain types of behaviour: for instance the members of a church congregation will display very similar behaviour patterns of standing, kneeling, sitting, praying, and singing. The nature of the behaviour setting is that of an ecological, situational unit, which extra-individually determines much of the behavioural variance.

The behaviour-setting concept was not elaborated much theoretically by Barker. However, Lévy-Leboyer (1979) points to three important consequences: (a) The environment is dependent upon its inhabitants and their regulatory behaviour (for instance organized activities). In turn, the physical setting determines the behaviour and prevents behaviours not related to its goal. (b) Because of individual differences between persons, different setting–person relationships may occur. (However, this interpretation by Lévy-Leboyer may only apply to differences in which the setting constrains behaviours outside the allowed range.) (c) Comparable settings may show ecological variability depending upon whether they are, for the purposes of the setting, over- or undermanned. The finding that undermanned settings allow for greater behavioural variability may again only mean that the behaviour setting's purpose distributes the acts necessary to fulfil that purpose among those present. Therefore, individual differences and ecological variability can still be subsumed under the guidance of the concept, namely that a setting's purpose explains a larger amount of the variability of behaviour of the individuals in it than anything else.

The concept's most important contribution is usually described as the 'discovery' of an independent entity determining behaviour that consists of a physical setting along with inherent behavioural prescriptions. Identifying the concept of the behaviour setting was a major step toward understanding behaviour not only from a person-centered psychological perspective but as embedded in an ecological context. Concentrating on the behaviour setting, however, was done at the cost of neglecting the psychological and social aspects.

Recently, several attempts have been undertaken to revive the behaviour-setting concept as a useful theoretical and empirical unit (Kaminski, 1985; Fuhrer, 1985). For instance, Kruse (1986) linked it to a more recent concept from social cognition, namely scripts, and used it as an example to point to parallels between the ecological and cognitive approach.

One could also look at the behaviour setting as a set of rules of social conduct shared by members of a social group, similar to role prescriptions. Behaviour settings could then be conceived of as aspects of the environment having physical and social properties that 'carry meaning in the form of shared behavioral expectations that grow out of social interaction' (Stryker's (1980) first proposition on symbolic interactionism (p. 53)). To take the parallel further: from interaction with others, one learns how one is expected to behave with reference to a particular behaviour setting; one is socialized into a behaviour setting. Behaviour settings also frequently assign positions to people acting in them and thus provide a social structure. The shared behavioural expectations created by a behaviour setting are role prescriptions.

A description of behaviour settings in the language of symbolic interaction and role theory can be useful for two purposes: (a) to consider the potential for behavioural variability for the individual in a setting, and (b) to point out the relevance of behaviour settings for the self-concept. A behavioural variability greater than that implied by Barker (and for reasons other than those implied by Lévy-Leboyer) in the behaviour setting can be theoretically deduced in the behaviour setting–role parallel when recognizing that roles, like settings, do not determine social behaviour but rather constrain the possibilities for alternatives: 'Roles are "made" rather than "played"' (Stryker, 1980, p. 54). In a behaviour setting, too, behaviour is the result of a role-making process. Behaviour settings differ in the degree to which they are open or closed with respect to the variations on behaviour they allow.

If behaviour settings can function like role prescriptions, behaviour in a given setting can become part of a person's behavioural repertoire formed by 'all the roles we are prepared to take in formulating our own line of action, both the roles of individuals and of generalized others' (Becker, 1968). A behaviour setting is a necessary prerequisite for the enactment of self-concept-relevant behaviours. A religious person may need a church to enact that religion, just as others need an art gallery, a theatre, or a shopping precinct to activate aspects of their self-concept. On the other hand, the socialization process within a given behaviour setting can be part of a larger socialization process providing necessary elements for an aspect of the self-concept. For the child, being socialized into church (as a social entity) also means being socialized in church (as a behaviour setting). The routines of conduct, the distribution of individuals within the church setting – all this is an expression of the rules and social structure of the church organization. In self-concept change, behaviour settings can be important mediators of new roles and behaviours.

In the context of environmental change in particular, the role of behaviour settings in the stability or change of the self-concept becomes relevant. The availability of behaviour settings, that is, the potential for constraint in change, varies with the molar, geographic environment. Obviously, rural small towns have different sorts of behaviour settings from metropolitan areas. Empirically, Barker and Schoggen (1973), after fourteen years of observation in a small town in the American Midwest and in an English town, found that Midwestern children had twice as many behaviour settings involving public expression of emotion, and fourteen times as many settings providing them with public attention than the children in the English town. The English town, on the other hand, provided its children with more settings related to sports and arts.

When considering self-concept change in an ecological context, behaviour settings are useful in demonstrating that within a stable environment, the possibilities for self-concept change are limited, although within complex environments, persons can select from among a broad range of settings. Changing environments can greatly alter the availability of behaviour settings, and thus facilitate self-concept change.

Place identity

The concept of place identity as a substructure of self-identity has theoretically been elaborated by Proshansky and his associates (Proshansky, 1978; Proshansky, Fabian, & Kaminoff, 1983). While acknowledging the role individual, interpersonal, and group processes play in the development of self-identity, they stress the contribution of the built environment to a person's personality development and that person's definition in relation to society. They define *place identity* as follows:

> To begin with, it is a substructure of the self-identity of a person consisting of, broadly conceived, cognitions about the physical world in which the individual lives. These cognitions represent memories, ideas, feelings, attitudes, values, preferences, meanings, and conceptions of behaviour and experience which relate to the variety and complexity of physical settings that define the day-to-day existence of every human being. At the core of such physical environment-related cognitions is the 'environmental past' of the person; a past consisting of places, spaces, and their properties which have served instrumentally in the satisfaction of the person's biological, psychological, social, and cultural needs. (Proshansky, Fabian, & Kaminoff, 1983, p. 59)

In many respects, Proshansky et al. emphasize that place identity is acquired and functions much like other aspects of one's self-concept. The meaning of places is mediated through social experiences, as well as what other people do, say, or think about a particular place. On a cognitive level, the processes involved in place identity are considered to be the same ones underlying the formation of other cognitive structures. However, while the processes are considered to be the same, the theoretical concept 'place identity' is necessary to point out that the physical environment shapes social experiences, and that specific schemata, scripts, or expectations exist in connection with the built environment. Therefore, some properties of the physical environment, for instance in regard to stability and change, can be linked to the relevant cognitive structures.

This can be exemplified when considering the function of place identity in mediating change.

A person can perceive discrepancies between his or her place identity and the characteristics of the physical setting, calling for the recognition of necessary change in the person–environment relationship, and for an assessment of the personal resources needed to affect that change. Several types of cognitions are identified by Proshansky et al. as mediating that change.

First, there are those cognitions that relate to changing the physical environment itself. Such cognitions, relating to personal skills to initiate change in the physical environment, and the interpersonal resources available or necessary, have been acquired in dealing with physical environments. These cognitions are important in an ecological approach to a person–environment system. In order to optimize the person–environment fit, a person has to make use of cognitions acquired in past dealings with this and other environments and in the social context that comes with environments: the physical world socialization. Thus, all experiences with an environment contribute to optimize the person–environment fit.

The second type of cognition refers to the physical world setting of interpersonal transactions. Interpersonal transactions are affected by the fact that persons occupy spaces, and that one's behaviour alters the actual nature of a physical setting. The meaning of a communication is determined by its setting, and the meaning of a setting can be altered by the specific interpersonal transactions taking place there. In particular, Proshansky et al. refer to skills using the physical setting as a medium to regulate privacy processes (see Altman, 1975).

Both types of cognitions change either the actual physical setting or the meaning of the physical setting. A third type of cognition is activated if the physical setting and the behaviour of others in it cannot be changed. Thus, these are cognitions affecting change in the person him- or herself to optimize the person–environment fit. They may involve cutting out some select sensory input from the physical setting, or in other ways reducing some specific impact certain effects of the environment may have on the individual while accepting others. Proshansky et al. state that these types of cognitions refer to certain types of environmental skills. These consist of the *environmental understanding* of the meaning of changes in the environment with regard to oneself, of *environmental competence*, that is, to be able to act in an appropriate way in relation to a physical setting, and of *environmental control*, that is, the ability to affect changes in the person–environment relationship.

Proshansky's theoretical analysis points to the necessity of including the physical environment in the understanding of processes of acquisition of and change in one's self-concept. In no way is the importance of the social process devalued; rather, social process is shown to be embedded, restricted, and enriched by the physical setting in which it takes place. Change in the self-concept is mediated through cognitions and processes that relate to the regulation of person–environment relationships which also determine the relationships to other persons and the experiences one has with regard to oneself.

An empirical illustration of the concept of place identity can be found in the work of Graumann and Schneider (Graumann & Schneider, 1986; Schneider, in press; Schneider, 1986). They found that the identity of a person is partially determined by that person's network of actual and biographical relevancy within a given neighbourhood. People attribute an inherent continuity to their physical setting, which thus lends stability to their identity. Physical settings, in particular those that themselves have some identity, such as old and distinctive parts of town, contribute to the identity of a person.

A different approach assessing the meaning of molar environments is possible on the basis of data from autophotography. Information available from photographs taken as part of one of the studies in the current research programme (see Chapter 11) can be analysed to yield an understanding of the meaning of urban environment for the self-concept and its role in change.

A study on the meaning of urban environments for the self-concept

The analysis of place identity at the same time stresses the relevance of the physical setting and points out that it functions similarly to other constituents of the self-concept. This is also the basic theoretical framework from which the role of urban environments for a person's self-understanding is considered here, namely as one element of an eco-system. These elements can usually only be considered as part of the whole system. The analysis here will assess the relative role of urban environments as compared to other aspects of the environment of a person that are considered by that person to belong to the self.

The method of assessment was autophotography (see Chapter 7). The set of photographs analysed for this purpose consisted of 707 photographs, taken by 101 adult subjects from a general population as part of a study of persons who had relocated (reported in Chapter 11). The data are reported here separately in the context of place identity, because they can be used to illustrate how autophotography allows one to assess some of the functions of urban environments for the self-concept. Relocating to a new city might conceivably make urban environments somewhat more salient.

The present data are based on 661 photographs (46 could not be analysed). Description of content refers to all 661 photographs. Of these, 52 (7.9 per cent)

The meaning of urban environments 119

depicted urban environments, which was one of 14 content categories into which the photographs were classified. Three of these categories referred to environments (urban, inside of living space, or nature), three to people, and eight to things. As mentioned before, research participants had to rank the seven photographs that they had taken according to their personal importance. One way to assess the relative importance of different contents is to compare the order of importance within content categories. Table 8.1 shows the absolute number of occurrences and the mean rank ordering of personal importance, as given by the subjects themselves for all content types within content categories (environments, persons, objects).

Table 8.1 *Occurrence and personal importance of photograph content*

Content category	Content type	N	Rank
Environments		**536**	**3.9**
	City	52	4.8
	Outside of building	17	4.5
	Inside living space	369	3.7
	Natural	42	4.3
	Park / garden	42	4.3
	Outside technical structure or environment	14	3.9
Persons		**129**	**3.0**
	Partner	24	1.9
	Family	27	2.1
	Friends	24	3.5
	Subject him- or herself	24	3.5
	Others	30	3.8
Objects		**62**	**3.9**
	Sports equipment	10	3.1
	Plants	10	3.7
	Books	35	4.1
	Personal possessions	7	4.6

Note: Low numbers refer to high rank. Category ranks are the mean of the individual ranks within category. Some photographs were assigned to more than one content category.

The table shows that, by number, environments are most represented (73.7 per cent), persons are much less depicted (17.7 per cent) and objects least of all (8.5 per cent). However, the average ranking of importance shows that people are considered to be much more personally important to a person, whereas the categories referring to the physical environment are less important, although not differing from one another.

The second step of analysis is based on the differences in the meaning assigned to the settings depicted. Comparisons are based on the functional dimensions described in Chapter 7: perspective, integration, self-presentation, symbolism, activity, memory, and reflection.

120 *Functions of the physical environment*

First, the types of environments were compared: urban, natural, and inside living space. Urban environments were rated as having less self-presentational value and as being less instrumental for specific activities than the average of all other categories. When comparing the perspective taken, urban environments are represented as more distant and less involved (2.5), whereas nature is represented as most immediate, from a perspective where the person is involved. The inside of a flat or house is photographed from an intermediate perspective (2.9; $p < .0001$). Urban environments serve least for self-presentational purposes (1.4), and inside living spaces most, as could be expected. Urban environments are also lowest in their activity value (1.1) as well as their reflection value (1.5). In summary, then, it seems that as compared to the two other categories of environments, urban environments consistently have the lowest scores for being functional for or expressive of the self-concept. This holds true even when all other categories of objects depicted are taken into account as well, as in Table 8.2.

The perspective taken is most distant when urban environments, furniture, or pets (that is, cats or dogs) are photographed; close-ups are used for sports equipment and books. Urban environments are slightly more integrated in their context than the average of the other categories, but not as much as furniture, pets, or natural environments. The self-presentational value of

Table 8.2 *Ratings on functional dimensions for physical environment*

Category	Perspective	Integration	Self-presentation	Symbolic value	Activities value	Memory value	Reflection
Environment							
City	2.5	3.1	1.4	1.9	1.1	1.1	1.5
Outside of building	3.0	2.5	2.0	2.3	1.3	1.3	1.7
Inside living space	2.9	3.3	2.1	2.1	1.9	1.1	1.7
Natural	3.3	3.3	1.6	2.2	1.2	1.0	1.8
Park/garden	3.0	3.2	1.6	2.7	1.5	1.1	1.7
Technical structure	2.9	3.0	1.6	2.0	1.3	1.1	2.0
Persons							
Partner				1.3			
Self			3.3				
Objects							
Paintings/art				1.4		1.5	1.9
Books	3.9						2.2
Pets	3.0	3.1				1.0	
Sports equipment	3.9				4.5		1.2
Furniture	2.9	3.4					1.2
Musical instruments			2.9		3.6		
Car			2.9				

Note: Ratings were done on 5-point scales, with '1' as low and '5' as high on that dimension. Ratings for persons and objects are presented as far as they are significantly distinct for the content category on that dimension.

urban environments is lowest (1.4), and is highest for cars and musical instruments (2.9 and 2.9). The symbolic value of urban environments is also very low (1.9) – only persons are lower (partner 1.3). Urban environments and art objects were considered to be least conducive to activities. The memory value of urban environments (1.1) was lowest, together with that for pets (1.0); however, the highest rating in the memory dimension for art objects was only 1.5. Urban environments are also relatively low on the reflection ratings (1.5), whereas books and objects of art are highest. Only sports equipment, furniture, and personal belongings, like a pair of glasses, are somewhat lower here. Again, even when compared to all possible objects depicted in the photographs, urban environments seem to be less functional to the self-concept than most other categories.

Next, on another level of analysis, it can be asked: for what kind of person or under what circumstances are urban environments more important? Even if they do not seem to be as relevant to the self-concept as some other aspects of the *Umwelt* of the self are, that does not have to mean that there may not be special circumstances or special kinds of persons for whom they are more relevant. Two-thirds of the research participants had not taken any photographs of urban environments at all, 26 per cent had taken one, and 11 per cent included more than one photograph of urban environments among the seven pictures descriptive of their self-concept. Further analyses compared the group of persons having any photograph of an urban environment to the group of persons having none. These groups did not differ on moving status, age, or sex. An interesting relationship was found when using the self-monitoring scale (Snyder, 1974) measuring the extent to which people orientate themselves to external social cues. Persons having photographs of urban environments are significantly higher on the self-monitoring scale, that is, more externally orientated in looking for social cues (10.9 versus 8.9, $p < .005$).

Participants in this study were also asked about significant life events in the past year. Two life events differentiated the groups that had or had not taken photographs of urban environments (although only at a level of significance better than .10): the 'urban environmentalists' indicated more frequently that they had had to make a new beginning in life during the last twelve months, and they were more likely to have undergone some severe illness. Based on the relationships to other life events, 'new beginning' is frequently used as a euphemism for something going wrong in people's lives. Persons for whom urban environments are important to their self-concept are more likely to be retired or unemployed, and less likely to be civil servants, workers, or housewives, whereas they are equally represented among middle-class white-collar workers, students, and apprentices. There is no relation to the number of times one has moved or to age.

Generally, when urban environments are seen in the context of all the possible aspects of the environment that may be of relevance to one's understanding and/or presentation of self, they seem to be of limited relevance. Only about one-third of all subjects considered urban environments as at all related to their self-concept, and of those, the large majority had only one such photograph. Of all photographs, only about 8 per cent were of urban environments.

Their meaning for the self-concept, as defined by the present theoretically based rating categories, was also consistently lower for urban environments than for most other categories. When urban environments are considered, they seemed to the raters to be less functional and meaningful for the self on several dimensions. However, the groups of people for whom urban environments do seem to be more expressive of their self-concept were in some ways different from others: they were more outward-looking in their search for social cues, they underwent a recent life event that was likely to be negative, and they were somewhat more likely not to be part of the work force. These life situations are times when people need more outside orientation because their internal stability has been questioned as a system for guidance. This seems to be the kind of person and the kind of situation for whom urban environments become more relevant: a person who has to look at what is around him or her; who has to look for orientation in the outside world.

These findings can be related to the ecological approach to self-concept change. According to this framework, some life events destabilize an element of the ecology of the self, for instance the social network, and question the self-concept. This is expected to lead to an outside orientation to find new aspects that can eventually be incorporated into a changed self-concept. An orientation to new aspects of social life could already be demonstrated in the life style of persons who had moved to a new location in connection with a self-concept-questioning life event (see Chapter 3). The present data extend these findings by demonstrating an outside orientation toward the physical environment after negative life events and by connecting this to a psychological state of being receptive to outside cues in social behaviour, namely self-monitoring.

While the above data seem to reduce the importance of the urban environment to a person's self-concept, they show that it is just in critical times, when one's sense of self is threatened, that a person relies more on this aspect of the physical environment. This does not seem to be in contradiction to an approach that emphasizes the role of place identity as one of several constituents of a person's self-concept, and it considers the function of perceptions that mediate changing person−environment relationships.

The meaning of urban environments

In summary, the molecular and molar physical environment has many functions in regard to a person's self-concept. Therefore, the relationship between a person and the physical environment is inextricably linked to that person's relationship to his or her social environment. As the relationship to one changes, the relationship to the other and among both change as well. A person's self-concept cannot be unaffected by changes in the environment. The person can either try to change the environment, or the place and role of others in it, or he or she can change the self-concept. Based on this is the general idea that the study of persons in the face of changes in the person–environment relationship, using relocation as an example, may be crucial for the understanding of the processes related to self-concept change.

9 Anticipation of transition from university

The anticipation of change in the person–environment relationship may itself be enough to start processes that either initiate self-concept change or instead solidify the present concept of self in the anticipation of necessary defensive maintenance. These may at first be changes in the way the environment is perceived, the functions it has for the self-concept, or the potential for functions it can have for future maintenance or change. Some aspects of the environment may only be relevant in transition between different states of the social and physical environment or in the individual's transition between environments. Two studies will be reported, one on the perception of the environment after transitions and in anticipation of change, the other one on commitment and interpersonal strategies in the anticipation of discontinuity of the self-concept. To study the relevant processes, both studies used transitions in connection with university exams and anticipation of the future after the exams.

Perceptions of the environment at times of transition

Something that has been of interest throughout this research is the role the physical environment plays in transitions and in the process of self-concept change. Information from several sources can be summarized suggesting that a person's relationship to his or her physical environment changes and that this change in relationship manifests itself through changes in the way this environment is perceived.

Within the self-concept literature that has been reviewed in Chapter 4, localization of identity is considered as ranging from inside values, convictions, and memories, to the outside, where it is represented in possessions, environments, or places where one has grown up. The literature on the meaning of the physical environment for the self-concept, as reviewed in Chapter 8, supports this notion. There, identity is seen as formed through the experiences and possibilities the physical environment one lives in affords, and is experienced and expressed in the objects one owns, handles, displays, and keeps.

The notion that transitions and self-concept change are occasions where the relationships to one's physical environment are particularly likely to change also finds some support. The success of the transition to college was shown to be correlated with and to some degree predictable by the objects displayed in the student's room (Vinsel et al., 1980). The way a person adapts to a new environment seems to be mediated by the way that a person handles the physical environment. But in addition the anticipation of a future transition is expressed in changing perceptions of the environment, as demonstrated in a study by Wofsey, Rierdan, and Wapner (1979). There, students who had graduated from college drew pictures of the environment where they had spent the past few years of their life, namely the campus. Whether or not these students had plans for the future was related to the way they presented their environment: those with plans seemed to have distanced themselves already and presented general and more distant views of the college campus; those without plans for the future seemed to be seeing themselves much more as part of that environment, and drew details or themselves into the picture.

The study by Wofsey et al. suggests that a quasi-experimental approach is necessary to shed more light on some assumptions inherent in the ecological model of self-concept change. One of the basic assumptions is that the localization of identity shifts in the process of self-concept change. A disturbance in the ecological system changes the relationship with the physical environment as well as its meaning and function. Dissatisfaction with oneself is also assumed to be related to a greater reliance on the outside, defining oneself through relationships to the outside world and obtaining new information about oneself that may eventually be incorporated into the self-concept.

Graduation from university, as in the study by Wofsey et al., is a transition that lends itself to the study of changing self-environment relations. It is a transition potentially involving changes in many aspects of life: social relationships are affected, work relationships are affected, frequently relocations either to the old home residence or to a new place of work take place, and the end of an old segment of life should also imply a new one. This transition between end and beginning is appropriately captured in Wofsey et al.'s variable asking subjects whether they have concrete plans for the future. However, the variable 'graduation from college' includes not only the successful conclusion of one part of life, but the necessity of making plans for the future. Therefore, the variable 'graduation' confounds the effects of the conclusion of one life event with the effects of the necessity to make plans for the future. While one may actually be a reinforcement for the self-concept, the difficulty of the other may make the person question the continuity of his or her concept of self.

To separate these two potential effects on the self-concept, a research design was developed that made use of the common curriculum at German universities. This consists usually of two major exam periods, one half-way through the degree course, called the *Vordiplom*, and the other at the end, called the *Hauptdiplom*. Both exams signify the conclusion of a major achievement, just as graduation from college does. However, the *Vordiplom* has continuity built into it because it automatically leads to graduate studies toward the *Hauptdiplom* and usually implies little change in life style. Therefore, it signifies reinforcement without inducing uncertainty about the future. However, because it concludes a major part of studies, it can be used to relocate or transfer to another university, so that the *opportunity* for self-imposed change is given without the *necessity* for it. On the other hand, the *Hauptdiplom* signifies the conclusion of a major part of life where the creation of continuity requires active planning on the part of the individual.

Summarized, the design involves two variables: (1) conclusion of the *Vordiplom* versus conclusion of the *Hauptdiplom*, and (2) having plans for the future involving relocation versus no plans. The latter was made part of the design because (a) relocation is almost necessarily part of plans to continue studies at another university, and (b) even after the conclusion of the *Hauptdiplom* many students who continue to live at the same address may try to project their student life into the future. The relocation requirement in the plans for the future is thus meant to assure the agentic nature of the plans. Thus, the basic quasi-experimental design was a 2 x 2 factorial with the independent variables 'type of exam' and 'plans for the future'.

Method

Subjects were students at the University of Heidelberg recruited from courses in which there were two exams, one approximately half-way through (usually the *Vordiplom* or *Zwischenprüfung*) and another at the end, the *Diplom* or *Magister* exam. Participants in the research were at first recruited with the assistance of administrators in charge of exams who were asked to pass out leaflets to exam candidates. Because this yielded very few subjects, a second approach was to have signs posted at different places near classrooms, exam administration offices, and cafeterias, asking for participation in a study and offering a small financial reward. Despite all this effort, fewer than forty subjects finally participated in the study. The low response rate may be due to several reasons: one is a general lack of interest or even distrust among students toward social science research. Another may be that times of transition, such as exams, are very demanding and therefore allow little time for additional activities, especially if they are relatively time-consuming, as participation in the current study was. Finally, there is no control possible over how many students were actually reached, and among those, how many considered themselves eligible for participation. The results of this study have to be considered with caution and within the context of the other studies yielding related information.

Because this study concentrated on the relationship to the physical environment, the instructions to participants varied in that respect from the standard autophotography instructions as used in the studies. Rather than leaving the content completely to the subject, the instructions asked for eight pictures, of which four were to depict objects, and the other four were to be pictures of environments. All other instructions were the same. The rating method used was the same as described in Chapter 7.

Results

Thirty-seven subjects participated in the study, of whom 20 were male and 17 female. The age ranged from 21 to 32, with the median at 24 years of age. Sixteen (43 per cent) had completed an interim exam (*Vordiplom* or *Zwischenprüfung*), and 21 a final exam (*Hauptdiplom* or *Abschlußprüfung*). More than 75 per cent had finished their exam within four weeks before the data collection, and all within ten weeks. Twenty-eight (75 per cent) indicated having some plans for the future; however, frequently these plans were for further study not involving relocation. For the purpose of the present design, the additional variables are of interest: 16 (43 per cent) had specific plans to move away, 13 knew exactly where they would move to, and 9 already knew they were admitted to another university or had a firm job at the new place of residence.

The group of students who had some clear plans about the future consisted of several subgroups. It included those students who, regardless of the kind of exam taken, had plans to move away from Heidelberg. To assure that the plans for the future had some specificity, certainty about the place a student planned to move to was used as indicating sufficient certainty about future plans. The combination of *Vordiplom* and *Hauptdiplom* students was necessary mainly because of the small number of students with plans for relocation after an interim exam. It is also theoretically justifiable because both subgroups include persons who plan a significant change in their life that includes changes in their geographical and social environment. Finally, members of both subgroups have some degree of certainty about what these plans involve.

The final design involved three groups: (a) interim exam (*Zwischenprüfung* – ZP) students, (b) final exam (*Abschlußprüfung* – AP) students, and (c) those with plans for relocation (PR). Theoretically, it is assumed that the first group can expect a continuation of their present life style in the future so that no active self-concept maintenance is required. The second group cannot continue their present life style. Maintenance or change of the self-concept would require active planning, which they are unlikely to have undertaken. The third group are the most agentic one since they have specific plans for changes in the near future.

Data analysis utilized a regression approach to the one-way analysis of variance. Dependent variables were the subscales of the Satisfaction with Self Scale and the photograph ratings for content and function for the self. If the overall effects were found to be significant, post hoc comparisons were employed to determine specific differences between groups. A summary of the results can be found in Table 9.1.

Table 9.1 *Means of satisfaction with self and photograph ratings*

Variable	Interim exam	Final exam	Relocation	F
N	11	13	12	(2, 33)
Work satisfaction	1.78b	3.00a	2.38ab	4.37*
Number of pictures with mobile objects	4.00a	2.80b	2.50b	3.82*
Number of pictures classified as environments	3.10b	3.00b	4.60a	6.31**
Reflection objects	1.23b	1.56ab	1.93a	4.10*
Symbolism objects	1.41b	1.74b	2.47a	4.47*

** $p < .01$; * $p < .05$. Different letters indicate significant difference between means. Higher numbers on the SSS stand for dissatisfaction.

Students who have taken an interim exam are most satisfied with themselves as far as their studies are concerned. Least satisfied are those who have passed a final exam and graduated. For the first group, the immediate future is relatively clear; for the others, the uncertainty becomes obvious. These results confirm the theoretical interpretation of the meaning of the respective type of exams for the maintenance and change of the self-concept. Students with relocation plans fall between the other two groups as far as satisfaction with work is concerned, and a separate inspection of means for ZP and AP within relocation shows them to be very similar (2.2 versus 2.5 respectively). Uncertainty about the future may make students slightly less satisfied after the interim exam if they have relocation plans, and the same plans may create some more certainty for those who have graduated. The similarity of means for the two relocation groups also justifies the fact that they were combined for the purpose of the present analysis.

The next effect is on a variable indicating the number of objects that are potentially mobile among all eight pictures. Mobility was defined as being movable in a relocation. Interestingly, it is the group with the most stable expectations for the future who clearly depicted most mobile objects. One possible interpretation is that any kind of uncertainty about the future, be it imposed by others or by oneself, is accompanied by a reliance on more stable aspects of the environment.

Similar but more pronounced is the effect on the depiction of environments. Persons who are about to leave their present environment are much more likely to take a picture of environments rather than objects. The expectation of leaving makes the present environment more salient. It is important to note that the circumstances of the data collection are unlikely to have made the planned relocation especially salient.

The objects depicted also seem to have a different meaning and function for the self-concept for those who have plans for a relocation. The raters assigned those pictures of objects higher reflection and symbolism values, indicating that the meaning of these objects is socially mediated.

Not affected were some other variables that Wofsey et al.'s study had suggested, in particular the distance and perspective on one's environment. If the study had had a larger number of subjects, and a more equal distribution among conditions so that the original design could have been implemented, perhaps effects on those variables could have been obtained.

Overall, students who have taken their interim exam are most satisfied with themselves regarding work; they are less likely to see themselves in relation to stable aspects of the environment. On the other hand, those with particular plans for the future involving relocation are more orientated to the environment and to socially shared and understood symbols.

Anticipation of the transition from university: into working life or unemployment?

A university degree is no longer a guarantee of professional employment, as was the case at least in some countries after the Second World War. Students approaching graduation with a vocational degree frequently have very clear expectations about their diminished chances in the labour market, despite the fact that their training led very specifically to a given profession. Professional socialization, together with the costs incurred and the social network which accompanies a particular course of study, have made future occupation an aspect of the self-concept for many people.

Awareness of not being able to continue this aspect of self has implications when plans for the future have to be made, involving either maintenance or willingness to change. Such plans will have to involve the degree of determination with which plans are consistently pursued despite objectively slim chances of realization on one hand, and the consideration of alternatives on the other hand, especially those involving lower social and professional prestige.

In a *Diplom* thesis (Seeger, 1986; Seeger & Hormuth, 1988), Seeger attempted to assess the meaning of variables related to students' self-concept, their commitment to their professional career, and their willingness actively to consider alternatives in relation to their chances in the labour market. In particular, students from three different programmes awarding advanced professional degrees at the University of Heidelberg participated in the study: translators, economists, and physicists. The *Diplom* degree awarded in these fields is comparable on a formal level and requires approximately the same amount of time and preparation. However, according to West German labour statistics, students in these fields have very different chances of employment in degree-related fields of work. Translators (*Dipl.-Übers.*) have practically no chance of professional employment. Economists (*Dipl.-Volksw.*) are qualified and recruited for a wide variety of work. However, they have to show some flexibility because their studies do not prepare them for one specific profession. Physicists (*Dipl.-Phys.*) have statistically the best chances of employment in areas of work relatively closely related to their training. Thus, the anticipation of graduation makes the necessity for self-concept change salient in very different ways to students in the three fields of study.

In a questionnaire distributed to sixty-five students immediately before graduation, variables were included that addressed the perceived probability of realization of profession, satisfaction with self, psychological commitment, sociological commitment (social integration), and the willingness to consider alternatives and their implications (for instance in regard to prestige and income).

Group comparisons (see Table 9.2) showed that translators and physicists had a clear perception of their different opportunities. However, economists also perceived uncertainty about their chances. Accordingly, the professional goal was less psychologically meaningful to translators than to physicists, but it was the economists who were less satisfied with themselves in regard to their studies as compared to the physicists. The meaning of the professional goal and alternatives was also measured by their implications for professional and private lives. Theorists of self-concept change such as Hayden (1979) argue that persons only consider alternatives for themselves that carry a higher meaning as expressed in the number of alternative implications. The different groups differed not only in that translators considered their professional goal to have the least implications for their future life, but in that they were also the only ones considering less prestigious alternatives. On the other hand, economists had the most grandiose plans: their alternatives had many more implications and thus meaning for themselves. Thus, from a position where several possibilities are seen as realistic, self-concept change as suggested by Hayden is indeed considered as long as it builds on the present self-concept. However, where the professional self-concept is threatened, as is the case for translators, self-concept alternatives involving fewer implications have to be considered, a case that Hayden had not taken into account. Of particular interest is that the group having the clearest chances for professional realization in the future, the physicists, are considerably less satisfied with themselves in regard to their studies than the economists, who also perceive a good chance for professional employment. They differ in that their type of employment is clearly prescribed, whereas economists perceive the freedom to choose among different types of professional work. This involves the possibility of increasing the implicative links of their future profession to other interests.

Table 9.2 *Comparison of means of students anticipating graduation*

Variable	Translators	Economists	Physicists
Psychological commitment to goal	3.37a	3.17ab	2.47b*
Realization attempts	3.36a	3.55a	2.39b**
Self-realization in occupation	5.17a	4.53b	4.97ab+
Implications of professional goal	3.51b	3.82ab	3.95a*
Perceived probability of realization	3.59b	3.85ab	4.56a*
Consideration of alternative	3.23a	2.38ab	1.68b**
Implications of alternative	3.37b	4.21a	3.88ab*
SSS study	3.93ab	3.71b	4.74a*
SSS object	4.86a	3.78b	4.35ab*

** $p < .01$; * $p < .05$; + $p < .10$. Different letters indicate significant differences between means. Higher numbers on the SSS stand for dissatisfaction.
Seeger (1986).

Multiple regression analyses across all groups were used. It turned out that the first variables to be eliminated were those that related to practical considerations, such as the probability of realizing the profession or the desired alternative, as well as concrete steps in application or toward alternatives. Satisfaction with oneself was determined by the meaningfulness of the chosen profession and the alternatives, concentration on studies and exams, and the perceived possibility of bringing one's concept of self into future work, as can be seen from Table 9.3.

Overall, students' commitment to their professional goals is more related to psychological variables, such as satisfaction, commitment, and perceived probability of realization of goals. On the other hand, the willingness to consider alternatives is more related to social processes, the satisfaction with social, family, and partner relationships, and the degree to which they are embedded in a social network.

Table 9.3 *Predictors of satisfaction with self across all groups*

Predictor	beta	F (df)	r-square
Regression		7.66(8, 43)***	.64
Flexible self-presentation	.28	5.46(1, 50)*	
Sensitivity to others	−.20	3.95(1, 50)*	
Implications of profession	.35	4.89(1, 50)	
Implications of alternatives	−.56	28.42(1, 50)***	
Realization attempts	.24	7.32(1, 50)*	
Self-realization in profession	.21	3.89(1, 50)+	
Concentration on studies	.17	4.31(1, 50)*	
Relation between alternative and chosen profession	−.13	7.00(1, 50)*	

*** p < .001; * p < .05; + p < .10.
The analysis used data from Seeger (1986). The first two variables refer to factors of a modified self-monitoring scale by Lennox and Wolfe (1984), translated into German.

The two studies discussed in this chapter show that the anticipation of change leads to a restructuring of the ecology of the self. The course this restructuring takes and the variables involved are influenced by the alternatives available, in particular whether these alternatives build on the present concept of self, and thus enrich it, or whether they necessitate giving up aspects of self.

10 The experience sampling method

One of the basic requirements mentioned earlier for an ecological approach to the study of self-concept change is that of ecological validity. Another requirement is to study actual social interactions in the situations in which they take place. A method fulfilling both of these requirements was found in the experience sampling method which yields random self-reports of actual behaviour *in situ*.

The development of the experience sampling method (ESM), its conceptual base, its applications to a variety of research questions such as the interaction of persons and situations, and its use for the naturalistic extension of laboratory findings or for the study of the stream of behaviour have been described in detail elsewhere (Hormuth, 1986a). Issues referring to the analysis of experience sampling data and the validity of this type of self-report data are also critically discussed there. Of particular interest for present purposes is that the method allows the researcher to collect information about naturally occurring events and situations that otherwise could not be studied *in situ* or be created under experimental conditions.

The actual employment of the method, which has also been described by me elsewhere in detail (Hormuth, 1986; see also Larson and Czsikszentmihalyi, 1983), is summarized here. The procedure uses a signalling device, the beeper, and a booklet containing a number of identical questionnaires. Both have to be carried by research participants, preferably at all times during the day. Exceptions or times when the beeper's signal is turned off have to be recorded.

The beeper used in the present research has been specifically designed for use with this method by me. Some other investigators use commercially available wrist watches, random beepers, or pagers. These have various advantages and disadvantages. Their disadvantages are mainly those that restrict the investigator's choice of research design and control over the signals emitted.

A special beeper was therefore designed and made for this research programme that was programmable to emit a signal at any possible time point within a time period of over a week. In addition, it did need not to be handled by the research participant or the investigator in any way during that time. Programming was done via a lap-size computer that also provided a print-out of an individual's beep schedule. Individualization of beep schedules allows research participation by people with unusual daily schedules, such as nurses on night shift. Since the beeper has a range of more than one week, variations in daily life events between work days and weekend days can be taken into account.

For purposes of the present research, subjects had to fill out a short questionnaire eight times daily at random intervals averaging 90 minutes for a whole week. Within eight 90-minute intervals per day, the beeper was programmed to emit a signal at a randomly determined point in time. Beep times can thus be as much as nearly 180 minutes or as little as one minute apart – but both are very unusual.

The research participant also receives a booklet (DIN A 6) containing about 65 or 70 questionnaires each two pages long. The booklet fits easily into a pocket. The questionnaires are designed to take no more than two minutes to fill out with a small amount of practice. Coding keys for certain questions are in the front flap, which can be folded out and used to keep the page in place. The back flap contains a form to record times the beeper was turned off or not carried (the 'snooze report').

Items that describe the type of activity, the current location, and the other interactants in a situation are reported according to a coding system that was developed over the course of pilot studies. The coding system provides different categories for:

(a) *Type of location* (13 categories), for instance at home, in another private home, at work, in class.
(b) *Type of interactant* (12 categories), for instance alone, spouse or partner, other member of my household, neighbour, friend, colleague, stranger.
(c) *Type of activity* (17 categories), for instance, studying, working, commuting, sleeping, eating, walking, and
(d) *Topic of conversation* (19 categories), for instance the weather, food and drink, politics.

Theoretically, the combination of these categories allows the differentiation of tens of thousands of situations. Of course, some combinations may be unlikely. In any case, familiarity with the coding system enables research participants to give a very specific description of a situation in a very short time.

The other items are either answerable on 5-point scales or dichotomously (yes/no). These items refer either to the current state, that is, a description of the events and the respondent's state at the moment the beeper went off, or to the last occasion an event of a certain class (for example an interaction) took place before the signal occurred. Examples of the former are focus of attention on self or outside, pleasantness of thoughts, pleasantness of current activities, and voluntary or involuntary engagement in current activity. These are continuous events or states that are thus captured at a random point in time. On the other hand, there are discrete events that may not necessarily have taken place at the time of the signal. In particular, social interactions of different varieties occur frequently but alternate with times of solitude. Because one of the specific goals of this research was the investigation of naturally occurring interactions, the answers at the time of a signal were supposed to refer to the social interaction that took place most recently between the previous and the current signal. Thus, the problems of anticipation faced by other investigators who used equal reporting intervals or ask subjects to report *all* events of a certain class (say interactions) were presumably avoided.

Several reporting requirements, in particular that of the time of the beep, were added to help assess some aspects of the validity of the information obtained. These were items that could either be independently verified, for instance through comparison with a printed schedule, or related to information obtained with other tools of psychological investigation, for instance questionnaires, or compared to information obtained in other studies by this or other investigators.

Data analysis, validity, and usefulness of ESM

(Some of the following discussion is adapted from Hormuth, 1986.) There is no commonly agreed upon method for the analysis of data collected through experience sampling. The guiding principle has to be the useful reduction of the large amount of data typically obtained. The different approaches are determined by different research objectives, such as the stability of behaviour over situations or over different states of the individual. To date, other analyses, such as single case studies or time series, have rarely been undertaken.

The first step in data reduction is usually the aggregation of data, for instance over situations, over persons, or over persons in situations. Most investigators use the many observations contained in experiential sampling data to increase the stability of situational ratings. In so doing, they anticipate or adhere to Epstein's (1983) advice: 'an effective technique for ... identifying the more stable and broader structures of personality is to aggregate behavior over many situations, which simultaneously cancels out the specific component and compounds the general one' (p. 367). He discusses in detail the theoretical function and implications for reliability and validity of appropriate and inappropriate aggregation in personality psychology. On a variety of physiological and psychological data, Epstein demonstrates a rapid increase in the size of stability coefficients as the number of days over which the data are averaged increases to approximately five. Even after that, every day of observation added to the stability coefficients' size, although the increase is much less. Many of his considerations on aggregation are of particular relevance when one has to deal with the reduction of experience sampling data.

An assessment of the experience sampling method and the quality of the data obtained should focus on the role of the research participant. The quality of the data collected by experience sampling depends almost exclusively on that person. Reliability and validity can, to some extent, be determined by answers to the following questions: does the subject respond to the signals on time? Are the subject's objective circumstances influenced by participation? Is the subject's subjective perception of a situation influenced by the method? Is the subject capable of reporting and rating situations? Most of these questions still lack sufficient answers.

Signal compliance is one possible criterion for evaluating the quality of experience sampling data. To preserve the purpose of the random sampling of situations, signals have to be responded to immediately. If this were not the case, subjects would wait for another, more convenient situation that either allowed more time or was more comfortable to report on than the randomly sampled one. The basic purpose of the method would thus be threatened. Therefore, control of the timeliness of responses seems essential in its own right and is one of several ways to assess the validity of the data obtained.

The programme used in my research provides a printout of each subject's individual signal schedule. This can be compared to the time written down by the subject when responding. Its accuracy is, of course, only one bit of information that helps to assess the reliability of the whole report at a given time. In the study reported in the following chapter, of all 5,145 signals to which the subjects responded, 70 per cent were answered within three minutes, and 80 per cent within five. These seem to be response times within acceptable limits.

Responding to each signal on time can depend on a great number of factors and may show intra-individual as well as inter-individual variance. To determine whether subjects in general respond on time, the mean response time for each of 101 subjects was also calculated. Here, 10 per cent of all subjects respond on the average within 1.3 minutes, 20 per cent within two minutes, and 50 per cent within 4.5 minutes. These relatively low average response times on the subject level seem to indicate a willingness on the part of research participants to comply with the signal. Sometimes situational demands interfere, hence the greater time differences on the signal level.

Some signals are never responded to. The above data were collected in a study that provided a schedule with eight signals a day for eight days. Only one subject responded to all 64 signals. Fifty per cent of the subjects provided more than 53 reports, that is, a median response rate of 83 per cent, and 90 per cent, more than 38. These response frequencies are comparable to those obtained by other investigators, as far as such data are reported. Pawlik and Buse's (1982) subjects in a study employing a similar method responded on the average to 57 out of 66 signals (that is, 86 per cent). Csikszentmihalyi and Figurski (1982) obtained an average response rate of 80 per cent (45 out of 56 on the average), and Savin-Williams and Demo (1983) reported 78 per cent.

The research participants' perception of how they were able to comply with the demands of the experience sampling method was assessed through a post-sampling questionnaire. (Items relevant to the method in general are presented by Hormuth, 1986, Table 4.) Overall, it seems that subjects thought that experience sampling was not very difficult and not very disruptive. However, an *immediate* response to the signal was frequently thought to be difficult. It is encouraging that readiness to participate in such a study again was frequently expressed not only in the questionnaire but in personal conversations.

Compliance and timeliness, of course, are only one way of assessing the validity and reliability of self-reports *in situ*. Their presentation here should only be taken as an example of many different variables that have to be found to estimate the reliability and validity of the method.

The methodological problems lie mainly in the responsibility that is given to the research subject in collecting not only subjective data, like thoughts and feelings, but also objective ones, like the description of situations. Being left alone for long periods of time and being an untrained rater makes the reliability of responses difficult to determine.

Of course, this can become a strength when the purpose of the research is to assess the subjective perception of actual situations. The method is able to capture the situation as perceived and interpreted by the participant at the actual time it takes place – it will be less influenced by the cognitive biases that frequently accompany hindsight, and will not be mediated through the interpretation of a third person, the investigator. ESM is therefore particularly appropriate for empirical investigation from a theoretical standpoint that acknowledges the individual's interpretation of the meaning of situations. The problems outlined above, therefore, are from such a standpoint less problems of validity than problems of reliability.

No one method in psychology can capture a particular phenomenon in a perfectly reliable and valid way. Recent years have seen an enrichment in the tools of psychological research that provide access to some data that were heretofore unattainable and allow the validation of other data that were previously obtained using methods of empirically undetermined quality. However, these new methods, of which experience sampling is one, open up new questions that should not be ignored. Every method of obtaining information about behaviours and experiences has different weaknesses and strengths – so does experience sampling. To overcome the weaknesses that lie in the unknown validity and reliability of data provided and rated by research participants, the strongest approach that can be chosen by an investigator is a multiple method approach rather than reliance upon one specific method, no matter how appealing.

Therefore, in the present research on self-concept change and relocation, ESM was used in the context of a multi-method approach, including more conventional methods, such as personality questionnaire studies, surveys, and very different ones, such as autophotography. Quasi-experimental designs were employed to compare the experiences and behaviour in experimental and various control groups. Short-term and longitudinal ESM-designs were combined with longitudinal studies through postal surveys. The studies used varying populations (for instance, non-students as well as students) and different sampling procedures.

11 A quasi-experimental study of relocation and satisfaction with self

The results of the telephone survey reported in Chapter 3 showed the general appropriateness of the relocation paradigm and the differential effects of moving on activities and attitudes depending upon the circumstances of the move as they may be relevant to the person's self-concept. These results were sufficiently encouraging for major studies to be conducted that implemented more specific research designs and made use of more elaborate methods of data collection.

The present study was designed to be the first in the series discussed here with several methodological requirements in one study. A sample of people who have relocated should be obtained by using a procedure that is independent of the reason for the move – that is, the sampling procedure should not introduce a confounding factor, such as the voluntariness of the move. Further, a quasi-experimental control-group design should allow comparisons between persons who have relocated and those who have not. The methods of data collection should stress ecological validity.

Procedure and design

Sampling

In the first survey (Chapter 3), obtaining a telephone was identified as a public act close to the time of moving which is performed by the majority of households and yields publicly accessible information about the relocation. A sample had thus been created without having to identify more specific events for groups of people relocating, such as moving to a retirement home or graduation from university. This procedure avoids confounding the issue of reasons for with circumstances of the move. The act of obtaining a telephone is generally independent of the circumstances of the relocation.

Problems with the telephone sampling method for the most part involve the fact that the exact time of relocation is hard to specify. By the time information about new telephone listings becomes available, some relocations may be more than twelve months ago. Cooperation from the postal service to provide this information earlier for the present study could not be obtained. Other events had to be identified which usually coincide with a move. One such necessary act is the connection of utilities, that is, water, electricity, and gas. Therefore, the municipal utility company was approached with a request for cooperation. After a careful investigation of the legal conditions of disclosing such information, the utility company agreed to compile random samples of new customers as specified by the research design as long as no additional information had to be disclosed. This way, it was possible to implement the following design.

Design

The design included three groups: (a) One quasi-experimental group, consisting of persons who had moved from *outside*, that is from another town, to Heidelberg. Two different control groups were also part of the design: (b) A group of persons who had moved *within* the city. This controls for some of the effects of moving but allows greater stability in social relationships and in some aspects of place identity. (c) A third, true control group consisted of people who had not moved but had a *stable* residence. They were defined as having resided at the same address for a minimum of two years. The addresses of persons in the first two groups were supplied by the utility company from month to month, with a small random sample of households who had been at the same address for at least two years included every month.

Because the group of primary interest was that consisting of persons who had moved from the outside, the size of the three groups was not held equal. About 50 per cent were in Group A (movers from outside), and about 25 per cent each in Group B (within town movers) and control Group C (stable residence for two years). Thus, some analyses can compare the movers' group to the combined group of permanent residents of the same city, and it was possible to perform additional analyses on Group A using the somewhat larger N.

Methods and instruments

This study was the first of those described in this book in which the experience sampling method and the autophotographic method were employed. The detailed description of these methods can be found in Chapters 7 and 10.

The ESM questionnaire had two parts, the first concentrating on the individual's present state and activities, the second on the last social interaction. In total, the questionnaire had twenty-five items. It started out by asking for current thoughts, whether the focus of attention was on self or outside, and the pleasantness of those thoughts. Next, the present location, who was present at the time, and the present activity had to be indicated through the use of a coding key that was attached to the front flap of the booklet. The activity also had to be rated on pleasantness and on voluntariness. The next items concerned the last object handled by the respondent, the length of time this object was part of the respondent's property (since before/after the move), and the personal relevance of the object.

The second part of the questionnaire specifically addressed the description and perception of the most recent social interaction having taken place before the signal. First it asked for the number of persons present, and then specified the person *last* talked to. This person had to be identified (as spouse, friend, boss, etc.), whether this person was known from before the move or only since, and it was to be specified how important this interaction partner was to the respondent. It was asked who initiated the interaction and to what degree it was spontaneous or planned. The next items addressed the perceived personal intimacy and importance of the conversational content, the degree of self-disclosure and of the other's disclosure in the conversation, and the situational determinacy of the behaviour. Those items were thought to affect the degree to which an interactional situation can become self-concept relevant, namely by revealing personal information about oneself and displaying behaviour that would allow personal rather than only situational attributions. Finally, the perceived appropriateness of the interactional situation had to be rated by the respondent.

Summarized, the intention of the ESM questionnaire was to assess the variety of situations a person is in, and the function social interactions may have in a new environment.

Because mobility may be related to age, before the actual data analysis was undertaken it was tested whether there was a significant age difference between the quasi-experimental groups. This was indeed the case: $F(2,98) = 5.12$, $p < .01$. Movers from out of town were on the average 28.2 years old, movers within town 27.3, and those having the same address for at least two years, 36.3. Based on this result, all further analyses including the three groups as a factor were conducted introducing age as a covariate.

Effects of social structure on satisfaction with self

Before conducting analyses based on satisfaction with self and its relationship to everyday behaviour and interactions, the relationship between social commitment as a sociological variable involving social structure and satisfaction with self as a psychological variable had to be investigated. This can serve as a validation of the Satisfaction with Self Scale in regard to the conceptualization of social commitment as central to the stability of the self-concept.

The measure of commitment (see Chapter 6) listed thirteen different kinds of persons (spouse, parent, child, colleague, etc.). First, the respondent had to indicate whether during the past year any significant kind of change in relationship occurred with respect to any of these persons, and whether this change involved the beginning of a relationship or getting closer versus the end of a relationship or a greater distancing. Next, the degree to which this change in relationship affected the social network was assessed: respondents had to point arrows from the person who was mainly affected to all others who were secondarily affected. This was an attempt to determine the relative degree to which changes in relationships were isolated or rather involved larger areas of the whole network of social relationships.

Thus, two variables were created that could be entered into the statistical analysis: type of change (approach versus separation) and degree of impact (only one other person was affected versus two or more). These two variables were combined with type of relocation (from outside town, within town, stable residence for at least two years) to form a 2 (change) $\times$ 2 (impact) $\times$ 3 (relocation) factorial design, with the total SSS score and the scores of the SSS subscales as dependent variables. To account for unequal cell sizes, analyses followed the general linear model approach to the analysis of variance and used the Type III sum of squares (see SAS, 1982) which are computed regardless of the order in which variables are entered into the analysis. Age was taken into account as a covariate; however, the reported means are the true means.

Analyses were first conducted using the total SSS score as the dependent variable. Effects that were significant for the total score were then further analysed using the subscales as dependent variables. This, rather than a multivariate, approach was chosen because further analyses will be based on the total score rather than on a multivariate combination of the subscales.

In the present analyses, the interaction effect that was theoretically the most meaningful one, namely type of change by impact regardless of relocation, was also the only effect significant for the SSS–Total score. It also turned out to be significant on two subscales, 'Social' and 'Object'. Table 11.1 shows the obtained effects. No other effect was significant on the SSS–Total score in the $2 \times 2 \times 3$ ANOVA.

Which forms do these interactions take? Separation shows the clearest differences depending on the degree of social impact: a separation not affecting several other relationships is more likely to be associated with a higher degree of satisfaction with oneself, especially in regard to social relationships. It even creates a higher satisfaction. However, a separation that involves other people is associated with fairly high degrees of dissatisfaction, as theoretically expected. On the other hand, getting closer to another person does not produce such a difference.

Table 11.1 *Interaction of type of relationship change by impact on SSS*

Change impact	Approach 1	Approach 2+	Separation 1	Separation 2+	F (df)
Scale					
SSS–Total	2.3	2.2	2.0	2.6	7.55(1, 70)**
Social	2.0	1.9	1.6	2.1	5.92(1, 76)*
Object	2.4	2.0	1.9	2.5	6.29(1, 76)*

Note: Higher scores indicate higher dissatisfaction.
** $p < .01$; * $p < .05$.

A somewhat higher degree of dissatisfaction, especially with one's physical environment, is also found when a relationship becomes closer but does not involve others, that is, has no social impact. It may be just the fact that this one positive turn in social relationships leads to a general dissatisfaction because it stays isolated, that is, does not affect more of the other social relationships. But because it is a positive *social* event, the general dissatisfaction may express itself in the relationships to other elements of the ecology of the self.

In general, the interaction effects between relationship change and social impact follow the theoretical expectations and demonstrate the postulated link between the social structure and self-concept. The total score of the Satisfaction with Self Scale is validly related to changes in social commitment that are central to the self-concept, as defined through their links to other relationships.

Relocation status and satisfaction with self

After the link between satisfaction with self and social structure was established, the relationship between moving and self-satisfaction was of interest. To separate out the effects of changes in the social and physical environment from other effects of moving, three planned contrasts between the relocation groups were undertaken. The three contrasts were: (a) Outside + Within versus Stable, testing for general effects of moving, (b) Outside versus Within + Stable, testing for the effects of complete changes in the environment versus relative stability, and (c) Outside versus Stable, testing for complete changes versus absolute stability.

The analyses were conducted as a one-way analysis of variance, following the general linear model approach, using age as a covariate. By conducting separate analyses rather than using the ANOVA as described above, cases which had to be disregarded because of missing data on the commitment

Table 11.2 *Relocation status and satisfaction with self: overall effects and planned contrasts (F, df)*

Scale	Overall	Contrast A O + W versus S	Contrast B O versus W + S	Contrast C O versus S
SSS–Total	3.23(2, 87)*	5.26(1, 87)*	4.09(1, 87)*	6.44(1, 87)*
Global	3.20(2, 95)*	4.91(1, 95)*	4.38(1, 95)*	6.40(1, 95)*
Social	4.52(2, 94)*	6.19(1, 94)*	6.98(1, 94)**	8.92(1, 94)**
Family	2.56(2, 90)+	3.18(1, 90)+	4.16(1, 90)*	4.99(1, 90)*
Work	ns	ns	ns	ns
Object	ns	ns	ns	ns

Note: ** $p < .01$; * $p < .05$; + $p < .10$; O From outside; W Within city; S Stable residency.

measure could be re-entered into the data analysis. Table 11.2 summarizes the results of the significance tests for the overall analyses and the planned contrasts.

With the exception of the subscales 'Work' and 'Object', the results indicate significant effects on almost all contrasts involving the other subscales and the total score of the SSS. Table 11.3 contains the mean values which will assist in interpreting the meaning of the significant findings obtained.

Table 11.3 *Mean values satisfaction with self by moving status*

Scale	Outside	Within	Stable
SSS–Total	2.34a	2.24ab	2.00b
Global	2.77a	2.61ab	2.27b
Social	2.07a	1.86ab	1.63b
Family	2.37a	2.10ab	1.83b
Work	2.34a	2.42a	2.49a
Object	2.24a	2.22a	2.01a

Note: Significant differences are indicated by subscripts.

Relocation, whether involving a complete change of environment or only of some aspects of it, is in the present study always associated with higher degrees of dissatisfaction with oneself when compared to being at the same place for a longer period of time. This is expressed in general dissatisfaction with oneself, but also in the way social and family relationships are affected. A move seems to affect satisfaction with self through its impact on social relationships, not so much through the changes in work relationships or in the physical environment that are associated with a move. Whether the relocation involves a complete change or only a partial one seems to be mainly a matter of degree rather than quality of the changes affecting satisfaction with self.

Satisfaction with self and moving: results from ESM

The following analyses are based on a 3 (type of move) by 2 (median split of SSS) factorial design, analysed using a general linear model approach in consideration of the unequal cell size. Reported F-values are based on Type III sum of squares (SAS, 1982, p. 237). The Type III SS tests effects independently of the order in which they were entered into the analysis; they are also appropriate for unbalanced designs as they are not functions of cell counts. To enhance understanding of the effects of the covariate age, of the group, of SSS, and of their interaction, the first table (11.4) will show those variables where the covariate age has an effect, the second (11.5), all main effects for group, the third (11.6), all main effects for satisfaction with self, and the fourth (11.7), the interaction effects of moving status and satisfaction with self.

Table 11.4 *Effects of the covariate age on ESM data*

Item		F (df = 1, 91)
B03:	How pleasant were your thoughts?	8.01***
B11:	Did the handled object have personal meaning?	5.34*
B23:	What did the other person learn about you?	5.09*
B24:	Was your behaviour situationally appropriate?	4.33*
BP46:	% reports away from home doing chores	4.87*
BP55:	% presence of neighbours	5.66*
BP602:	% activities chores	17.49***
BP605:	% activities rested	7.52**
BP611:	% activities watched television	5.98*
BP617:	% activities something else	4.63*

Note: B-variables are items taken directly from the booklet. BP-variables indicate the percentage of a specific category within rating categories.
*** $p < .001$; ** $p < .01$; * $p < .05$.

The results indicate that the age of respondents is indeed a significant covariate on many items. Age differences seem especially significant on items that indicate specific activities. Because of the high prevalence of age effects as a covariate, and because of the differences in age among the quasi-experimental groups, all of the following effects to be reported will be controlled for age differences so as to assess the effects of moving and satisfaction with self. The presentation of results will concentrate on those at least significant at the 5 per cent level, unless the effect is close and of particular interest. Table 11.5 summarizes the main effects and means for group.

146 *A quasi-experimental study*

Table 11.5 *Main effects of moving on ESM data*

Item		Outside	Within	Stable	F(2,91)
B22:	Importance of conversation				
	(1 – very)	3.16	4.02	3.70	3.85*
B23:	Other learned about respondent				
	(1 – much)	4.13	5.04	4.58	3.40*
BP53:	% with relatives	4.00	6.00	19.00	7.33**
BP610:	% telephone call	1.70	1.40	3.40	4.65*

** p < .01; * p < .05.

Two items referring to the last conversation with another person showed significant difference due to moving status: the importance of the conversation and how much the person learned about the other. In both cases it is the group moving within the city who showed the highest scores, whereas for those moving from the outside, the conversations were least important and they learned less about the other person. A possible interpretation may be that for persons moving within a city, existing relationships take on new relevance, whereas persons who are new in a city are initially more engaged in contacts which are still superficial. The assumption that those people would engage more in contacts with the previously known social environment cannot be supported by the present data; rather, persons having a stable residence engage most in contact with relatives and make most telephone calls. Both effects are highly significant, even when controlled for age. Obviously, stability in residence comes with a long-existing social network that is more easily activated.

Table 11.6 presents the significant main effects and means for the median split on satisfaction with self, based on the same analyses as in the tables above.

Basically, only two ESM variables showed clear relationships with satisfaction with self. Persons who were less satisfied with themselves also liked their present activity less, and they considered their behaviour much less

Table 11.6 *Effects of satisfaction with self on ESM data*

Item		Satisfaction High	Satisfaction Low	F(1,91)
B07:	Liked activity (1 – much)	2.23	2.84	5.35*
B24:	Behaviour situationally appropriate (1 – much so)	1.74	2.35	7.43**

** p < .01; * p < .05.

Satisfaction with self and moving

situationally appropriate. They feel unsure of themselves in social situations; orientation on situational cues (high self-monitoring) would be an appropriate behavioural strategy in that state.

Table 11.7 reveals the interactive effects of moving group and satisfaction with self.

Table 11.7 *Interactive effects of SSS and moving on ESM data*

Item	SSS high SSS low	Outside	Within	Stable	F (2, 91)
BP43:	% visiting others	9.2	3.4	5.7	
		5.5	12.8	6.4	4.02*
BP51:	% with partner	39.0	40.0	47.0	
		55.0	41.0	34.0	2.88+
BP617:	% did something else	25.0	18.0	13.0	
		17.0	20.0	24.0	4.24*

* $p < .05$; + $p < .10$.

Whereas satisfaction with self does not influence the number of visits to others by persons with a stable residence, it shows a contrary effect on those moving from the outside or within. Persons moving within the city visit others more when they are dissatisfied with themselves, and stay at home much more when satisfied with themselves. The opposite, though not quite so extreme, is true for people who are new to the city. They are more likely to venture outside when satisfied with themselves.

Interesting too is the effect on the variable 'did something else', indicating the percentage of activities not covered by the other coding categories. This may be considered an indicator of more innovative, different kinds of behaviour. Among those new in town, this category is rated most frequently by those satisfied with themselves, whereas the effect is reversed for those who have not moved. They are more likely to do something else when dissatisfied.

Finally, dissatisfied persons new in town spend most time with their partners, and dissatisfied long-term residents spend the least amount of time with their partners ($p < .07$). Taking all this information together, being new in town is associated with exploratory behaviour for people who are satisfied with themselves. The dissatisfied new residents stay at home, with a person they know, and stick to activities they know. However, the same kinds of behaviours that were interpreted as exploratory for new residents can have very different meaning for people for whom the environment did not change. Within a few weeks after the move, dissatisfaction with self does not seem to lead to active attempts to make use of new opportunities – it is the satisfied ones who are more willing to take on the new environment. The present design is not able to answer the question whether this pattern of results will last.

These interpretations, of course, rely on very limited information. They can be validated or invalidated in the light of different analyses within the same study, the information obtained from different methods, and through different studies.

To shed light on the contribution of different spheres of life on the effects of moving, the SSS subscales that represent different life spheres have been analysed. The analyses follow the same approach as before. The SSS subscale main effects of (a) a median split on the different SSS subscales and (b) moving group as factors will be reported in the following tables as well as their interaction effects. Again, all analyses were conducted using age as a covariate.

Table 11.8 *Main effects for SSS subscale Global on ESM data*

Item		Global satisfaction		$F(1, 91)$
		High	Low	
B07:	Liked activity (1–much)	2.10	2.99	11.86***
BP53:	% with relatives	6.40	10.60	5.16*

*** $p < .001$; * $p < .05$.

The Global subscale essentially shows a similar effect to that of the total score. There is clear evidence that people who do not like themselves also do not like what they are doing. Persons who are not satisfied with themselves also spend considerably more time with their relatives, that is, in a familiar and safe social context.

Table 11.9 shows the interaction effects between moving group and SSS–Global. When considering the interaction, the effects of the variables 'with partner' and 'did something else' are similar to those obtained using the total score of the SSS. The main effect for liking an activity has to be specified: differences are practically non-existent among long-term residents, somewhat clearer for relocators within the city, and most pronounced for persons who have moved from the outside. Changes in the person–environment relationship have probably made this effect most salient.

The next tables (Table 11.10 and Table 11.11), based on the same type of analysis, analyse the effects of satisfaction with self in the sphere of social relationships, that is, is based on the subscale 'Social'.

Table 11.9 *Interaction effects for SSS–Global and moving group*

Item	SSS–Global high SSS–Global low	Outside	Within	Stable	F (2,91)
B07:	Liked activity (1–much)	1.92	2.04	2.47	
		3.29	2.69	2.56	3.78*
BP51:	% with partner	44.00	42.00	52.00	
		52.00	39.00	28.00	4.56*
BP617:	% did something else	23.00	17.00	12.00	
		18.00	20.00	22.00	3.55*

* $p < .05$.

Table 11.10 *Main effects for median split on SSS–Social on ESM*

Item	Social satisfaction		F (1,91)
	High	Low	
B07: Liked activity (1–very)	2.26	2.82	3.59+
B21: How personal was conversational content (1–personal)	4.29	3.74	4.81*
B24: Behaviour situationally appropriate (1–conforms)	1.73	2.39	5.13*

* $p < .05$; + $p < .10$.

The most clearly significant effects of SSS–Social is on two variables related to the last social interaction. Persons low on SSS–Social consider conversations less personal and less situationally appropriate. General dissatisfaction with oneself in the social sphere becomes actualized in individual social situations. Dissatisfied persons also tend to like their present activity somewhat less ($p < .07$).

Table 11.11 shows the interaction effects for SSS–Social and moving status.

Table 11.11 *Interaction effects for SSS–Social and moving group on ESM*

Item	SSS–Social high SSS–Social low	Outside	Within	Stable	F (2,91)
B03:	Thoughts pleasant (1–pleasant)	3.40	3.69	3.53	
		2.66	2.94	3.58	3.25*
BP54:	% with friends and acquaintances	4.00	0.60	0.60	
		2.40	6.50	1.20	3.40*
BP59:	% with other persons	1.50	0.70	2.10	
		0.90	2.80	0.40	2.99+

* $p < .05$; + $p < .10$.

150 A quasi-experimental study

As in the previous analysis, changes in the person−environment relationship seem to make the association between pleasant thoughts and satisfaction with self on the social sphere salient. The time spent with friends and acquaintances is a variable of immediate relevance to SSS−Social. The interaction effect shows that newcomers have to be satisfied with themselves to spend more time with friends, whereas those who lived in the same city, with presumably unchanged access to friends, spend more time with friends and acquaintances when dissatisfied with themselves in the social sphere. This is especially true for movers within the city. The pattern of results is repeated for the two moving groups on the variable 'with other persons' ($p < .06$).

The next analyses used the median split on the SSS subscale 'Family'. The main effects are shown in Table 11.12, and the interaction effects in Table 11.13.

Table 11.12 *Main effects for median split on SSS−Family on ESM*

Item		Satisfaction with family		$F (1,91)$
		High	Low	
B07:	Liked activity (1−very)	2.15	2.87	10.08**
B19:	Importance of other person (1−very)	1.73	2.12	3.63 +
BP614:	% played game	1.40	0.70	4.74*
BP616:	% did sports	1.40	0.30	7.87**

** $p < .01$; * $p < .05$; + $p < .10$.

Persons who are satisfied with themselves in the family sphere like what they are doing more, they also engage more in activities that can be taken up in a family context, such as playing games and sports. The only significant interaction effect (Table 11.13) is on the variable 'time spent with relatives'. Here, people who have not moved are most likely to spend a lot of time with relatives when they are satisfied with their family relationships. The opposite is true for persons who moved within the city. Perhaps they are dissatisfied because they have to spend more time with their relatives than they want to. Newcomers, on the other hand, spend relatively little time with relatives, possibly because they are removed in space. For long-standing residents, a clear relationship exists between satisfaction with the family and time spent with relatives.

The next analyses are based on a median split of the SSS subscale 'Work'. Results of the SSS−Work main effect are presented in Table 11.14.

Satisfaction with self and moving

Table 11.13 *Interaction effects for SSS–Family and moving group on ESM*

Item	SSS–Family high SSS–Family low	Outside	Within	Stable	F (2, 91)
BP53:	% with relatives	3.8 4.8	1.8 11.4	24.9 9.7	5.00**

** $p < .01$.

Table 11.14 *Main effects for median split on SSS–Work on ESM*

Item		Satisfaction with work		F (1, 91)
		High	Low	
BP43:	% visiting	5.7	8.9	5.54*
BP50:	% alone	7.2	0.6	3.49+
BP52:	% with member of household	11.2	18.9	3.45+
BP607:	% reading newspaper	2.1	3.9	4.94*

* $p < .05$; + $< .10$.

Only two effects are marked (the others are significant at $p < .07$): persons dissatisfied with themselves in regard to their work spend more time visiting others and reading newspapers. Through lack of additional information, these effects seem interpretable only if they take place during working hours and are a distraction from work. Otherwise, dissatisfaction with work does not seem to influence other life spheres, nor does it clearly interact with changes in the person–environment relationship as exemplified in moving status.

The next analyses are based on the median split of the SSS subscale 'Object'. The main effect for SSS–Object shows that satisfaction with their physical environment affects the places where people spend their time. Persons satisfied with their physical environment are more likely to go outside for relaxation and hence spend less time at home; but they also spend more time at their place of work.

Table 11.15 *Main effects for median split on SSS–Object on ESM*

Item		Satisfaction with objects		F (1, 91)
		High	Low	
BP41:	% at home	50.7	58.8	4.15*
BP42:	% at workplace	21.1	11.0	7.78**
BP47:	% outside relaxation	3.9	2.1	4.54*

** $p < .01$; * $p < .05$.

The interaction effects, as presented in Table 11.16, again demonstrate reverse effects for persons moving from the outside, who spend more time in restaurants and bars and doing chores when dissatisfied, as opposed to those who stayed within the city, for whom those activities seem to be more frequent when they are satisfied with their relationship to the physical environment. Dissatisfaction with a new environment perhaps leads to attempts to distract oneself.

Table 11.16 *Interaction effects for SSS–Object and moving group on ESM*

Item	SSS–Object high SSS–Object low	Outside	Within	Stable	F (2, 91)
BP44:	% at restaurant or bar	0.8	3.0	1.0	
		2.4	0.8	1.0	3.09*
BP602:	% chores	9.7	10.9	15.2	
		15.6	7.1	7.5	3.83*

* $p < .05$.

The results show that the objective environment and the possibilities for behaviour in it are perceived and used very differently, depending on moving status and satisfaction with self. Persons moving from the outside, that is, those for whom the environment is strange and new, are only likely to explore in the first few weeks from a position of strength and satisfaction with oneself. The social and physical environment seems to play a very different role for those who have moved within the city: when dissatisfied, they are more likely to go out and leave the new home. For them, the home is the new environment, whereas the city is familiar and provides continuity. For persons who have moved from another town, their own home provides relative continuity.

Results from autophotography

The procedure of rating photographs has been explained in detail in Chapter 7. Chapter 8 gave an example of an analysis and an interpretation of a set of photographs that was taken from the present study. To complement the analysis presented there, a further step in the data analysis of autophotography followed the 2 × 3 factorial design SSS–Median split by moving status. Dependent variables were, first, the content of the pictures and then the ratings of functionality dimensions for the self-concept. As in all similar previous analyses, the GLM approach to the ANOVA was used, age was entered as a covariate, and the F-value was computed on the basis of the Type III sum of squares. Because of the diverse meanings of categories, a multivariate analysis of variance was not deemed to be appropriate.

No main effects significant at least at the .05 level were obtained for satisfaction with self. Therefore, Table 11.17 presents the means according to moving status. On these means, planned contrasts were computed as described above, namely (A) Outside + Within versus Stable, (B) Outside versus Within + Stable, and (C) Outside versus Stable. Subscripts in the table of means (Table 11.17), which also shows the overall effect, refer to the planned contrasts if the overall effect was significant at least at the 10 per cent level or the planned contrast significant at least at the 5 per cent level. The F-values and significance levels are presented in Table 11.18.

Table 11.17 *Means of photograph ratings by moving status*

Category	Outside	Within	Stable	F(df)
Memory (environments)	1.07	1.32	1.02	2.47(2, 74) +
Art	0.30a	0.38a	0.74b	3.58(2, 90)*
Pets	0.25a	0.25a	0.74b	4.64(2, 90)*
Musical instruments	0.30a	0.04b	0.04b	5.04(2, 90)**
Singular object	1.86a	1.75a	2.30b	2.93(2, 90) +
Picture of self	0.14a	0.42b	0.78b	2.81(2, 90) +

** p < .01; * p < .05; + p < .10. Significant differences are indicated by subscripts.

Table 11.18 *Planned contrasts of photograph ratings by moving status*

Variable	O + W versus S	O versus W + S	O versus S
Art and paintings	6.68(1, 90)*	3.82(1, 90) +	6.96(1, 90)**
Pets	8.63(1, 90)**	5.02(1, 90)*	9.05(1, 90)**
Musical instruments	ns	9.98(1, 90)**	6.04(1, 90)*
Single object	5.86(1, 90)*	ns	4.68(1, 90)*
Self	ns	5.37(1, 90)*	4.90(1, 90)*

** p < .01; * p < .05; + p < .10.

A single object was depicted in isolation most often by persons who had not moved at all. On the other hand, pictures of oneself were mainly taken by persons whose residence had been stable. This is particularly interesting, because it may be interpreted in contradiction to the self-awareness prediction as an indication that the self is not particularly salient when moving to a new locale. However, it is only one suggestion in this direction and has to be compared to other related variables.

Table 11.19 shows the effects for the interaction of SSS by moving status. Only interaction effects at least significant at the 5 per cent level are reported.

154 A quasi-experimental study

Table 11.19 *Means of photograph ratings for interaction SSS by moving status*

Category	Satisfied Dissatisfied	Outside	Within	Stable	F(df)
Non-mobile objects		2.83	1.46	3.44	
		2.85	3.27	0.80	3.98(2, 90)*
Paintings and art		0.22	0.69	0.61	
		0.37	0.00	1.20	4.07(2, 90)*
Books		0.65	0.38	0.44	
		0.22	0.91	0.60	3.22(2, 90)*
Sports equipment		0.26	0.46	0.00	
		0.07	0.00	0.40	4.20(2, 90)*

* $p < .05$.

The depiction of non-mobile objects is not affected by satisfaction with self among movers from the outside of town. Movers within the city and non-movers show opposite effects: the former depict more non-mobile objects when dissatisfied, the latter more when satisfied. Possibly, it is an aspect of the new home or a view from it that indicates dissatisfaction, and a familiar aspect of the old environment that indicates satisfaction produced by stability.

Paintings and pieces of art are affected in the opposite way: they are photographed mainly by the satisfied movers within the city and the dissatisfied non-movers. In both cases dissatisfaction with some aspects of the environment may be counteracted by the enjoyment of art.

Books as well as sports equipment are photographed more frequently by the satisfied movers, and less so by the satisfied stable persons. These items are salient when stable persons are dissatisfied. Reading books and doing sports are both considered activities that may be functional in changing oneself because they provide new experiences. The person who has moved from outside has already had to process many new experiences, and additional ones can only be taken on when one is in a position of strength. On the other hand, the person who has lived in the same place may only feel the necessity to acquire new experiences when dissatisfied with himself or herself.

Behavioural and perceptual predictors of satisfaction with self

The main focus of the foregoing analyses was the interaction effect between satisfaction with self and moving status, testing the assumption that different relationships between environment and person may result in different ways of making use of the environment to cope with a certain status of the self-concept. The appropriate way to address that question is through the analysis of an interaction in a factorial design. However, to do this the continuous variable 'satisfaction with self' had to be dichotomized to yield a factor with two levels. While this allows the necessary analysis of an interaction, it makes only limited use of the information contained in the variable 'satisfaction with self'. To be able to obtain more information about the relationship between SSS and the respective ESM variables regarding behaviour as well as the autophotography ratings, multiple regression analyses were conducted regardless of the interaction with the different quasi-experimental moving groups. These regression analyses were conducted using only select subsamples of the variables. In particular, these variables were (a) the variability of behaviour, (b) the assessment of interactional situations, and (c) the self-relevant dimensions of autophotography ratings.

The first regression was conducted using SSS on the criterion side of the regression and entering on the predictor side the variables (B19, B21–B24) that evaluated the perceived importance and self-disclosure character of social interactions. Only one variable remained in the model at the .10 threshold, namely the item 'How important was this person to you?', $F(1, 89) = 2.79$, $p < .10$, beta = .097. However, the variance explained in satisfaction with self was only 3 per cent. The direction of the beta-value indicates that the greater importance of the other person is related to greater satisfaction with self.

The next analysis investigated whether behavioural variance may be related to satisfaction with self. Behavioural variance, that is, the range of different behaviours, was statistically defined as the mean variance of the percentage of categories used within one rating variable. This could be applied to several variables: 'activities', 'locations', and 'other persons present'. A high variance indicates that the person was engaged in a wide variety of behaviours during the ESM week.

The behavioural variance of locations, companions, and activities was entered into the regression analysis with satisfaction with self. The range of persons present when responding to the signal, that is, the variance of companionship, showed a highly significant relationship to satisfaction with self, $F(1, 89) = 7.34$, $p < .01$, beta = 7.14. The direction of the beta-value indicates that greater variance is related to greater dissatisfaction. The variance explained is 7.6 per cent. Considering the many potential effects on satisfaction with self and the very different approaches to measurement, this percentage can be considered of interest. Satisfaction with self is, according to this analysis, related to the range and variability of social interactions one has with others.

The next analysis considered the dimensions of the photograph ratings as functional to self-concept-related processes, for instance self-presentational, symbolic, and so forth. These analyses were conducted separately for each of the three different categories of possible photograph content, namely objects, environments, and persons. For the photographs having objects as main content category, four dimensions combined explained 13.4 per cent of the variance, $F(4,77) = 3.00$, $p < .03$. The best four predictors of SSS were (a) degree of integration, $F(1,77) = 3.75$, $p < .06$, beta .15, (b) activity value, $F(1,77) = 3.50$, $p < .07$, with a beta of .15, (c) reflection value, $F(1,77) = 6.79$, $p < .02$, beta .28, and (d) symbol value, $F(1,77) = 5.13$, $p < .03$, beta $-.13$.

Integration, activity, reflection, and symbolism of photograph content are related to satisfaction with self, such that high integration, activity, and reflection and low symbolism relate to high satisfaction with self.

When *environments* were the main content of the photograph, only the degree of integration was related to SSS, $F(1,74) = 3.66$, $p < .06$, beta $-.20$. This variable explained 4.7 per cent of the variance. Finally, when *persons* were considered to be the main content of the photograph, a more significant relationship emerged again, $F(3,56) = 4.07$, $p < .015$, r-square .18. The three variables contributing to this effect were (a) degree of integration, $F(1,56) = 3.88$, $p < .06$, beta $-.21$, (b) reflection, $F(1,56) = 4.35$, $p < .05$, beta .31, and (c) symbolism, $F(1,56) = 6.15$, $p < .02$, beta $-.17$.

Over all three types of content, the dimensions reflection and symbolism had the most stable relationship to satisfaction with self, reflection being positively related and symbolism negatively. Indeed, when the multiple regression was conducted regardless of content across all categories, the combination of these two variables proves to be significant, $F(2,88) = 3.99$, $p < .025$, variance explained r-square $= .083$. The effects for the two variables were (a) for symbolism $F(1,88) = 5.88$, $p < .02$, beta $-.18$, and (b) reflection $F(1,88) = 7.08$, $p < .01$, beta .36.

Reflection was described initially as: 'a social message, an invitation for the viewer to share in the thoughts and reflections of the person who took the picture. Thus, the picture presents part of the individual's self and reveals it to another' (Chapter 7). On the other hand, the symbolic value of a picture was defined as a presentation of symbols that are societally shared. The stable positive relationship of satisfaction with self to reflection and negative relationship with symbolism may indicate that persons who are more satisfied with themselves rely more on their own personal interpretations of the world around them and less on the common meanings. Taken further, for persons satisfied with their self-concept the world around them has acquired meaning through personal interaction and not by simply accepting the meanings already provided for.

In general, the results of the present study have indicated a completely different meaning and function that environment and behaviour can have at different stages in the person–environment relationship. For persons who have lived in the same city for a while, an orientation toward the outside seems to be more associated with dissatisfaction with the self-concept. Those who are new to an environment are more likely to be orientated toward the social and physical outside environment when they are satisfied with themselves. Satisfaction with self was found to be associated with a stable social network and a view of the world that communicates one's personal meaning.

What implications do these findings have for the theoretical approach taken here? Seemingly contrary to one of the assumptions guiding this research, persons in a new environment are not as likely to seek out new experiences as an opportunity to change a self-concept that they are not satisfied with. On the other hand, persons for whom the external environment has been stable are more likely to make use of its opportunities when dissatisfied.

The data for newcomers have to be considered from the point of time after the move when they were collected, namely within six to eight weeks after the move. Both from an earlier elaborated theoretical standpoint that presumed an initially heightened resistance to change, and from an empirical standpoint, based on the data of the first telephone survey demonstrating the resistance to change, eight weeks may be too early to accept the opportunities of a new environment. Therefore, two more studies will be presented that tried to follow the course of development in a new environment longitudinally over twelve and eight months respectively.

12 Relocation as transition and change in a physical and social context

By now, the different elements of the ecological system in which the self-concept develops and changes have been put together. On this basis, it is possible to consider the transactions of persons as they move in and through the ecological system and how this affects change.

Over the last few years, a number of studies have addressed changes in the self-concept and in person–environment relationships, many of them published recently, after my own research had been conceived and some of it had already been conducted (1980–5). Basically, such studies can be seen as belonging to one of two groups: studies specifically concerned with self-concept change, and those that make use of changes in the person–environment relationship as a general framework for the study of personal change and development. Some make specific use of relocation as a major transition affecting the social and physical context of a person. Therefore, a short overview of psychological research on relocation will first be given.

Relocation as a subject of psychological research

In modern societies, more people move more frequently. In Germany, between 40 and 50 per cent of the population relocate over a five-year period (Horstmann, 1979). In the US, 16 per cent of the population had moved between March 1982 and March 1983. Overall, however, the mobility rate in the US is declining, from about 20 per cent between 1960 and 1961 to about 16 per cent between 1982 and 1983 (US Bureau of the Census, 1984). Of those moves, about half take place between countries rather than within, that is, they mostly involve a completely new and different environment.

Psychological research has long been concerned mainly with the consequences of involuntary relocation. Besides work-related relocations and those taking place in connection with urban renewal, persons committed to institutions and the relocation of whole institutions have been studied. Only recently has the topic of relocation gained more general interest within psychology. Three approaches can be distinguished: (a) One approach concerns itself with the reasons, motives, and decision processes leading to a decision to move; (b) Another studies the psychological consequences of a move and the coping strategies employed; (c) Finally, relocation is studied as a paradigmatic life event involving complex changes in the person–environment relationship.

Social scientific research on mobility probably started with the work of Ravenstein in 1885 (cited in Franz, 1984). He tried to interpret the flow of migration by formulating laws and typologies of migration. He was not interested in the individual motives for migration, but in the economic and social conditions of the degree and direction of migration. Ravenstein's work was influential for sociological and economic research on relocation.

On the other hand, psychological research is focused on the individual processes leading to a relocation of residence. Such research was first undertaken in the context of decision theoretical approaches, starting with relatively simple utility models and later developing models that tried to take the decisional freedom of a person into account. Lately, attempts have been made to integrate the sociological-economic and individual level of analysis in relocation decisions (Gatzweiler, 1975). However, because of the necessity for longitudinal research designs to test related hypotheses, few empirical realizations of this approach have been undertaken. Even in sociological migration research, cognitive models based on individual decision making (for example Esser, 1980) are competing with those seeking societal status tensions as a source of migration (Hoffmann-Nowotny, 1970). These theoretical approaches are compared by Nauck (1988).

Another area of investigation involves the processes related to *disassociation* from the old environment: changes in the perception of the environment, in attitudes toward the old and new environment, and other variables in the changing person–environment system. Wapner and associates developed a four-stage model of the transition from an old to a new environment (see, for instance, Wofsey, Rierdan, & Wapner, 1979). During the first phase, the individual is still integrated in the old environment and has no plans for change. The second phase is the anticipation phase: the old environment is perceived as more distant and decreases in emotional and personal relevance. In the third phase, after the move has occurred, a complete distancing from the old environment is observable, but the person still feels alien and isolated in the new environment. This is the critical phase of relocation. The newcomer seeks orientation in the new social and cultural patterns and tries to construct a new environment for himself or herself. The environment is now perceived in a neutral and non-committal way. Finally, the fourth phase indicates complete integration and is thus comparable to the first one: the new environment has become an old one.

Little research has been done on the personality correlates of relocation. In a study of Indian migrants to Canada, Winchie and Carment (1988) found occupational dissatisfaction, sensation seeking, interest in world news, and belief in a predictable world to discriminate between applicants for immigration and visitor visas. Achievement motivation contributed little, and risk taking and previous mobility nothing, to the discrimination. These differences suggest that persons seeking a new location are not out for adventure, but to better themselves under conditions involving calculable risk. The authors even suggest that previous mobility may produce personality changes. This argument is very much in line with the use of relocation as a paradigm for self-concept change.

Most studies on the *consequences* of relocation concentrate on the negative ones. Relocation is supposedly involved in depression, alcoholism, delinquency, or even suicidal tendencies (see Fischer & Fischer, 1981). However, frequently relocation takes place in connection with other critical life events (for example divorce, the death of someone close, graduation, change of job). Therefore, it is difficult to determine whether such influences are actually due to relocation or to the other stressors involved. Studies that allow a clear distinction between these effects are rare. Many reported negative consequences are likely to be produced by cumulative stress surrounding a relocation (Fischer & Fischer, 1985). The degree of stress of a move is also determined by individual social, intellectual, and financial resources that can assist in coping.

The information on the negative consequences of involuntary relocation, as reviewed by Heller (1982), is somewhat clearer. Involuntary relocation takes place especially in connection with urban renewal (Tessin, Knorr, Pust, & Birlein, 1983), in connection with changes in work (job change, promotion), and in institutional settings. Involuntary relocation could frequently be associated with a higher susceptibility to illness and other emotional, physiological and behavioural reactions; some studies also report a higher mortality rate following relocation. The seriousness of consequences depends on the initial psychological and physical state, on a long anticipation phase, and on the degree to which the person being relocated can contribute to the decision and relocation process and its outcome.

The new environment also influences the coping process. The stranger the new environment is perceived to be, the more serious are resistance to change and resulting stress. One factor that contributes positively to coping consists of continued ties to the old social network (Bourestone & Tars, 1974) and its gradual replacement by a new social network (Jones, 1980). New environments providing a better quality of life may also make the coping process easier. Summarized, reviews of the literature on involuntary relocation do not allow general statements on the consequences.

A study linking the process of adaptation to the individual experiences brought into the new environment has also been conducted by Wohlwill and Kohn (1973), based on adaptation-level theory. They assumed that the processing of new environmental stimuli is to a large degree determined by the adaptation level formed by the earlier environment. They studied persons who had moved to a medium-sized city, and compared the perception of the same city of persons who had moved there from a large metropolitan area to those from a rural community. They demonstrated that the perception of variables in the physical environment (noise, pollution) and the social conditions (crime and need for security) differed for those groups.

Fischer and Fischer (1985) also emphasize the role of the individual's family context. Psychological consequences of a relocation can be different for different members of the same family with different degrees of contribution to the decision process and the actual move, often wives and children. Involvement in the decision also influences different social integration processes of family members. Fischer and Fischer tried to provide a family-orientated theory of transition to develop specific hypotheses regarding these issues; an empirical investigation has not yet been undertaken by them.

Stokols, Shumaker, and Martinez (1983) studied the effects of repeated relocation among highly mobile populations. Mobility could be related to symptoms of illness, especially (a) among highly mobile persons who show few exploratory behaviours in regard to the new environment, (b) among less mobile persons who are little satisfied with the new environment, and (c) among persons in low-quality housing with little hope for improvement. Highly mobile persons also show little personal involvement in the new neighbourhood and community. Brett (1982) also points to dissatisfaction in social relationships as a consequence of frequent relocation. On the other hand, Newmann and Owen (1982) show improvements in material conditions for highly mobile populations.

The transition of roles concurrent with a move was the topic of a study by Rosch and Irle (1984). They studied cognitive variables and indicators of health status among immigrants with a German background from Poland into West Germany. While in Poland, these persons were considered Germans; when in Germany, as Polish. The clearer they perceived this role transition, and if in addition they attributed the source of problems in the new environment to themselves, the higher the probability of illness.

To summarize, relocation is the focus of a variety of stress factors. Whether they come to bear depends on a great variety of individual and social conditions. Much attention has been on outcome studies, but there has been too little on studies of the processes of coping with change.

Relocation as a research paradigm for transitions

The general paradigmatic nature of transitions between environments has been recognized only recently (Fischer & Fischer, 1981, 1985; Hormuth, 1984; Stokols, Shumaker, & Martinez, 1983; Wapner, 1981, 1987).

Jones (1980) studied relocation as an adjustment process for the self. Her study involved interviews with thirty newcomer families in an Australian city. The theoretical background and the analytic inductional method she employed were explicitly based on the approach of the Chicago school of symbolic interaction. In some respects, the study has close parallels to the approach taken here. In particular, her findings can be related to some of those obtained here.

Jones found that for newcomers contact through letters with relatives and friends outside the city was of special importance. Having a correspondence relationship with others had, according to Jones, special functions for the change and maintenance of the self-concept. These special functions were related to the special nature of communication through letters, which allows a high degree of control over the communication. That way, responses can be elicited that support the person's present view of self. If the person was trying to maintain his or her self-concept, relationships by correspondence increased in intimacy and could thus support the previous concept of self. If, on the other hand, the persons changed aspects of their self-concept, the freedom to provide information selectively in letters made it possible to maintain a high degree of control over the other's response and to elicit support for specific aspects of the self-concept.

Jones also described how the establishment of social structures in the new environment was functional in the maintenance or change of the self-concept. The re-establishment of support systems through seemingly normal networks was seen by her as essential in providing continuity. Persons in search of continuity established social networks that built on the similarities of persons from the new and old environments. Networks were made up of new others who served similar functions to others in the old networks. That way, the actual persons may have been exchanged but their functions for the self-concept remained similar, as when one interviewee remarked that she seemed to establish mother-like relationships everywhere she moved.

The social network was also identified as a mediator for change by Jones. It served this function either by the newcomer's choice or by necessity. However, if a network was not re-established in its old function and was different in the new environment, it was not necessarily the case that people were following a plan for change; some took advantage of new opportunities and support structures. Hence over the course of the year during which Jones conducted interviews, changing aspects of the self were emerging. Choice entered into self-concept change when social support for an emergent new aspect of self was either accepted or rejected. Change was not predictable, but persons considered opportunities as they came along and decided to build a social support structure for that aspect of self or to forgo the opportunity.

Of particular interest is Jones's interpretation of the self as an adjustment process. Change in the self was perceived as such by the investigator, but not by the persons being investigated. Instead, if they had changed after the first year, they reconstructed their past retrospectively so that the present concept of self seemed a continuation of the past self-concept: 'the process of retrospectively constructing the past to fit the present situation was the key to the maintenance of continuous identity in a changing situation' (Jones, 1980, p. 92). Jones interprets this process as a search for meaning *sensu* Mead: persons simultaneously took the perspective of the past and the present. The self served as an adjustment process converging both perspectives and thus providing the feeling of stability while the person was going through a transition.

The variables and processes studied by Jones are surprisingly close to the ones that are being considered here. It was mainly her methodological approach that was different. It allowed access to some information that the studies reported in this book could not yield. In particular, the dialectic of change and stability is of importance because it points to some relationships between social processes related to the self-concept that are related to change and cognitive processes that favour stability. Following her suggestions may help in explaining why some studies have difficulties finding self-reported self-concept change amidst social and environmental change.

Figure-ground relationships in new environments

Using a different approach, Stewart, Sokol, Healy, and Chester (1986) conducted a series of longitudinal studies to test hypotheses regarding internal adaptation to external life changes. Their studies involved transitions to, between, and from school, into marriage, and into parenthood. They maintain that:

> life changes precipitate an internal process that begins with a heightened awareness of the external and interpersonal environment and a shift in the relation of the self to that environment ... When we experience a major change – even, say, of location (as on vacation) – we are suddenly more aware of the environment we are in ... Moreover, it carries with it a reduced sense of self. In a way, the ground (environment) has become the figure, and we, who were formerly figures, are now reduced in salience and clarity. (Stewart et al., 1986, p. 144)

Curiously, they go on from this perspective to propose a similarly curvilinear adaptation process as implied in the self-awareness perspective, namely initial resistance toward the strange environment, followed by a period of acting in the new environment and learning from it. However, their empirical data refer not to behavioural adaptation but only to emotional development. The sole measure of adaptation and change consisted of a TAT-type projective test assessing four dimensions: (a) relationships to authority, (b) relationships to other people, (c) inner feelings, and (d) orientation to action. In general, Stewart et al.'s results are quite consistent with the model proposed here. An emotional stance of confusion and rejection, along with actions taken to protect the self, is later followed by individual initiative and assertiveness toward the new environment.

The hypothesis that the new environment absorbs attention and focuses it away from self directly contradicts the one proposed in Chapter 4 above as derived from the interpretation of the figure–ground principle and its relationship to self-awareness theory. Stewart et al. do not present a direct empirical test of their hypothesis; it is taken as a basic assumption that leads in turn to the curvilinear hypothesis of adaptation. Indeed, their projective test does not provide for an assessment of self-focus. The self-awareness hypothesis in my own research has a similar status: self-awareness is considered a prerequisite for self-concept-relevant processes to occur. However, while Stewart et al. did not make their hypothesis subject to empirical testing, the previous study included an item in the ESM booklet asking for the direction of attention: self versus outside.

A comparison among the groups based on the percentage of attention focused on oneself did not show any differences. To allow a test of an additional hypothesis that the attention of persons in a new environment fluctuates more between self and outside, an index was constructed that assessed the degree to which succeeding answers to this focus of attention item either alternated or stayed the same. This index showed that for the group of persons moving from the outside the degree of fluctuation of attention was more than 50 per cent higher than for the other two groups (who did not differ), but the very high variance within groups kept the F-value at less than 1.

These results, along with a number of problems associated with the measurement of focus of attention in general (Wicklund, 1975) and the measurement of focus of attention through experience sampling in particular (Hormuth, 1986, pp. 284–6), do not allow an empirical decision between the two hypotheses. At best, the way of measuring focus of attention was inappropriate. A measure of chronic level of self-consciousness was not included in any of the studies presented here because the focus of attention hypothesis was considered to be a basic assumption guiding this research rather than a hypothesis to be tested. In this respect, the present research does not differ from that of Stewart et al. Their results, however, can as well be explained through the present hypothesis that self-awareness initially makes the difference between the self-concept and the new environment salient and therefore leads to an actualization of previously existing standards and the rejection of new ones. This, basically, seems to agree with the proposition of Stewart et al. that transitions make the person–environment relationship salient.

On a theoretical level, the difference between an assumption that the environment is dominating and one that proposes that the self-concept becomes salient is the difference between an adaptive and an agentic approach to change. If the environment is dominating, the person's change follows the parameters, that is opportunities and constraints, as set by the new environment. A process of adaptation takes place, and when the individual recognizes the changes that have taken place, self-concept change results. This is the process of self-concept change as proposed by Becker (1964), and indeed, Stewart et al. finally conclude that the processes they studied in connection with changes in the environment, in daily routines, and in the interpersonal or social world were processes of adaptation, and did not necessarily demonstrate developmental attainment, or growth.

The findings of Stewart et al. that 'changes precipitate a shift toward a receptive emotional stance and that after change there is a shift toward more autonomous or assertive stances' (p. 149) are further complicated by the fact that most subjects underwent new, additional transitions so that a new phase of helplessness and receptivity toward the environment interferes with the adaptation process.

This finding points to a general problem in the longitudinal naturalistic study of change: over time, the common quasi-experimental condition may be only one event among many in research participants' lives so that the variance added over time makes the detection of specific processes increasingly difficult. Therefore, longitudinal studies of the changes in behaviour and self-concept which follow transitions may at some point have to make use of design techniques that reduce variance produced by other events. This can consist either of the identification of shared transitional events, of samples from homogeneous populations, or the use of quasi-experimental design reducing within-group variance and capitalizing on the between-group variance. However, to counteract the possible confounding factors introduced either way, all strategies should be part of a multiple-study approach. This approach has, to some degree, been followed by Stewart et al., because among their studies they were able to differentiate between types of transitions with different probabilities of continued change. This is also the approach taken in the present research programme.

Attitude and self-concept change following life transitions

Another series of longitudinal studies related to self-concept change was undertaken by Mummendey (1986). The primary aim of these studies was the investigation of the attitude–behaviour relationship, but self-concept-relevant variables were also included. These consisted of a measure of the evaluative aspect of the self-concept in one study or an ideal–real self comparison in another study. One study was of soldiers recruited in the army; the other, of young mothers. The soldiers' results showed that self-concept evaluation decreased considerably when they were confronted with the military environment and increased again only slowly. For young mothers, the discrepancy between real and ideal self was large immediately preceding childbirth, but was quickly reduced to normal levels again. However, again in both studies the results were not as clear-cut as expected; Mummendey attributes this to a variety of other influences.

The results match the present framework well. Transition to motherhood is a transition that quickly requires agentic change. The actual role transition has, to some degree, taken place before childbirth. In Stewart's terminology, the receptive stance would have occurred before childbirth. Therefore, self-concept change has already started in anticipation of the event. On the other hand, for soldiers the new, almost total change in social and physical environment puts them in a role that can to a much lesser degree be made but has to be played. Because of these constraints, agentic change cannot take place, and the phase of resistance may not be overcome.

A very interesting comparison could be presented by Mummendey that highlights the importance of the previous ecological system in self-concept change. Groups of soldiers who made frequent journeys home were compared to those who visited home infrequently. A visit home could make the previous self-concept salient, whereas staying in the military environment (an almost 'total' environment) had a continuous deindividuating effect. The data show a linear decrease in self-concept evaluation when the former environment was not made salient through frequent home visits. On the other hand, those soldiers visiting home showed curvilinear change: an initial increase in self-concept evaluation was followed by a decrease to the same point as in the other group. The data present evidence that the awareness of differences between the former and the present person–environment relationship produces initial resistance to change followed by adaptation.

Seemingly completely different results were obtained in a longitudinal study of self-concept stability by Filipp and Klauer (1986). Their longitudinal design involved three years of measurement of the self-concept of adult males. The measurement instrument consisted of rating scales as well as spontaneously generated statements about the self-concept. As compared to the studies summarized above, practically no significant changes of aspects of the self-concept were found, despite a great variety of life events that had taken place in these men's lives.

Filipp and Klauer argue that the self-concept is a process that facilitates stability rather than change. This, indeed, is similar to the argument which I presented earlier. The self-concept is a cognitive structure linking new experiences to old ones and thereby provides for stability rather than change. However, the sole reliance on measures of self-concept taken at several points neglects the processes, the behaviours, and changes in evaluations that demonstrate processes of coping with life events. This neglect may well yield the apparent stability. In addition, Filipp and Klauer did not take steps to reduce the variance introduced by many different life events, as was done in the previously cited studies. Therefore, change that may occur at the individual level may not be detectable among a sample of more than 100 persons. But the study is important as a reminder that stability is the rule. On the other hand, studies like the ones presented in this book and the ones summarized above capitalize on change because they are interested in the processes surrounding change rather than in the outcome.

Stability versus change as reaction to a new environment may also be the result of individual differences. A personality variable mediating stability versus change in new environments has been described by Whitbourne (1986): 'Openness to experience' is described as 'the disposition to welcome new and unusual experiences without anxiety'. Whitbourne applied this personality trait specifically to the study of identity change in adult life. Openness to experience was thought to be a mediator in a process of identity flexibility where an adult contemplates alternatives to his or her current identity commitments. Identity flexibility as a process of anticipation with openness to experience as mediator should predict whether or not the opportunities inherent in a life change will be realized. Over a twelve-month period, it turned out that actual age was the most important predictor of contemplation of change; greater age seemed to limit the opportunities perceived. As far as actual change was concerned, education, independent of age, was the best predictor. However, identity flexibility was also related to actual change: the majority (63 per cent) of those who said they would make a change actually did change during the course of one year, and the minority (15 per cent) of those who said they would not changed nevertheless.

Whitbourne interprets the finding that identity flexibility is important in predicting change, however, as possibly related to variables of social constraint (age) and social resources (education) rather than to openness to the experience of actual change. This has some affinity to an ecological view of the self-concept in which changes in the self are related to the possibility for changes in the person−environment relationship. Social structural variables were in Whitbourne's study more powerful predictors than personality variables.

A consistent programmatic approach to the study of transitions and change has been presented by Wapner (1981, 1987). His studies involve critical transitions of persons-in-environments. The environment refers to its physical, interpersonal, and socio-cultural aspects. The programmatic research encompasses a wide variety of transitions, and is undertaken from a holistic, systems-orientated developmental perspective. Wapner considers this complex approach as necessary if one tries to understand humans in their complexity operating in everyday life settings. His is also a multi-method approach. The methods employed range from controlled experimentation to a descriptive, phenemenological methodology. Theoretically, he draws on developmental, social, sociological, and phenomenological approaches.

Wapner considers the study of critical transitions of persons in environments as paradigmatic. His assumptions are very similar to the ones guiding the present research: '(1) the person-in-environment is the unit to be analyzed, (2) the person-in-environment system operates in dynamic equilibrium directed toward long- and short-term goals, and (3) a disturbance in one part of the person-in-environment system affects other parts and the transactional system as a whole' (Wapner, 1981, p. 224).

The review of studies of transitions and change in a social and physical context re-emphasizes the necessity to study development over time, that is, to conduct longitudinal studies. In addition, the state of the individual before undergoing a transition and the expectations of it determine the way the new life situation is approached and made use of in the development of the self-concept. The following two chapters describe longitudinal studies encompassing approximately the first ten to twelve months in a new environment.

13 A longitudinal questionnaire study over one year

The studies described above addressed change through a cross-sectional approach or only at one point in time soon after relocation. Cross-sectional studies can only suggest changes in individuals over time: they cannot replace longitudinal studies. However, it is very difficult to sample for longitudinal studies requiring special populations who undergo major life transitions, such as persons who have just moved to a new environment. Accessibility of the population is one problem. Events or actions have to be identified that are common to people moving into a new town, that are public, or provide some public information about the fact of arrival of newcomers, and that are as close as possible to the time of arrival in the new environment.

Getting a telephone and access to electricity and gas are two such events that have been made use of in the studies described in earlier chapters. Both have advantages and disadvantages. The telephone book does not give any information about how long ago the arrival occurred; it does not distinguish between new arrivals in town and other people who have new telephone numbers; and the information is several weeks or months old by the time it becomes available. While more recent newcomers could also be reached in the studies making use of telephone listings, this happens more by chance than by planning. Listings of households with new connections to electricity and gas are a very good and up-to-date source of information. However, because of the voluntary nature of the cooperation by the local utility company, no permanent or extensive use of this source of information can be made.

The most common source of information for social scientists obtaining samples in Germany is city registration offices. German law requires the registration of persons immediately after taking up residence. In theory, if everyone obeyed the law, every town and every city would have a complete listing of all persons living in that town. However, because the law is not strictly enforceable, this is not the case. There are also some incentives to register late or not at all and thus legally keep the old residence. People can then take advantage of geographical differences in insurance rates, may prefer to continue to be eligible to vote or be elected in another town, or may delay their registration for other reasons. Hormuth and Brückner (1985) have already argued that there is no reason to assume that city registration data are superior to some other means of sampling, for instance, telephone listings. As compared to other means of sampling, samples from registration offices can become very expensive because of fees charged by city offices for compiling samples according to a social scientist's instructions.

Registration is an event concomitant with relocation but of limited informativeness. However, it is an event with different biases from those associated with the other events, and samples of some informativeness can be obtained that way. Given that registration is likely to be delayed, a study of the effects of moving making use of that information should constitute a conservative test through the lack of precision in sampling right after arrival. Some subjects may have moved several months before they register; others may register sooner. In any case, this should increase the variance of effects but not exclude the possibility of detecting effects. Therefore, a low-cost sampling procedure was devised to make use of registration requirements to sample for a longitudinal questionnaire study.

The city registration offices of small towns surrounding Heidelberg, ranging in size from a few thousand to almost 50,000 inhabitants, were approached to collaborate in obtaining volunteers for participation in a questionnaire study. Rather than providing names and addresses of persons registering, which was refused by practically all of them on the basis of (inadequate) legal arguments, they agreed to make leaflets available in the registration offices. These leaflets described the basic purpose of the study and asked people to volunteer by writing to the investigator's address provided.

A sample of about fifty persons volunteering to participate in a study was obtained. Unfortunately, there was no control possible over the participation rate of cooperating city offices. Because the sample grew rather slowly, a second sample was added from computer records of the Heidelberg city registration office. Persons from those lists received letters asking for their cooperation in the study.

Design of the study

The study was designed as a longitudinal questionnaire study, involving four waves over one year. Subjects who indicated their interest in participation first received one questionnaire, without being aware that this was to be part of a longitudinal study. They were instructed to fill out the questionnaire provided in the mailing, and were asked whether they were also willing to receive three similar questionnaires over the next twelve months. Hence commitment to participation in a longitudinal study was not implied when they responded to the first questionnaire.

Design of the study

Willingness to participate in the longitudinal study was indicated by returning a separate postcard containing one's name and address. This was done to insure that no identification of questionnaires was possible, and persons who provided their names that way received the next three questionnaires. Keeping mailing lists and questionnaires completely separate necessitated other ways to connect questionnaires of the same person at different times. To avoid any identification, and to use a method that made concern for the protection of privacy obvious to research participants, the respondents were asked to provide a neutral but unique code. This code consisted of the first letter of the mother's first name, the second letter of the father's first name, the last letter of the place of birth, and the third letter of the month of birth. This code could easily be reconstructed by a person, but only by that person. Subjects were aware that data protection was under their own control, and not that of the investigator. At the same time, the connection of longitudinal data was possible without making any identification necessary.

The questionnaire included the main instruments used in the previous studies:

> A life event questionnaire including twenty life events.
> The measurement of commitment, as described in Chapter 6.
> A list of seventeen objects and things, tools and personal property that had to be rated in regard to personal importance on a five-point scale.
> A list of activities. Respondents were asked to indicate for twenty-four social and solitary activities the frequency with which that activity was performed over the last four weeks.
> The Self-Monitoring Scale in an adaptation of a translation by Amelang and Borkenau (1982).
> The Satisfaction with Self Scale (SSS), as described in Chapter 7.
> Background information on the respondent, such as sex, age, living arrangements, education, occupation, and type of move undergone.

This form of the questionnaire was provided for the first mailing. The second, third, and fourth questionnaire also contained the scale of personal values that was initially used in the first telephone survey.

Sample and return rate

The first wave had 86 respondents initially. Of those, 48 per cent were male, and 52 per cent female. Their mean age was 30.2 years (SD = 11.6), ranging from 19 to 91 years. They had already lived at their present address for an average of 5.3 months, showing that a relatively long time had indeed passed between moving and registration; 70 per cent were single, but only 37 per cent lived alone; and 70 per cent rented a flat.

There was practically no possibility of influencing the return rate with the exception of one reminder postcard. Additional reminders, though methodologically necessary, would have been prohibitively expensive. In addition, respondents in this study had no incentive to participate. The participants in the first wave were not even aware initially that the design of the study was longitudinal. Only after they had agreed to participate were they informed that three more mailings were planned.

The first wave had 86 respondents (100 per cent), the second, 66 (76.7 per cent), the third, 64 (74.4 per cent), and the final one 50 (58.1 per cent) − a 23.3 per cent loss from the first to the second wave, a 3 per cent loss from the second to the third, and a 21.9 per cent loss from the third to the fourth mailing.

Changes over time

Repeated measurements analyses were conducted over all four measurement points. Because of subject loss and missing data, only the data of forty subjects were complete and could be entered into these analyses. Analyses were conducted as repeated measurements multivariate analyses of variance.

The first repeated measurements MANOVA was conducted on the factors of Things, as obtained at Measurement 1. Things were grouped in factors that were called 'Antiques', 'Stereo', 'Home', 'Books', and 'Leisure time'. The multivariate repeated measurement effect was non-significant ($p < .20$); univariate effects were significant for Antiques, $F(3, 117) = 3.82$, $p < .02$, and for Books, $F(3, 117) = 4.06$, $p < .01$. The means are shown in Table 13.1.

Table 13.1 *Changes in the importance of things from T1 to T4*

Factor of things Time	T1	T2	T3	T4
Antiques	2.33	2.22	2.18	2.04*
Books	3.51	3.44	3.48	3.20**

** $p < .01$; * $p < .05$.

The personal importance of possessions making up these factors decreased over the course of the year. Antiques and Books are the two groups of possessions that are most capable of providing continuity; other items referring to the encouragement of new experiences and activities did not change in personal relevance over time.

The next multivariate analysis combined the factors from the scale of important values: 'House', 'Action', 'Close relationships', 'Risk', and 'Old age'. 'House' is a factor consisting of variables that indicate the importance of owning a home. 'Action' is an orientation toward activity. 'Close' refers to the importance of having close social relationships. 'Risk' indicates a willingness to take on some risk, both financial and personal. 'Old age' refers to concern about providing for the future, in particular for old age.

These factors were only assessed at the second, third, and fourth measurement points (Table 13.2). The multivariate repeated measurement effect was significant, $F(12, 146) = 2.18$, $p < .02$. Univariate effects were obtained on the factors 'Old age', $F(2, 78) = 4.24$, $p < .02$, and 'Risk', $F(2, 78) = 5.44$, $p < .01$. Marginally significant were the effects of time on 'Action', $F(2, 78) = 2.92$, $p < .06$, and 'Close relationships', $F(2, 78) = 2.65$, $p < .08$.

Table 13.2 *Changes in important values from T2 to T4*

Factor	T2	T3	T4
Old age	3.56	3.43	3.27*
Risk	3.64	3.57	3.41**
Action	2.53	2.65	3.23+
Close	3.53	3.16	3.18+

** $p < .01$; * $p < .05$; + $p < .10$.

The pattern of results indicates an initial need for security and closeness to friends and family. From this position of security, however, the respondents also seemed to be willing to take on some risk. Later, the willingness to take a risk is replaced by an actual willingness to engage in action.

Multivariate analyses of the twenty-three activities listed were conducted in different clusters which were obtained by grouping conceptually similar behaviours together. The first cluster combined activities that are centered around the house and may involve the immediate family (ACT 1, 2, 4, 9, 13, 14). The multivariate repeated measurement effect was significant, $F(18, 325) = 2.18$, $p < .005$. Univariately, the effect on 'Home improvements' was clearly significant – $F(3, 120) = 6.56$, $p < .001$; and marginally significant were the effects on 'Games with the family', $F(3, 120) = 2.17$, $p < .10$, and on 'Reading magazines', $F(3, 120) = 2.32$, $p < .08$. The means are shown in Table 13.3. The time immediately after a move is obviously the most active one for home improvements. However, activities undertaken with the family increase over time, and solitary activities, such as reading magazines, decrease slightly in frequency.

Table 13.3 *Changes in frequencies of home-centered activities T1 to T4*

Activity	T1	T2	T3	T4
Home improvements	15.05	3.76	6.39	4.10**
Games with family	1.17	1.49	2.20	2.05+
Reading magazines	12.80	10.41	11.71	9.59+

** p < .01; + p < .10.

The next cluster of activities combined those behaviours that are usually performed without another person necessarily being present (ACT 3, 8, 10, 11, 12, 23). Such solitary activities are telephone calls, reading books, and so forth. Neither the multivariate repeated measurement effect nor any of the univariate effects yielded significance.

Another cluster of activities combined those social behaviours that involve being where others are, without necessarily involving a specific other person, that is, generally social behaviours (ACT 5, 6, 7, 15, 17, 21), for instance, going to the cinema, going to a new restaurant, or attending church activities. By creating non-committal social contact, these behaviours may sometimes be attempts at getting to know new people.

The overall multivariate repeated measurement effect was highly significant, $F(18, 308) = 2.60$, $p < .001$. The univariate analyses showed significant effects for the behaviours 'Going to new restaurant', $F(3, 114) = 8.18$, $p < .001$, and 'Going to church', $F(3, 114) = 2.93$, $p < .04$. The means for these variables are shown in Table 13.4. As in the first study reported, the second quarter is crucial for such activities. After the settling in period, social activities are undertaken in which the new environment and the people in it are explored. After the first half-year, these activities decrease again to stable values. Fluctuations in church attendance are more difficult to interpret. For instance, seasonal influences are a possible explanation because for a relatively large part of the total sample T3 may have been around Christmas time or Easter. Because new subjects were added constantly, this effect is not very clearly expressed.

Table 13.4 *Changes in the frequency of social activities from T1 to T4*

Activity	T1	T2	T3	T4
New restaurant	1.39	3.23	1.31	1.13**
Church	0.62	0.44	0.64	0.31*
Dinner with friends	3.40	6.16	4.29	4.58*

** p < .01; * p < .05.

The final cluster of activities consisted of social activities with friends (ACT 16, 18, 20, 22) – inviting friends, going out with friends, and so forth. While the overall effect was non-significant, 'Going out for dinner with friends' yielded a univariately significant effect, $F(3,111) = 3.22$, $p < .03$. The means are included in the Table 13.4 above. The pattern of means on this variable is similar to 'New restaurant' with a peak at T2. While 'New restaurant' then declines slightly (because the probability of finding a new restaurant decreases as a new town becomes more familiar), 'Going out with friends for dinner' also peaks at T2, but stays higher at T3 and T4 than at the beginning. Such behaviours show a curvilinear development over time. When these data are interpreted along with behaviours around the home, it seems that the first few months are spent more around the home, followed by an exploration phase in which social activities away from home show high frequencies. In many respects, these findings are replications of the ones obtained in the cross-sectional telephone survey (Chapter 3).

Effects of self-monitoring and satisfaction with self

Self-monitoring and satisfaction with self were entered as continuous variables into the repeated measurement MANOVAs. In effect, this computes a multiple regression on the mean value of the dependent variables over all four measurement points, that is, does not constitute a regression on change, but rather on a stable aggregation.

Self-monitoring yielded a significant regression for the cluster of generally social behaviours (cinema, restaurant, church, sports event), $F(6,32) = 2.91$, $p < .03$. To be better able to determine the individual contributions of the specific behaviours to this effect, a multiple stepwise regression on the same variables was conducted, yielding, of course, the same overall effect. It may seem that the multiple stepwise regression as used here reverses predictors and criteria, because the 'dependent' variable was measured at an earlier time. However, the multiple regression is in principle reversible as long as the beta-values are not being considered.

The overall effect in the first step explained 35.3 per cent of the variance. In the significant final step, $F(3,35) = 5.91$, $p < .003$, three variables remained significant and explained 33.6 per cent of the variance on self-monitoring:

Church, $F(1,35) = 10.38$, $p < .003$.
Charitable acts, $F(1,35) = 5.12$, $p < .03$, and
Sports events, $F(1,35) = 3.89$, $p < .06$.

High self-monitoring goes along with high attendance at church and at social events, but less with charitable activities. No similar effects were found on the other behavioural clusters. The behaviours related to low self-monitoring involve social activities that may make one feel a member of a social group without necessarily involving any direct contact or commitment. Low self-monitoring seems to be relevant only to *non-committal* general social behaviours, but not necessarily to those involving specific other persons or just oneself.

To assess the effects of satisfaction with self on the change taking place between different measurement points, individual multivariate analyses were conducted for the differences between measurement points which tested (a) whether the difference was significantly different from zero, and (b) whether this difference was due to satisfaction with self at the earlier of the two measurement points that were compared. It was tested as a regression of SSS at T1 on the difference of the dependent variables between T1 and T2. The groups of variables entered into the multivariate analyses were the same as in the overall test of the effect of the repeated measurements. However, in contrast to the overall repeated measurement analyses presented above, the present analyses could be based on larger cell counts.

Effects of SSS on the *importance of things*, using the six factors into which objects were clustered, showed a significant overall difference between the first and the second measurement, $F(6,54) = 2.96$, $p < .02$ ($N = 61$). The univariate analyses show effects for the factors 'Photographs', $F(1,59) = 5.28$, $p < .03$, and 'Leisure time' objects, $F(1,59) = 10.81$, $p < .002$, with the importance of Photographs declining and that of Leisure time increasing.

The effect of SSS as a covariate in this analysis, that is, the regression of SSS on the dependent variables, showed an overall multivariate significant effect of SSS on change from T1 to T2, $F(6,54) = 2.75$, $p < .03$, with still significant univariate effects on the factors 'Photographs', $F(1,59) = 5.92$, $p < .02$, and 'Leisure time', $F(1,59) = 11.24$, $p < .002$. Change effects from T2 to T3 and T3 to T4 were non-significant.

The regression shows that the change in the importance of things during the first four months (i.e. from T1 to T2), largely due to change in the importance of Photographs and Leisure time objects, was influenced to a significant degree by satisfaction with oneself at Time 1. The dissatisfied person may retreat into memories, whereas the satisfied person pursues active interests during leisure.

The finding that satisfaction with oneself had a significant effect on changes in the meaning of things during the first three months, but not later, may be given the interpretation that through destabilization of the environment satisfaction with self affects the relationship between a person and his or her environment. Once this environment is stabilized, which seems to be the case after about three to five months, satisfaction or dissatisfaction with oneself is less likely to lead to a re-evaluation of the meaning of physical aspects of the environment.

Effects of SSS on *activities* were again tested using different multivariate clusters. The first cluster combined those variables having to do with *home and family*. No overall effect for change from T1 to T2 was found (p < .20), and the multivariate regression of SSS testing for change on these variables was also non-significant (p < .20). Individual change effects on the next cluster of activities, namely *solitary* activities, were non-significant between all measurement points.

Generally, social activities showed no multivariate effects. The change in charitable activities between T1 and T2 increased significantly, $F(1,58) = 5.08$, $p < .03$, and was influenced by satisfaction with self, $F(1,58) = 6.68$, $p < .02$. Charitable activities are one way to meet other people and give purpose to life — both are attempts to overcome dissatisfaction with self. Charitable activities may also be for some a new outlet not available in their old environment. Social activities with *friends* were unaffected by satisfaction with self.

The scale assessing *values* associated with risk and stability was only included in the second, third, and fourth measurement because it had been improved from the first study in a survey that was conducted after the first measurement was planned. Therefore, only differences between T2 and T3 and between T3 and T4 can be determined. Based on the above results, where most of the change took place between T1 and T2, this is likely to be a conservative test of the change of values in a new environment and its relationship to satisfaction with self. However, because these data are not available for T1, an interpretation linking changes in these values to other preceding changes in behaviours should be avoided.

Changes in values between T2 and T3 were significantly different from zero, $F(6,40) = 2.75$, $p < .03$, with univariate effect on 'Risk', $F(1,45) = 6.20$, $p < .02$, and marginally significant on 'Home', $F(1,45) = 3.43$, $p < .075$. Values regarding the ownership of a home increased, and those associated with risk taking decreased. These changes are related to satisfaction with self. The overall multivariate regression effect is highly significant, $F(6,40) = 3.35$, $p < .01$. Taking SSS into account, the F-values increased considerably for 'Risk' $F(1,45) = 7.56$, $p < .01$, and for 'Home' $F(1,45) = 4.06$, $p < .05$. Higher satisfaction with self seems to lessen the degree of fluctuation that these values undergo in a new environment.

Changes were still marginally significant between T3 and T4, $F(6,35) = 2.18$, $p < .07$, with a decrease in 'Risk' contributing most to this change, $F(1,40) = 8.48$, $p < .006$. Only the change in risk-related values was significantly affected by satisfaction with self, but remained clear, $F(1,40) = 6.17$, $p < .02$.

Because of the lack of a measurement of values at T1, one may only speculate whether values show changes at times that behaviours no longer change. Some of the changes in values involve the whole first year. These changes in values and attitudes are related and partially determined by satisfaction with oneself. Persons entering a new environment with lesser self-concept satisfaction are more subject to changes, and seem to be more unsure of themselves in the face of new information.

Overall assessment

To summarize, it was found that changes in the relationship to the environment and in some behaviours take place after moving to a new environment. Most of these changes take place during the interval between the first and the second measurement, with a subsequent stability setting in. The overall effects have shown that this is due on some variables to a strong change between T1 and T2 and following smaller differences. Regression analysis, conducted as part of the multivariate analyses, demonstrated that these changes are to some degree related to satisfaction with oneself.

As a result of this longitudinal study, it can be concluded that satisfaction with self is a moderator of reported changes over time. This supports the notion that the necessity for orientation in a new environment as it takes place during a move is indeed taken as an opportunity for changes related to satisfaction with one's self-concept. Self-monitoring and satisfaction with self are variables that are relevant to the way a person orientates himself or herself in a new environment and changes over time. Self-monitoring explained more than one-third of the variance of social activities that indicate an attempt at social integration in a new environment. Satisfaction with self was related to the degree of stability versus fluctuation between withdrawal and security on the one hand ('Photographs', 'Home') and outgoing activities and exploration of new possibilities ('Leisure time', 'Risk') on the other hand.

However, the influence of satisfaction with self on actual behavioural variables could not be established as clearly. Either the constraints of a new environment allowed less behavioural variance through satisfaction with self, or, because of the relatively crude measure taken in the present study, such effects could not be detected. The next study to be reported employs experience sampling and so takes a different approach to the assessment of actual behaviour in a new environment.

The current study was not able to determine whether such changes as were found are related to a state of the self-concept as it was before the move took place, or whether the changes are not only changes within the new environment but also originated from the situation as it was while it was still stable. To follow persons from an initially stable situation through an environmental transition until the new situation was restabilized was a methodological barrier that could not yet be broken, both because of problems associated with identifying persons who would undergo such a transition, and because of the cost involved in doing so. Finally, the current study had several problems with sampling which made the sample a very divergent one. The actual move had been a relatively long time ago for most participants by the time of the administration of the first questionnaire, and this varied greatly within the sample. For these reasons, the tentative conclusions about the relationship between satisfaction with self and change over the first year in a new environment can be considered preliminary because they are based on data that contain a great deal of variance irrelevant to the questions asked.

14 A longitudinal study of students' transition to university

The previous study was one attempt at longitudinally describing the adaptation to new environments. Problems of access to samples, problems of follow-up, and problems of diverse populations, as they have been discussed earlier, are prohibitive in conducting a study encompassing all the stages of a transition from the anticipation of change through the early phase in a new environment and including the adaptation over a longer cycle. Such a study could address the role of expectations with which a person approaches a transition, as well as how satisfaction with self influences behaviour and adaptation once the environment is actually entered into. A longitudinal approach could also shed light on the question of whether the newness of an environment enhances or restricts choices available to a person, and whether increasing familiarity leads to a self-imposed restriction to certain possibilities or to a continually increasing range of behaviours.

To obtain a random sample of an adult population planning to move was found to be an almost impossible task given the limited possibilities of this research project. Given the multi-method, multi-study approach chosen here, it seemed justifiable to conduct one such study on a more specific, easily accessible sample, within the context of other studies that make use of different types of samples. Therefore, it was decided to conduct a longitudinal study on students entering university. The study was only of students for whom the transition to university also included a relocation, that is, their previous residence was not the location of the university. Furthermore, access to the chosen population had to be possible before they had actually made the transition so that their expectations concerning the relocation and the transition could be assessed. The study was to include one measurement when the new environment was still relatively unfamiliar, a second when some familiarity had been gained, and a third when a new cycle had taken place, when certain events were repeated for the first time.

Overview of the design

The study included four measurement points: (a) a few weeks before the beginning of the students' first semester, (b) within the first half of the first semester, that is, the first six weeks, (c) within the second half of the first semester, that is, the second six weeks, and (d) at the beginning of the second semester. Since the academic year began in mid October, the pre-measurement was conducted by post in late September and early October; the first measurement was between mid October and before the Christmas break; the second measurement after the Christmas break and before mid February; and the third measurement between the end of April and early June.

The population consisted of new students of the University of Heidelberg not yet living in Heidelberg. A sample of 350 newly registered students was drawn immediately after registration in September and several weeks before classes commenced. Only students whose primary place of residence was not within Heidelberg or its vicinity (i.e. not within easy commuting distance) were included in the sample. This was intended to increase the likelihood that the transition to university would be accompanied by an actual relocation.

The *pre-measurement* consisted of a questionnaire. Before they moved to Heidelberg, access to the students was only possible by mail. A questionnaire was mailed to assess the students' satisfaction with themselves, their relationship to their social and physical environment, and their expectations in regard to transition to university and relocation. In addition, they were asked whether they would participate in a longer study involving several measurements during the first few months at university.

The first measurement included experience sampling and autophotography. The experience sampling addressed the current activity with special emphasis on social interactions. Instructions for autophotography were the same as in previous studies, asking for an answer to the question 'Who am I?' through photographs.

The second measurement included only experience sampling, whereas the third measurement again included experience sampling together with autophotography. Finally, several questionnaires, to be described in detail later, concluded the data collection.

To assure a continued high participation rate, students were promised DM 100 for participation in the longitudinal study. No remuneration had been offered for filling out the questionnaire. After the second measurement, when more than two-thirds of the actual work had already been done, students were informed in writing that additional funds had become available that made it possible to raise the remuneration to a total of DM 120, DM 50 to be paid after the second measurement when the beeper was returned. The additional DM 70 was paid at the conclusion of the study. That way, an additional incentive was created (less than half of the money was paid after more than two-thirds of the data collection was concluded) for students to participate until the end of the study. This resulted in a drop-out rate that was relatively low for a longitudinal study lasting almost ten months: the initial questionnaire was answered by 131 students, the first measurement was concluded by 98, the second by 92 students, and the third by 75.

The initial return rate of more than 37.4 per cent is reasonable for a mail-out questionnaire without reminder. Because of the high cost of postage, a reminder could not be sent out. The first drop (pre-measurement to T1) from 131 to 98 is due to the considerably different level of involvement in the study, and is therefore relatively low. The loss of participants from T1 to T2 is relatively small, 6 per cent. Between T2 and T3 the loss was 18 per cent. However, there was a two-month semester break, and several students did not return to university after that, so that the actual drop-out rate was quite low.

Instruments

The pre-measurement questionnaire consisted of several parts which were to serve as predictors for the adaptive process to the new environment. It contained standard instruments as used in the other studies as well as some that were specially constructed. Standard instruments included were the Satisfaction with Self Scale, the Self-Monitoring Scale, Changes in Relationships, Life Events, Importance of Things, and Personal Values. Designed for this study were scales to assess specific expectations for the new life situation regarding continuity and change.

Specific expectations for the new situation were first clustered on a theoretical basis according to content, yielding two clusters consisting of six items each. Both clusters were then subjected to separate factor analyses. The emerging factors are shown in Table 14.1 (translated from the German). Percentage of variance explained refers only to the individual clusters of two factors each.

The ESM booklet

At the measurement points T1, T2, and T3, the students carried beepers and booklets with them. The booklet was designed to assess primarily current activities and the perception of the interactional situation that preceded the signal.

Overview of the design

Table 14.1 *Factors of expectations for the new environment*

Factor/Item	Loading	Variance explained
Expectation of continuity		32.0%
+ For me personally things will mostly stay the same even after I begin my studies.	.71	
− By starting my studies I have a whole new part of life ahead of me.	−.73	
+ My external circumstances will remain the same, even after I begin to study.	.81	
Readiness for change		29.0%
+ By studying, I expect to change myself considerably.	.49	
+ I am ready to adjust myself to the new milieu.	.81	
+ I will be able to make use of new challenges and opportunities.	.87	
New relationships		27.6%
− It is more important for me to keep contact with my old friends than to start new friendships.	−.63	
+ I think I will meet more interesting people at my new place of study than I am used to from home.	.79	
+ In my new environment, I want to do as much as possible to get to know new people.	.76	
Adaptation to studies		20.0%
+ Because of my studies, I will at first have to forgo some of my leisure activities and personal interests.	.61	
+ Through my studies, most of the changes will take place by themselves, without my having to do much about it.	.75	
+ As regards my studies, it would be important to change my style of working significantly.	.43	

The current activities were described using a coding key extended on the basis of the experiences in the previous ESM study and adapted to a student population. It contained coding keys for the following questions:

> *Where* were you at the time of the signal?
> Who were you *with*?
> *What* did you do?
> *Who* did you talk to last?
> *What* did you talk about?

Each coding key had approximately twenty different categories.

The other part of the ESM questionnaire referred to the perception of the immediately preceding conversation. The items are listed in Table 14.2. Of these items, P21 to P24 specifically addressed the actually perceived and the desired self-disclosure and other-disclosure. In other words, they were related to the actual and ideal exchange of information about oneself in a conversational situation. On the other hand, P19, P20, and P25, referring to degree of intimacy, importance of the content, and desired future contact, are more general items to assess the importance of the interactional situation to the individual.

Table 14.2 *ESM-items regarding the perception of social situations*

Item number	Item wording
P19	How personal was the conversation?
P20	How important was the content of the conversation to you?
P21	Did the other person learn something about you through this conversation?
P22	Would you rather that the other person had learned more or less about you?
P23	Did you learn something about the other person through this conversation?
P24	Would you rather that you had learned more or less about the other person?
P25	Would you like to have contact again with that person soon?

Note: Items were answered on a five-point scale, with '1' expressing strongest agreement, and '5' total disagreement. On P22 and P25, '1' referred to 'more'.

The data analysis will first describe the starting point, that is, provide the descriptive analysis of the pre-measurement results. Some predictors will then be chosen from the pre-measurement and applied to the actual social behaviour and the perceptions during the measurement points T1, T2, and T3. In addition, change between these points will be assessed.

Description of the sample

Pre-measurement refers to the questionnaire that was mailed to new students after registration in September but before the beginning of classes in mid October. The questionnaires were mailed to their home addresses outside the greater region around Heidelberg.

The questionnaire was returned by 131 students. Of these, 39 per cent (51) were male, and 61 per cent (79) were female (one respondent did not indicate his or her sex). The median age was 19, with a range from 18 to 44. Ninety-nine per cent of the respondents were single. Thirty-two per cent indicated that they lived alone in a household, 6 per cent lived with a partner,

50 per cent with their parents, and 12 per cent shared accommodation with others (*Wohngemeinschaft*). However, this information does not mean that almost one-third of the students lived in a one-person household before they attended the university. When asked how long these living arrangements had existed, 34 per cent indicated 'one month', meaning that the question was answered by this group as referring to the living arrangements chosen for the university town. Another 28 per cent stated that their living arrangements had been the same for nineteen or twenty years, obviously referring to the fact that they had been living with their parents for that time. This also coincides with the reported household size, namely a one-person household for 34 per cent, two persons for 14 per cent, and three and more for over half of the respondents, namely those living with their family or sharing their accommodation. Twenty per cent indicated that they lived with children under 18 years of age. Thirty-seven per cent lived in a house that was owned by their families, 3 per cent in a rented house, 33 per cent in a rented flat, another 3 per cent in a condominium, and 24 per cent were subletting. Again, 38 per cent were obviously already referring to their new living arrangements.

Respondents were also asked how many times they had moved in their lifetime. Fifteen per cent had never moved before, 29 per cent had moved once, 18 per cent twice, 15 per cent three times, and the rest, 23 per cent, between four and nine times.

Effects of moving on the perception of interactional situations

The ESM questionnaire contained a series of questions addressing the respondent's perception of actual interactional situations. Of particular interest were the actual and desired degree of intimacy of the interaction, the actual and desired self-disclosure character of the situation, and whether further interactions with the present interaction partner were desired (see Table 14.2).

Responses to these items were aggregated within each of the three one-week periods. To test for changes over the whole period of the longitudinal study, a repeated measurement analysis was conducted (BMDP4V). This analysis, of course, can only rely on the means of those participating in the study through all three measurement points. To allow a comparison of the means of that group (n = 73), they are presented in Table 14.3, along with the results of the repeated measurement analysis.

The repeated measurement effect is clearest on those variables describing the actual intimacy, importance, and degree of self-disclosure and self-disclosure reciprocity of the interaction. Over a period of ten months, conversations came to be seen as more personal and more important, other

Table 14.3 *Means and standard deviations of P19 to P25 over T1 to T3*

Item	T1: Mean (SD)	T2: Mean (SD)	T3: Mean (SD)	F (df)
All				2.53 (14,276)**
P19	4.01 (.74)	3.80 (.75)	3.81 (.83)	4.72 (2,144)*
P20	3.59 (.63)	3.37 (.65)	3.41 (.61)	6.74 (2,144)**
P21	4.43 (.80)	4.14 (.82)	4.07 (.81)	13.35 (2,144)**
P22	3.67 (.66)	3.54 (.61)	3.58 (.70)	2.99 (2,144)+
P23	4.31 (.80)	4.02 (.84)	3.97 (.90)	11.53 (2,144)**
P24	3.40 (.69)	3.26 (.70)	3.30 (.80)	2.94 (2,144)*
P25	2.15 (.66)	2.11 (.56)	2.06 (.56)	1.22 (2,144)ns

For the wording of variables, please refer to Table 14.2.
** p <.01; * p <.05; + p <.10.

people learned more about the respondent, and the respondent learned more about other people. A possible interpretation of this effect is that various interaction partners became increasingly familiar and/or the ratio of familiar persons among all interaction partners increased over time as social relationships stabilized. Later analyses, looking at the variance in the types of interaction partner, will shed more light on these interpretations.

In the next step of the data analysis, regression analyses of 'satisfaction with self' on P19 through P25 at the different points in time were performed, as well as on the differences between the measurements: T1−T2, T2−T3, and T1−T3. Again, because the 'dependent variable' was assessed earlier in time, correlation coefficients rather than beta-values are used to assist in the interpretation. Those results reaching significance in the multivariate regression along with the corresponding correlations are presented in Table 14.4.

The results indicate some interesting relationships between the Satisfaction with Self Scale before moving and starting a course at the university on one hand, and the perception of actual social interactions on the other hand. Those relationships are naturally strongest at the first measurement point. However, it should be noted that the first measurement point was, on average, two months after the SSS was answered. After two months, satisfaction with self is a highly significant predictor for the perception of social experiences in a new environment. In particular, persons who are more satisfied with their self-identities consider their interactions to be more personal and the content of conversation to be more important, attribute more self-disclosure to their part of the conversation, and prefer to have contact with the other person again. These relationships are weaker at the third measurement point, and non-significant after ten months.

The regression of SSS on the mean of all three measurement points demonstrates convincingly the relationships between satisfaction with self

Perception of interactional situations

Table 14.4 *Regression of SSS on P19 to P25 at T1 through T3 and differences between T1 and T2 resp. T3*

Item	T1	T2	Mean	T1–T2	T1–T3
df	1,95		1,71	1,88	1,71
All	(df7,89) 2.59*	2.01+	2.01+		1.91+
P19	9.70** $r=.30**$		5.67* $r=.27*$	3.22+	5.45** $r=-.27*$
P20	11.45** $r=.33**$		2.97+ $r=-.26*$	6.15*	11.67** $r=-.38**$
P21	4.29* $r=.21*$	2.83+	4.43* $r=.24*$		
P25	4.70* $r=.22*$	3.22+	5.65* $r=.27*$		6.63* $r=-.29*$

Note: No significant relationships for P (T3) and P (T2–T3).
** $p<.01$; * $p<.05$; + $p<.10$.

and perception of actual social interactions: the more satisfied with themselves before attending the university, the more personal respondents consider their social interactions (P19), the more they convey about themselves to another in a conversation (P21), and the more they look forward to more contact with their interaction partner (P25) throughout the first nine months.

Satisfaction with self also proved to be a significant predictor for change. Differences between the first measurement and the third measurement point are significantly predicted by SSS on three variables: P19 (How personal), P20 (How important), and P25 (More contact). The direction of the correlation coefficients shows the predicted kind of relationship: it is the initially more dissatisfied persons for whom interaction becomes more satisfactory; for the initially more satisfied, interaction becomes less satisfactory. (The possibility that this is due to regression to the mean has been considered and is unlikely.) Items P21 to P24, which refer to the self-disclosure character of the situation, showed no significant relationships between SSS and change. The strength of the relationships and the differentiation between the different items make it unlikely that the findings can be due solely to regression effects. It seems possible that satisfaction with self created different expectations with regard to new social experiences. Over the course of several months, high expectations may have become more realistic, and lower expectations led to slowly increasing satisfaction with social interactions.

Effects of specific expectations

After testing for the effects of satisfaction with self before entering the new environment, the effects of the more specific factors regarding expectations for the new life situation can be assessed. These variables, 'Expectation of continuity', 'Readiness for change', 'New relationships', and 'Adaptation to studies', can be related to the perception of the actual social situations encountered, namely the items that address the actual intimacy (P19), importance (P20), and degree of self-disclosure by the research subject (P21) and his or her interaction partner (P23), as well as expectations of desired intimacy (P22 and P24) and future interaction (P25). Relationships obtained can shed light on the questions of how individual social encounters are used to fulfil expectations for the new life situation. Table 14.5 shows the results for 'Readiness for change'.

Table 14.5 *Regression of 'Readiness for change' on social experiences*

Item	T1	T3–T1
All	$F(7,89) = 2.04+$	ns
P21	$F(1,95) = 4.18*$	
	$r = -.21$	
P22	$F(1,95) = 4.32*$	
	$r = -.21$	
P23	$F(1,95) = 5.41*$	
	$r = -.23$	
P25	$F(1,95) = 3.46+$	
	$r = -.19$	

* $p < .05$; + $p < .10$.

Persons who expect to change in the new life situation feel at Time 1 that the other person learned more about them, and that they would like to reveal even more about themselves. They also think that they learned something about the other person, and that they would like to meet the other person again. Readiness for change is a significant predictor specifically for those variables indicating the degree of personal exchange between two interaction partners. It is not a significant predictor for change on these variables between Time 1 and Time 3.

Table 14.6 shows the results for the factor 'Expectation of continuity'.

This factor expresses the feeling that the transition would not change much for the respondent. The overall effect is significant, with marginally significant effects on two variables, namely on P22 and P23, that is, the variables expressing the desired degree of disclosure from themselves and the actually felt degree of disclosure from the other person. High expectation

Effects of specific expectations

Table 14.6 *Regression of 'Expectation of continuity' on social experiences*

Item	T1	T3–T1
All	F (7,89) = 2.34*	ns
P22	F (1,95) = 3.46+ r = .19	
P23	F (1,95) = 3.05+ r = .18	

* p <.05; + p <.10.

of continuity accompanies low desired self-disclosure and low perceived other-disclosure, and discontinuity is related to high degrees of desired self-disclosure and perceived other-disclosure. Obviously these results entail that staying the same in a new environment can only be achieved at the cost of closing personal exchange: in other words, embarking on a totally new stage of life also has to involve the exchange of information by which persons get to know each other. Continuity and change are mediated through openness and the lack of it in social encounters. Again, change on these variables over time seems to be unrelated to 'Expectation of continuity'.

Table 14.7 shows the results for 'New relationships', the factor expressing openness for new relationships.

Table 14.7 *Regression of 'New relationships' on social experiences*

Item	T1	T3–T1
All	ns	ns.
P21	F (1,95) = 4.41* r = –.21	
P23	F (1,95) = 4.86* r = –.22	

* p <.05.

The overall effect is not significant; but two univariate analyses yield a significant effect, on P21 ('Did the other person learn something about you?') and P23 ('Did you learn something about the other person?'). The actual openness to new relationships is related to the actual perceived level of self-disclosure of both, but not to the desired level. Again, change over time was not affected by expectations regarding new relationships.

Also, no effects at all were obtained with the specific expectations regarding 'Adaptation to studies'. However, it could be that the variables used here were not specific enough to the study situation, and an analysis specifically using study-related interaction partners may shed some light on the realization of this expectation.

It can be seen from the above that the most global assessment was undertaken using the Satisfaction with Self Scale. Through the theoretical basis from which it was constructed, this scale emphasizes the way in which the self-concept is connected to the social environment in which it exists. Indeed, satisfaction with oneself before entering the new life stage significantly predicts how one perceives, acts in, and wishes individual social encounters to be. The overall relationship is significant, and so is a range of variables addressing several aspects of a social encounter, especially those variables regarding the overall evaluation of the situation by the respondent: how important and how personal the interaction was, and whether future contact is desired. However, most of those variables that address the actual exchange of information – that is, desired self-disclosure and perceived and desired other-disclosure – are not significantly related.

Satisfaction with self is also a good predictor of *change* between the first and second semester on those variables assessing the personal nature and importance of a conversation, as well as hopes for future interaction. One of the basic premises of this research has thus found support: maintenance versus change in new environments is mediated by self-concept-related variables.

The more specific expectations for the new life situation and environment were not found to be mediators of adaptation over time. In fact, they pointed quite specifically to the aspects of a social encounter that are mediators of readiness for change, expectation of continuity, and openness to new relationships. With these specific expectations, it was not the general satisfaction with and importance of a conversation, but rather the more specific actual and desired amount of personal information being exchanged that was influenced.

Situational variance and satisfaction with self

Variability in behaviour is another type of information that can be obtained from the experience sampling data. Various questions can be put: after they have moved, do people meet many different kinds of people or do they have a fairly stable circle of friends and acquaintances? Does the number of people one interacts with decrease or increase over time? Does the range of locations within a new place of residence become larger with increasing familiarity or does behaviour after a settling in period take place within a more restricted range of locations? How great is the range of topics addressed in conversations?

To investigate these kinds of questions, the precoded answers to the following questions were taken into account:

> Location (P4): Where were you when the signal was heard?
> Partner (P5): Who were you with?
> Activity (P6): What did you do?
> Conversation partner (P12): Who was the last person you talked to?
> Conversation topic (P18): What did you talk about?

All these questions were answered by the respondents by using a coding key that provided for a large variety of possible locations, interaction partners, and activities. Each individual code provided for about twenty alternatives. To help in assessing the variability of behaviour, the following analyses are based on the variance within the categories 'Location', 'Partner', 'Activity', 'Conversation partner', and 'Conversation topic'. Variances were computed on the basis of the percentage of occurrences of different situations within each coding key per category. A large variance indicates greater behavioural diversity; a smaller variance indicates more stable behavioural patterns.

The first set of analyses studied the variability of behaviour within the three measurement points as a repeated measure analysis encompassing about ten months. Table 14.8 provides the variance of the five different variables at T1, T2, and T3. All analyses were conducted as multivariate repeated measurement designs that looked at the effects of the repeated measurement separately and conducted the regression of SSS on the repeated measurement design.

With the exception of the variance in conversation partners, there was great change in variability of behaviours over the three measurement points.

The variance of locations was greatest at T2 and somewhat reduced again at T3. New students started out with a smaller range of places to be in a new environment, and after several months, toward the end of the first

Table 14.8 *Situational variance over T1, T2, and T3*

Item	Variance at	T1	T2	T3	(df)	F
Interval					10,280	6.94**
VP4	Locations	221	292	237	2,144	14.69**
VP5	Partners	251	253	217	2,144	4.23*
VP6	Activities	44	50	59	2,144	9.70**
VP12	Conversation partner	114	119	116	2,144	.18 ns
VP18	Conversation topic	28	31	40	2,144	6.66**

Note: 'V' before the variable number refers to the variance.
** $p < .01$; * $p < .05$.

semester, became familiar with a greater range. After they had explored those, they restricted themselves at the beginning of the second semester to fewer locations. These were presumably the locations preferred after an initial period of exploration.

A restriction in behavioural variability also occurred with regard to the persons the students were with. Little change over the course of the first semester was followed by a smaller variance in the second semester. This can be interpreted as an indicator of stabilization in interpersonal relationships. While the range is still large (as compared to specific conversation partners), the reduction is very clear. It is also clear from the large difference in variance between 'partner' and 'conversational partner' that only a small fraction of those indicated as being present were also conversational partners. Obviously, the category 'partner' includes a variety of persons who were only incidentally present, for instance fellow students in a class.

However, the range of activities respondents engaged in showed a clear and continuous increase. Fewer people and fewer locations allowed a greater variety of behaviours to take place as familiarization set in, possibly indicating greater behavioural competence with time. This was paralleled by an increase in conversational topics. The same variety of conversational partners provided at T3 for a greater variety of topics of discussion.

Overall, the picture emerges of a decrease in *outside* sources of behavioural variance with a concurrent increase in the use of *internal* resources: locations and partner decrease in variance up to T3 with conversational partners staying the same. Activities and conversational topics increase in variability. These require initiative and are indicative of agentic behaviour. The next step in the analysis investigates whether behavioural variability and changes therein are related to satisfaction with self before entering the new environment.

The multivariate analysis also allows the test of the regression of satisfaction with self on behavioural variance. These statistics are summarized in Table 14.9. The mean represents a stable aggregation of the overall behavioural variance: the difference accounts for the change over the longitudinal study. The following analysis tested for the contribution of satisfaction with self by entering this variable into the regression before the other variables.

Satisfaction with self is related significantly to those mean values of variables that have to do with actual social interactions (P12: With whom did your last conversation take place?; P18: What did you talk about?). The regressions of SSS on the mean of other variables were not significant. The investigation of correlations of the variances with SSS shows that those more dissatisfied with themselves showed less variance in their interactional behaviour, and those more satisfied showed more interactional variance.

Table 14.9 *Regression of SSS on behavioural variance*

Item		Mean of T1 + T2 + T3	Difference from T1−T3
All		F (5,67) = 3.07*	F (5,67) = 2.25 +
VP4	Locations	ns	F (1,71) = 5.30*
VP5	Partners	ns	ns
VP6	Activities	ns	ns
VP12	Conversation partners	F (1,71) = 11.91**	ns
VP18	Conversation topics	F (1,71) = 6.86*	ns

** $p < .01$; * $p < .05$; + $p < .10$.

These correlative relationships are similar at all three points for VP12, conversational partners, which remained stable, and strongest at T3 for VP18, conversational content, which increased in variability at T3. The relevant correlations are presented in Table 14.10.

Table 14.10 *Correlations of variance in conversational behaviour with SSS*

Item		T1	T2	T3
VP12	Conversational partner	−.22*	−.27**	−.27*
VP18	Conversational topic	ns	ns	−.26*

** $p < .01$; * $p < .05$.

The results of the analyses based on experience sampling point, through a number of interesting relationships, to the importance of actual social experience in the realization of personal goals, and to the role of the evaluative element of the self-concept in adaptation and change. The course of adaptation over time, as it could be measured on a variety of variables, is influenced by satisfaction with self as far as social experiences are concerned. Other behaviours also change over time with increasing familiarity; however, they do so independently of this self-concept-relevant variable.

Finally, the results of autophotography and their relations to the expectations with which the new environment was entered into are also assessed.

Results from autophotography

As described in the overview of the design, all subjects received cameras at the time of the first beeper measurement in order to take seven pictures of aspects of their social or physical environment that were considered to be self-concept relevant. The same was done at T3. The following analyses concentrate first on the photographs taken at T1.

Photographs were rated (see Chapter 7) by two raters first by content and classified as being mainly depictions of objects, environments, or persons. In a second step, the functionality for the self-concept was rated on the following dimensions: perspective, integration, self-presentation, activity, reflection, memory, and symbolism. In addition, the internal–external localization in regard to the person was rated. In the rating of content categories, inter-rater correlations varied from a minimum of $r = .76$ to a maximum of $r = .91$. For the functionality dimensions, inter-rater correlations were not always satisfactory: Perspective $r = .56$, Integration $r = .49$, Self-presentation $r = .50$, Activity $r = .71$, Reflection $r = .61$, Memory $r = .68$, Symbolism $r = .47$, and Localization $r = .26$. On the original functionality dimensions, most correlations were around or above $r = .50$, which, considering the experimental nature of the procedure, is satisfactory. On 'Localization', the correlation was quite low; this could imply that it is not well defined for the raters, or that it is a theoretically vague concept difficult to operationalize. Because of the low rater agreement, ratings on this concept are not included.

The first set of analyses consisted of multivariate analyses of variance employing a repeated measurement design (BMDP4V). These analyses were conducted to test for change between T1 and T3 (no photographs were taken on T2) on (a) the amount of environmental, object, or person-related content of the photos, and (b) the functionality for self-concept dimensions. Localization of identity was not included in the two MANOVAs. The means and results of the repeated measurement analysis are summarized in Table 14.11.

Table 14.11 *Change in photograph content and functionality between T1 and T3*

Category/Dimension	M(T1)	M(T3)	F(df)
Content (multivariate)			ns
Objects	37.9	35.5	ns
Environments	56.6	59.0	ns
Persons	5.4	5.1	ns
Function of self (multivariate)			29.9 (6,69)**
Perspective	3.31	3.50	29.3 (1,74)**
Integration	2.31	2.83	50.4 (1,74)**
Self-presentation	2.45	2.01	40.9 (1,74)**
Activity	1.44	1.49	1.2 (1,74)ns
Reflection	1.56	1.62	.6 (1,74)ns
Symbolism	2.25	1.99	6.5 (1,74)**
Memory	1.30	1.11	15.4 (1,74)**

** $p < .01$.

The results show that while no change could be noted for the relative content of the picture, the content depicted changed considerably in meaning between the two measurement points, according to the raters.

When people are totally new to the environment, a more distant perspective is taken, whereas several months later the pictures show a closer perspective. Items depicted are also less isolated and more integrated in their context after the environment became familiar – possibly an indirect support of the figure–ground hypothesis proposed here. However, the self-presentational value of the pictures decreases over time; perhaps a greater self-assurance diminishes the need for self-presentation in a new environment. Also the symbolic value of the pictures is considerably smaller, as is the memory value to some extent.

Overall, it seems that the pictures taken immediately after being in a new environment make more use of the categories that include information about what kind of a person one is and was before: self-presentation, symbolism, and memory. These functions of things for the self-concept are, as defined here, mainly functions making use of generally shared information that presents a clear picture of oneself. Over time, these functions of the physical environment decrease, and the person feels more a part of the environment. The presentation of self is now less important.

The next analyses, using stepwise regression, should detect whether satisfaction with self before entering the new environment was related to the content and meaning of the pictures depicted at T1 and T3, and also to the difference between the two measurement points.

Satisfaction with self was not significantly related to the content of the photographs at T1 or T3, or to the differences in content between T1 and T3.

The difference in the meaning categories between T1 and T3 was significantly related to SSS, with two variables remaining in the regression, namely self-presentation and symbolism. Results of the last step in the regression and the relevant correlations are shown in Table 14.12. SSS was not related to the meaning of the photographs taken at T3 or T1.

Table 14.12 *SSS and differences in meaning of photographs from T1 to T3*

Variable	F (df)	r-square	r
Regression	3.31 (2,73)*	.09	
Self-presentation	4.24 (1,74)*		.08
Symbolism	6.10 (1,74)*		−.17

* p <.05.

The higher the initial satisfaction with self before entering the new life situation, the steeper the decrease in self-presentation from T1 to T3. The higher the initial satisfaction with self, the slower the decrease in symbolism between the two measurement points. Both are variables that connect the person's self-concept, as expressed in the pictures, to his or her social environment; however, whereas self-presentation serves as a 'front' to the social environment, symbolism may be an expression of the acceptance of socially shared values.

These two dimensions in combination explain 9 per cent of the variance of SSS. While from one perspective this may be thought of as low, the indirect approach of the method and the completely different method of collecting data have to be considered. Also, a time period of more than ten months is covered by the analysed difference.

The results obtained through autophotography show a change in the perception of the environment and its meaning over time. Most of this change is due to adaptation rather than to the state of the self-concept before entering the new life situation. However, when the self-concept influenced change over time in the perception of the self-concept-relevant aspects of the social and physical environment, it was through those functions which linked the individual to the social environment. Persons low on satisfaction with self attempt to present themselves longer, but they accept socially shared symbols sooner.

In short, the present study was able to be much more specific in its findings than some of the others. In particular, the methods used, and the variables made possible through the use of these methods, show convincingly the kind of direct influence that expectations about the future life situation and evaluations of one's own state before entering this life situation have on the perception of individual social interactions. It was the starting point of the present research that social interactional situations are the basic element mediating self-concept change, either adaptation or development, in new environments. The present study has borne out this conviction; it has, however, also shown that specific expectations influence information exchange in the beginning, and that the more global assessment of oneself, while related to more global evaluations of the interactional situation, is nevertheless clearly related to the form that change over time in a new environment takes.

15 Conclusion

The empirical work described in this book was based on particular theoretical assumptions, as stated in Chapter 1, and was embedded in a context of theory and research on the self-concept encompassing cognitive social psychological approaches, sociological approaches, and contributions from environmental psychology.

The basic theoretical assumptions, forming an ecological model for self-concept change, were the following:

> A person's understanding of self is formed through social experiences.
>
> Social experiences take place in a context of and in interaction with *others*, as the sources of direct social experiences, with *objects*, as symbols and representations of social experiences, and with *environments*, as the settings of social experiences. This complete system was labelled the ecology of the self.
>
> Social experiences and their meaning for the self-concept are reflected in self-related cognitions.
>
> The way self-related cognitions are organized and the way a person's social and physical environment are structured only rarely undergo radical change, assuring the basic stability of the self-concept.
>
> The self-concept is stable to the degree to which the ecological system of the self is stable. Change in the self-concept is only possible concurrently with or subsequent to change in the ecological system of the self-concept of a person.
>
> The mechanism that provides stability for the cognitive structure and for the person's self-concept within a social and environmental structure is one of implicative links.
>
> By the linking of new experiences to existing ones, the new experiences are provided with meaning. By the linking of social relationships to others, social commitment is created.

These basic assumptions were supported and specified through a review of the literature. The similarity of principles operating on the social structural level and on the cognitive level was demonstrated. The function of the molecular and molar physical environment for the self-concept was also seen from the perspective provided by these assumptions, which completed the review of the elements of the ecological system of the self.

To study these processes in a way appropriate to an ecological approach in theory, a methodological approach was chosen emphasizing ecological validity, access to direct social experience, and the perception of one's environment in times of change. This necessitated the development and adaptation of a number of varied methods and measurement instruments appropriate to the theoretical and methodological framework chosen. These were employed as part of a multi-method, multi-study research programme. Relocation was chosen as a quasi-experimental research paradigm for the study of changing person–environment relationships.

The empirical contributions focused on effects of the changing self–environment relationship on social behaviours and experiences, and on the perception of the social and physical environment's function for the self-concept. The aim was not to measure the amount of change in a person's self-related cognitions, but to study the processes mediating such change.

At the end of this research programme, the theoretical and the methodological approaches have to be evaluated. Can the findings obtained be understood within the theoretical framework, and do they support it or even specify it? Have the methods fulfilled expectations, and did they complement each other? Because the ongoing discussion of findings has already tried to address these questions to some degree, and critical evaluations of the methods employed have been provided elsewhere (Hormuth, 1986a, Hormuth & Brückner, 1985), the following considerations provide a summary assessment rather than a detailed review.

The empirical findings provided data that illustrated the changes a person's social behaviours and experiences undergo, and how the perceptions of the relationship between self and environment are affected. In general, persons in a new environment show a curvilinear development on those variables indicating the acceptance of the new person–environment relationship. These variables are, for instance, those that indicate the importance of ties to the old home environment, and activities with familiar others, that is, family and friends. Social integration in the new environment starts out with non-committal or organized social activities.

In a new environment, people's behaviour first takes place in a greater variety of settings, but with a smaller range of other people. Over time, the relevant settings for behaviour become established, and the variety of social partners increases. Social interactions become more important and meaningful, and more personal information is exchanged. When a person is new in an environment, socially provided and shared meanings of the environment are accepted and made use of in self-presentation. Over time, aspects of this environment acquire more personal meaning.

Conclusion

These summary statements describe the process of adjustment to a new person–environment relationship on self-concept-relevant variables in a global way. The description fits in with existing knowledge and theoretical assumptions of processes following transitions. However, the information obtained in the studies presented here goes beyond the previously known because some of the relevant variables studied had not been previously considered or were even inaccessible, for instance the perception of actual social situations.

More relevant from the present theoretical standpoint is the mediation of adjustment processes through self-concept-relevant variables. These variables were chosen in such a way as to emphasize the individual's place in a social and physical context, and to be sensitive to the implications for stability and change.

In one study, the relevant variable consisted of the perceived changes in commitment concomitant with the move. Commitment was conceptualized as the centrality of social relationships to the self-concept. Centrality is established through the links to other social relationships that stabilize the social structure as it is relevant to one's self-concept. In other studies, the relevant variable was measured through a questionnaire assessing satisfaction with self. The questionnaire was constructed to reflect the different life spheres in the ecology of the self that are potentially subject to interdependent relationships between self-concept and environment, that is, the person's self-concept is influenced through this life sphere, which is in turn influenced by that person's self-concept. It was possible to demonstrate the relationship between the variable measured through the Satisfaction with Self Scale on one hand, and change in commitment, as defined above, on the other hand. Thus, the variables chosen emphasized the close link between social and environmental structure and the self-concept.

The variables were thought to be sensitive to implications for stability and change because the beginning or end of a commitment breaks up the existing social structure and thus implies the need to restructure one's environment. Dissatisfaction with the existing self-concept was also thought to imply a readiness for change and openness to new experiences.

It was assumed that change has to be preceded by a questioning or dissatisfaction with the present concept of self, as an indicator of the necessity to change, and by a break-up of the social and environmental structure supporting the current concept of self. A self-concept that a person is satisfied with and that has been reinforced should lead, if the opportunity is given, to further development of the existing aspects of self. It was expected that change under the above conditions could be agentic in a new social and environmental context offering new opportunities. Agentic means being based on decisions by the individual to select among the different possibilities the new environment affords. The process by which this agentic change takes place was presumed to involve initially exposure to a great variety of possible experiences, followed by a later concentration on some which become linked to other elements in the ecology of the self to provide new structure and stability.

The data indicate that, indeed, the variables Commitment and Satisfaction with Self determined to some degree the behaviours, experiences, and perceptions of persons in a new environment and the course these took over time. However, at variance with the hypothesis that dissolution of existing structures for a self-concept one is dissatisfied with should lead to agentic change if one is given the opportunity, these persons were less likely in the beginning to seek out new experiences, and were in general more likely initially to withdraw in a new environment.

These findings do not directly support the present hypotheses and have to be accounted for. The main element responsible for the initial withdrawal seems to be low self-esteem related to the events questioning the previous self-concept. These events, too, were social experiences. Consequently, the probability with which a person is willing to engage in future social interactions was reduced. Further, low self-esteem not only has evaluative consequences, as they are measured through the Satisfaction with Self Scale, but emotional ones too. The emotional consequences of low self-esteem are likely to be responsible for the avoidance of social contact and the withdrawal from new experiences. Low self-esteem thus hinders the awareness of the possibilities inherent in the new person–environment relationship. The theoretical model has underestimated the emotional component and overestimated the degree to which the opportunity to restructure actively the ecology of the self is perceived.

Two questions follow from the above statement: how is the new environment perceived, and the individual in it; and can agentic change take place after familiarization with the environment has set in?

In the beginning, the new environment is likely to be little structured in the perception of the individual moving into it. Indeed, the assessment by Stewart et al. (1986) cited earlier, namely that the experience of a new environment is 'confusing and anxiety provoking, partially due to a lack of understanding, or successful mapping, of the external environment' (p. 144), seems to be appropriate (see also Wapner, 1987). The acceptance of this statement does not imply the acceptance of Stewart et al.'s conclusion that such a state would necessarily reduce self-awareness. Rather, it may further strengthen the consequence of low self-esteem, namely a self-imposed restriction.

The empirical data show also that this state does not last. In general, persons low on satisfaction with self showed more exploratory behaviours and openness after some time. People whose relocation was related to the end of a social commitment went out much more frequently after a few months, seeking social experiences. Charitable activities, for instance, were identified as ones in which persons dissatisfied with themselves engaged more over time. In short, the findings suggest that after the initial strangeness of the new environment has been overcome, persons are willing to make new social experiences. However, these new social experiences are not likely to lead immediately to a new commitment.

The further development of the theoretical model will have to focus on the emotional consequences of the conditions that necessitate self-concept change, and on a clearer identification of the conditions that hinder or support the perception and enactment of environmental opportunities.

An assessment of the *methodological* approach chosen here reveals the advantages of access to completely new kinds of information in self-concept research, for instance subjective social experiences *in situ*, or the perception of the self-concept-relevant environment. The multi-study, multi-method approach has provided the chance to identify general patterns of results and separate them from isolated findings that make little sense in the context of the complete research programme. On the other hand, the new methods employed, experience sampling and especially autophotography, still need to become known better in regard to their reliability and validity. Within the course of the present research programme, some pertinent information could be obtained, and improvements could be implemented in later studies. As part of a multi-method approach, the methods yield information that can be interpreted in the context of that obtained using the respective other operationalizations and modes of data collection.

This research programme has obtained information that is far from exhausted. The analyses described in this book have only addressed questions regarding the development of self-concept-relevant behaviours, experiences, and perceptions over time, and their relationship to a condition that should lead to self-concept change. Further specification is possible, and can, for instance, provide additional information on the nature of social situations. To conduct such analyses in the present context would have gone beyond the purpose and scope of the book.

In present-day social psychology, the self-concept has become one of the central topics of study: in my opinion, rightly so. The self-concept constitutes the cognitive representation of a person's social experiences, and, in turn, it influences that person's perceptions of and acts toward his or her environment. As a concept of social psychological theorizing and research, it is therefore uniquely qualified to provide a link between a person's social cognitions and that person's social and physical context. For cognitions to be social, it has to be possible to relate them to social structure and social action.

This programme of research has emphasized the external sources of self-related, that is, social cognitions, has investigated behaviour leading to social cognitions, and has stressed their subjective perception. It has tried to complement other research that addresses essentially the same issues of self-concept maintenance and change, but investigates these either on a mainly cognitive or on a mainly social structural or environmental level. To provide a link between these approaches, between social reality and social cognition, is a task for the ecological approach in social psychology.

References

Allport, G. W. (1937). *Personality.* New York: Holt.
Altman, I. (1975). *The environment and social behavior.* Monterey, CA: Brooks/Cole.
  (1976). Privacy: a conceptual analysis. *Environment and Behavior,* 8, 7–29.
Altman, I. & D. A. Taylor (1973). *Social penetration: the development of interpersonal relationships.* New York: Holt, Rinehart, & Winston.
Amelang, M. & P. Borkenau (1982). Über die faktorielle Struktur und externe Validität einiger Fragebogen-Skalen zur Erfassung von Dimensionen der Extraversion und emotionalen Labilität [Factorial structure and external validity of some questionnaire scales that assess dimensions of extraversion and emotional lability]. *Zeitschrift für Differentielle und Diagnostische Psychologie,* 3, 119–46.
Archer, R. L. & W. B. Earle (1983). The interpersonal orientations of disclosure. In P. B. Paulus (ed.), *Basic group processes,* pp. 189–214. New York: Springer-Verlag.
Aronson, E. (1968). Dissonance theory: progress and problems. In R. P. Abelson, E. Aronson, W. J. McGuire, T. M. Newcomb, M. J. Rosenberg, & P. H. Tannenbaum (eds.), *Theories of cognitive consistency: a sourcebook,* pp. 5–27. Chicago: Rand McNally.
Backman, C. W. (1985). Interpersonal congruency theory revisited: a revision and extension. Presented at the Annual Convention of the American Sociological Association.
Barker, R. G. (1965). Explorations in psychological ecology. *American Psychologist,* 20, 1–13.
  (1968). *Ecological Psychology.* Stanford, CA: Stanford University Press.
Barker, R. G. & P. Schoggen (1973). *Qualities of community life.* San Francisco: Jossey-Bass.
Baumeister, R. F. (1982). A self-presentational view of social phenomena. *Psychological Bulletin,* 91, 3–26.
Becker, H. S. (1960). Notes on the concept of commitment. *American Journal of Sociology,* 66, 32–40.
  (1964). Personal change in adult life. *Sociometry,* 27, 40–3.
  (1968). The self and adult socialization. In E. Norbeck, D. Price-Williams, & W. M. McCord (eds.), *The study of personality: an interdisciplinary appraisal,* pp. 194–208. New York: Holt, Rinehart, & Winston.
Bem, D. J. (1967). Self-perception: an alternative interpretation of cognitive dissonance phenomena. *Psychological Review,* 74, 183–200.
  (1972). Self-perception theory. In L. Berkowitz (ed.), *Advances in experimental social psychology,* Vol. VI, pp. 1–62. New York: Academic Press.

References

Berscheid, E., E. Graziano, T. Monson, & M. Dermer (1976). Outcome dependency: attention, attribution, and attraction. *Journal of Personality and Social Psychology*, 34, 978–89.

Bossong, M. (1983). Selbstbild, wahrgenommene Beurteilung durch den Ehepartner und soziales Verhalten [Self-image, perceived judgment by spouse, and social behaviour]. Diplomarbeit, Psychologisches Institut der Universität Heidelberg.

Bourestone, N.C. & S. Tars (1974). Alterations in life patterns following nursing home relocation. *Gerontologist*, 14, 506–10.

Bower, G.H. & S.G. Gilligan (1979). Remembering information related to one's self. *Journal of Research in Personality*, 13, 420–32.

Brett, J.M. (1982). Job transfer and well being. *Journal of Applied Psychology*, 67, 450–63.

Brückner, E., S.E. Hormuth, & H. Sagawe (1982). Telefoninterviews: Ein alternatives Erhebungsverfahren? [Telephone interviews: an alternative method of data collection?] *ZUMA-Nachrichten*, 11, 9–36.

Brunswik, E. (1949). *Systematic and representative design of psychological experiments*. Berkeley and Los Angeles: University of California Press.

(1952). *The conceptual framework of psychology*. International encyclopedia of unified science, Vol. I, No. 10. Chicago: University of Chicago Press.

Bryson, G. (1945). *Man and society: the Scottish inquiry into the eighteenth century*. Princeton: Princeton University Press.

Burke, P.J. (1980). The self: measurement requirements from an interactionist perspective. *Social Psychology Quarterly*, 43, 18–29.

Callero, P.L. (1985). Role-identity salience. *Social Psychology Quarterly*, 48, 203–15.

Carver, C.S. & M.F. Scheier (1978). Self-focusing effects of dispositional self-consciousness, mirror presence, and audience presence. *Journal of Personality and Social Psychology*, 36, 324–32.

(1981). *Attention and self-regulation: a control theory approach to human behavior*. New York: Springer-Verlag.

Clagett, A.F. (1988). Theoretical consideration of integrating social structure into symbolic interactionism: selected methodological insights. *Social Behavior and Personality*, 16, 97–108.

Cook, T.D. (1985). Post-positivist critical multiplism. In L. Shotland & M.M. Mark (eds.), *Social science and social policy*, pp. 21–62. Beverly Hills, CA: Sage.

Cook, T.D. & D.T. Campbell (1979). *Quasi-experimentation: design and analysis issues for social research in field settings*. Boston: Houghton Mifflin.

Cooley, C.H. (1902). *Human nature and the social order*. New York: Charles Scribner.

Crowne, D. & D. Marlowe (1960). A new scale of social desirability independent of psychopathology. *Journal of Consulting Psychology*, 24, 349–54.

Csikszentmihalyi, M. & T. Figurski (1982). Self-awareness and aversive experience in everyday life. *Journal of Personality*, 50, 15–28.

Csikszentmihalyi, M. & E. Rochberg-Halton (1981). *The meaning of things: domestic symbols and the self*. Cambridge, UK: Cambridge University Press.

Darroch, R.K. & M. Miller (1981). Environmental psychology: coming and going. *Australian Psychologist*, 16, 155–71.

Diener, E. & T. K. Srull (1979). Self-awareness, psychological perspective, and self-reinforcement in relation to personal and social standards. *Journal of Personality and Social Psychology*, 37, 413–23.

Duval, S., V. H. Duval & R. Neely (1979). Self-focus, felt responsibility, and helping behavior. *Journal of Personality and Social Psychology*, 37, 1769–78.

Duval, S. & V. Hensley (1976). Extensions of objective self-awareness theory: the focus of attention–causal attribution hypothesis. In J. H. Harvey, W. J. Ickes, & R. F. Kidd (eds.), *New directions in attribution research*, Vol. I, pp. 165–98. Hillsdale, NJ: Erlbaum.

Duval, S. & R. A. Wicklund (1972). *A theory of objective self-awareness*. New York: Academic Press.

(1973). Effects of objective self-awareness on attribution of causality. *Journal of Experimental Social Psychology*, 9, 17–31.

Elliott, G. C. (1986). Self-esteem and self-consistency: a theoretical and empirical link between two primary motivations. *Social Psychology Quarterly*, 49, 207–18.

Epstein, S. (1973). The self-concept revisited: or a theory of a theory. *American Psychologist*, 28, 404–16.

(1983). Aggregation and beyond: some basic issues on the prediction of behavior. *Journal of Personality*, 51, 360–92.

Esser, H. (1980). *Aspekte der Wanderungssoziologie* [Aspects of the sociology of migration]. Darmstadt: Neuwied.

Felson, R. B. (1985). Reflected appraisal and the development of self. *Social Psychology Quarterly*, 48, 71–8.

Fenigstein, A. (1979). Self-consciousness, self-attention, and social interaction. *Journal of Personality and Social Psychology*, 37, 75–86.

Fenigstein, A. & C. S. Carver (1978). Self-focusing effects of heart-beat feedback. *Journal of Personality and Social Psychology*, 36, 1241–50.

Fenigstein, A., M. F. Scheier & A. H. Buss (1975). Public and private self-consciousness: assessment and theory. *Journal of Consulting and Clinical Psychology*, 43, 522–7.

Festinger, L. (1954). A theory of social comparison processes. *Human Relations*, 7, 117–40.

(1957). *A theory of cognitive dissonance*. Stanford, CA: Stanford University Press.

Filipp, S.-H. (no date). Eine deutschsprachige Übersetzung der Self-Consciousness Scale [A German translation of the Self-Consciousness Scale]. Psychologisches Institut, Universität Trier.

Filipp, S.-H. & J. Brandstädter (1975). Beziehungen zwischen situationsspezifischer Selbstwahrnehmung und generallen Selbstbild [Relations between situation-specific self-perception and general self-image]. *Psychologische Beiträge*, 17, 406–17.

Filipp, S.-H. & T. Klauer (1986). Conceptions of the self over the life span: reflections on the dialectics of change. In M. M. Baltes & P. B. Baltes (eds.), *Aging and control*. Hillsdale, NJ: Erlbaum.

Fischer, M. & U. Fischer (1981). Wohnortwechsel und Verlust der Ortsidentität als nichtnormative Lebenskrisen [Relocation and loss of place-identity as a non-normative critical life event]. In S.-H. Filipp (ed.), *Kritische Lebensereignisse*, pp. 139–53. Munich: Urban & Schwarzenberg.

Fischer, M. & U. Fischer (1985). Ökopsychologische Analyse mobilitätsbedingter Anpassungsprozesse bei Individuum und Familie [Ecopsychological analysis of adaptation processes of individual and family caused by mobility]. In W. F. Kugemann, S. Preisner, & K. A. Schneewind (eds.), *Psychologie und komplexe Lebenswirklichkeit*, pp. 253–76. Göttingen: Hogrefe.

Fishbein, M. J. & J. D. Laird (1979). Concealment and disclosure: some effects of information control on the person who controls. *Journal of Experimental Social Psychology*, 15, 114–21.

Franz, P. (1984). *Soziologie der räumlichen Mobilität* [*The sociology of spatial mobility*]. Frankfurt on Main: Campus.

Froming, W. J., G. R. Walker & K. J. Lopyan (1982). Public and private self-awareness: when personal attitudes conflict with societal expectations. *Journal of Experimental Social Psychology*, 18, 476–87.

Fuhrer, U. (1985). Das Konzept 'Behavior Setting': Überlegungen zu seiner für Psychologie relevanten 'Aufbereitung' [The concept 'behaviour setting': some thoughts about its adaptation relevant to psychology]. In P. Day, U. Fuhrer, & U. Laucken (eds.), *Umwelt und Handeln: Ökologische Anforderungen und Handeln im Alltag*, pp. 239–61. Tübingen: Attempo.

Gangestead, S. & M. Snyder (1985). On the nature of self-monitoring: an examination of latent causal structure. *Review of Personality and Social Psychology*, 6, 65–85.

Gatzweiler, H. P. (1975). *Zur Selektivität interregionaler Wanderungen* [*The selectivity of interregional migrations*]. Bonn.

Gecas, V. (1982). The self-concept. *Annual Review of Sociology*, 8, 1–33.

Gecas, V. & M. L. Schwalbe (1983). Beyond the looking-glass self: social structure and efficacy-based self-esteem. *Social Psychology Quarterly*, 46, 77–88.

Gergen, K. J. (1977). The social construction of self-knowledge. In T. Mischel (ed.), *The self: psychological and philosophical issues*. Totowa, NJ: Rowman & Littlefield.

Gibbons, F. X. & R. A. Wright (1983). Self-focused attentions and reactions to conflicting standards. *Journal of Research in Personality*, 17, 263–73.

Goffman, E. (1959). *The presentation of self in everyday life*. Garden City, NY: Doubleday-Anchor.

Gollwitzer, P. M. (1986). Striving for specific identities: the social reality of self-symbolizing. In R. F. Baumeister (ed.), *Public self and private self*, pp. 143–59. New York: Springer-Verlag.

Graumann, C. F. (1974). Psychology and the world of things. *Journal of Phenomenological Psychology*, 4, 348–404.

(1985). Memorabilia, mementoes, memoranda: toward an ecology of memory. Paper presented at the International Symposium in memory of Herrmann Ebbinghaus, Berlin, GDR.

Graumann, C. F. & G. Schneider (1986). Städtische Umwelt: Identität und Identifikation [Urban environment: identity and identification]. In M. Krampen (ed.), *Environment and human action*, Proceedings of the 8th International Congress of IAPS, Berlin, 1984, pp. 237–40. Berlin: Hochschule der Künste.

Greenwald, A. G. & A. R. Pratkanis (1984). The self. In R. S. Wyer & T. K. Srull (eds.), *Handbook of social cognition*, Vol. III, pp. 129–78. Hillsdale, NJ: Erlbaum.

Hastie, R. (1981). Schematic principles in person memory. In E. T. Higgins, P. Herman & M. P. Zanna (eds.), *Social cognition: the Ontario symposium*. Hillsdale, NJ: Erlbaum.

Hastie, R. & D. Carlston (1980). Theoretical issues in person memory. In R. Hastie, T. F. Ostrom, E. Ebbesen, R. Wyer, D. L. Hamilton, & D. Carlston (eds.), *Person memory: the cognitive basis of social perception*. Hillsdale, NJ: Erlbaum.

Hayden, B. (1979). The self and possibilities of change. *Journal of Personality*, 47, 546–56.

Heller, T. (1982). The effects of involuntary residential relocation: a review. *American Journal of Community Psychology*, 10, 471–92.

Hoelter, J. W. (1983). The effects of role evaluation and commitment on identity salience. *Social Psychology Quarterly*, 46, 140–7.

(1985). The structure of self-conception: conceptualization and measurement. *Journal of Personality and Social Psychology*, 49, 1392–1407.

Hoffmann-Nowotny, H.-J. (1970). *Migration. Ein Beitrag zu einer soziologischen Erklärung* [Migration: a contribution to a sociological explanation]. Stuttgart.

Hormuth, S. E. (1979). Self-awareness, internal standards, and response dominance. Doctoral dissertation, University of Texas at Austin, 1979. *Dissertation Abstracts International*, 40, 1424–B.

(1982). Self-awareness and drive theory: comparing internal standards and dominant responses. *European Journal of Social Psychology*, 12, 31–45.

(1984). Transitions in commitments to roles and self-concept change: relocation as a paradigm. In V. L. Allen & E. van de Vliert (eds.), *Role transitions: explorations and explanations*, pp. 109–24. New York: Plenum.

(1985). Experiment und Quasi-Experiment in der Psychologie: Die Notwendigkeit eines multiplen Methodenansatzes [Experiment and quasi-experiment in psychology: the necessity of a multiple methods approach]. Vortrag auf dem 1. Hamburger Symposium zur Methodologie der Sozialpsychologie.

(1986a). The sampling of experiences *in situ*. *Journal of Personality*, 54, 262–93.

(1986b). Lack of effort as a result of self-focused attention: an attributional ambiguity analysis. *European Journal of Social Psychology*, 16, 181–92.

(in press). Selbstaufmerksamkeit: Bedingungen des Auftretens und Konsequenzen für die Performanz [Self-awareness: conditions for its occurrence and consequences for performance]. In J. P. Janssen, E. Hahn, & H. Strang (eds.), *Konzentration und Leistung*. Göttingen: Hogrefe.

Hormuth, S. E. & R. L. Archer (1986). Selbstenthüllung im Lichte der sozialpsychologischen Selbstkonzeptforschung [Self-disclosure in view of social-psychological self-concept research]. In A. Spitznagel & L. Schmidt-Atzert (eds.), *Sprechen und Schweigen: zur Psychologie der Selbstenthüllung*. Bern: Huber.

Hormuth, S. E. & E. Brückner (1985). Telefoninterviews in Sozialforschung und Sozialpsychologie: Ausgewählte Probleme der Stichprobengewinnung, Kontaktierung und Versuchsplanung [Telephone interviews in social research and social psychology: selected problems of sampling, contacting, and experimental design]. *Kölner Zeitschrift für Soziologie und Sozialpsychologie*, 37, 526–45.

References

Hormuth, S. E., N. M. Fitzgerald & T. D. Cook (1985). Quasi-experimental methods in community psychology research. In E. C. Susskind & D. C. Klein (eds.), *Community research: methods, paradigms, and applications*, pp. 206–49. New York: Praeger.

Hormuth, S. E. & M. Lalli (1988). Eine Skala zur Erfassung der bereichsspezifischen Selbstzufriedenheit [A scale to assess life-sphere specific satisfaction with self]. *Diagnostica*, 34, 148–66.

Horstmann, K. (1979). Zur Soziologie der Wanderungen [The sociology of migration]. In R. König (ed.), *Handbuch der empirischen Sozialforschung*, 2nd edn, Vol. V. Stuttgart: Enke.

Houts, A. C., T. D. Cook, & W. R. Shadish, Jr (1986). The person–situation debate: a critical multiplist perspective. *Journal of Personality*, 54, 52–105.

Jackson, S. E. (1981). Measurement of commitment to role identities. *Journal of Personality and Social Psychology*, 40, 138–46.

(no date). A test of the impact on cognition of commitments to role identities. Unpublished manuscript: University of Maryland, College Park, MD.

James, W. (1890). *The principles of psychology*. New York: Holt (reprinted 1950, New York: Dover Publications).

Joas, H. (1988). Symbolischer Interaktionismus. Von der Philosophie des Pragmatismus zu einer soziologischen Forschungstradition [Symbolic interactionism: from the philosophy of pragmatism toward a sociological research tradition]. *Kölner Zeitschrift für Soziologie und Sozialpsychologie*, 40, 417–46.

Jones, E. E. & T. S. Pittmann (1982). Toward a general theory of strategic self-presentation. In J. Suls (ed.), *Psychological perspectives on the self*, Vol. I, pp. 231–62. Hillsdale, NJ: Erlbaum.

Jones, W. L. (1980). Newcomers' biographical explanations: the self as an adjustment process. *Symbolic Interaction*, 3, 83–94.

Kaminski, G. (ed.) (1985). Ordnung und Variabilität im Alltagsgeschehen [*Order and variability in everyday events*]. Göttingen: Hogrefe.

Kelly, G. A. (1955). *The psychology of personal constructs*. New York: Norton.

Kiesler, C. A. (1971). *The psychology of commitment*. New York: Academic Press.

Kihlstrom, J. F. & N. Cantor (1984). Mental representations of the self. In L. Berkowitz (ed.), *Advances in experimental social psychology*, Vol. XVII, pp. 1–47. New York: Academic Press.

Kinch, J. W. (1963). A formalized theory of the self-concept. *American Journal of Sociology*, 68, 481–6.

Klinger, E. (1975). Consequences of commitment to and disengagement from incentives. *Psychological Review*, 82, 1–25.

Koffka, K. (1935). *Principles of gestalt psychology*. New York: Harcourt, Brace.

Kruse, L. (1980). Privatheit als Problem und Gegenstand der Psychologie [*Privacy as a problem for and subject in psychology*]. Bern: Huber.

(1986). Drehbücher für Verhaltensschauplätze oder: Scripts für Settings [Scripts for settings]. In G. Kaminski (ed.), *Ordnung und Variabilität im Alltagsgeschehen*, pp. 135–53. Göttingen: Hogrefe.

Kuhn, M. H. & T. S. McPartland (1954). An empirical investigation of self-attitudes. *American Sociological Review*, 19, 68–76.

References

Laird, J.D. & S. Berglas (1975). Individual differences in the effects of engaging in counter-attitudinal behavior. *Journal of Personality*, 43, 286–304.
Larson, R. & M. Csikszentmihalyi (1983). The experience sampling method. In H. Reis (ed.), *New directions for naturalistic methods in the behavioral sciences*. San Francisco: Jossey-Bass.
Layder, D. (1982). Grounded theory: a constructive critique. *Journal for the Theory of Social Behavior*, 12, 103–23.
Lennox, R.D. & R.N. Wolfe (1984). Revision of the Self-Monitoring Scale. *Journal of Personality and Social Psychology*, 46, 1349–64.
Lévy-Leboyer, C. (1979). *Psychologie et environment*. Paris: Presses Universitaires de France (English translation 1982: *Psychology and environment*. Beverly Hills, CA: Sage).
Lewin, K. (1926). Untersuchungen zur Handlungs- und Affekt-Psychologie. II: Vorsatz, Wille und Bedürfnis [Experiments in the psychology of action and affect. II: Intention, volition, and need]. *Psychologische Forschung*, 7, 330–85.
  (1935). *A dynamic theory of personality*. New York: McGraw-Hill.
  (1943). Defining the 'field at a given time'. *Psychological Review*, 50, 292–310.
Lück, H. & E. Timaeus (1969). Skalen zur Messung manifester Angst (MAS) und sozialer Wünschbarkeit (SDS–E und SDS–CM) [Scales to assess manifest anxiety (MAS) and social desirability (SDS–E and SDS–CM]. *Diagnostica*, 15, 134–41.
McClelland, D. (1951). *Personality*. New York: Sloane.
McCuster, A. (1985). The satisfaction with the self or the readiness for self-concept change of Americans living in the Heidelberg area. Diplomarbeit, Psychologisches Institut der Universität Heidelberg.
McGuire, W.J. & C.V. McGuire (1981). The spontaneous self-concept as affected by personal distinctiveness. In A. Norem-Hebeisen, M.D. Lynch & K. Gergen (eds.), *The self-concept*. New York: Ballinger.
  (1982). Significant others in self-space: sex differences and developmental trends in the social self. In J. Suls (ed.), *Psychological perspectives on the self*, Vol. I. Hillsdale, NJ: Erlbaum.
McGuire, W.J. & A. Padawer-Singer (1976). Trait salience in the spontaneous self-concept. *Journal of Personality and Social Psychology*, 33, 743–54.
McPhail, C. (1979). Experimental research is convergent with symbolic interaction. *Symbolic Interaction*, 2, 89–94.
Marks, S. (1977). Multiple roles and role strain: some notes on human energy, time, and commitment. *American Sociological Review*, 42, 921–36.
Markus, H. & K. Sentis (1982). The self in social information processing. In J. Suls (ed.), *Psychological perspectives on the self*, Vol. I, pp. 41–70. Hillsdale, NJ: Erlbaum.
Mayer, F.S., S. Duval, R. Holtz, & C. Bowman (1985). Self-focus, helping request salience, felt responsibility, and helping behaviour. *Personality and Social Psychology Bulletin*, 11, 133–44.
Mead, G.H. (1934). *Mind, self, and society from the standpoint of a social behaviorist*. Edited and with an introduction by Charles W. Morris. Chicago: The University of Chicago Press.

Mischel, W., E.B. Ebbesen & A.R. Zeiss (1973). Selective attention to the self: situational and dispositional determinants. *Journal of Personality and Social Psychology*, 27, 129–42.

Modick, H. (1977). Dreiskaliger Fragebogen zur Erfassung des Leistungsmotivs [Questionnaire consisting of three scales to assess the achievement motive]. *Diagnostica*, 23, 298–321.

Moreland, R.L. & J.M. Levine (1982). Socialization in small groups: temporal changes in individual–group relations. In L. Berkowitz (ed.), *Advances in experimental social psychology*, Vol. XV, pp. 137–92. New York: Academic Press.

Mullen, B. (1983). Operationalizing the effect of the group on the individual: a self-attention perspective. *Journal of Experimental Social Psychology*, 19, 295–322.

— (1984). Participation in religious groups as a function of group composition: a self-attention perspective. *Journal of Applied Social Psychology*, 14, 509–18.

Mummendey, H.D. (1986). Attitude and self-concept change following behavior change: a research project on mothers' and soldiers' behavior and attitudes. *German Journal of Psychology*, 10, 157–77.

Nauck, B. (1988). Sozialstrukturelle und individualistische Migrationstheorien: Elemente eines Theorienvergleichs [Social structural and individualistic theories of migration: elements of a comparison between theories]. *Kölner Zeitschrift für Soziologie und Sozialpsychologie*, 40, 15–39.

Newman, S.J. & M.S. Owen (1982). Residential displacement: extent, nature, and effects. *Journal of Social Issues*, 38 (3), 135–48.

Pawlik, K. & L. Buse (1982). Rechnergestützte Verhaltensregistrierung im Feld: Beschreibung und erste psychometrische Überprüfung einer neuen Erhebungsmethode [Computer-assisted registration of behaviour in the field: a description and first psychometric validation of a new assessment method]. *Zeitschrift für Differentielle und Diagnostische Psychologie*, 3, 101–18.

Prelinger, E. (1959). Extension and the structure of self. *The Journal of Psychology*, 47, 13–23.

Proshansky, H.M. (1976). Environmental psychology and the real world. *American Psychologist*, 31, 303–10.

— (1978). The city and self-identity. *Environment and Behavior*, 10, 147–69.

Proshansky, H.M., A.K. Fabian & R. Kaminoff (1983). Place-identity: physical world socialization of the self. *Journal of Environmental Psychology*, 3, 57–83.

Ritsert, J. (1980). Die gesellschaftliche Basis des Selbst: Entwurf einer Argumentationslinie im Anschluß an Mead [Societal basis of the self: concept of a line of argument following Mead]. *Soziale Welt*, 31, 288–310.

Robinson, J.P. & P.R. Shaver (1969). *Measures of social psychological attitudes.* Ann Arbor, MI: Institute for Social Research.

Rosch, M. & M. Irle (1984). Immigration as role transition: a cognitive analysis of its impact on health. In V.L. Allen & E. van de Vliert (eds.), *Role transitions: explorations and explanations*, pp. 97–107. New York: Plenum.

Rose, A.M. (1962). A systematic summary of symbolic interaction theory. In A.M. Rose (ed.), *Human behavior and social processes: an interactionist approach*, pp. 3–19. Boston: Houghton Mifflin.

Rosenberg, M. (1965). *Society and the adolescent self-image*. Princeton, NJ: Princeton University Press.
(1979). *Conceiving the self*. New York: Basic Books.
(1981). The self-concept: social product and social force. In M. Rosenberg & R. H. Turner (eds.), *Social psychology: sociological perspectives*, pp. 591–624. New York: Basic Books.
Rotter, J. B. (1966). Generalized expectancies for internal versus external control of reinforcement. *Psychological Monographs*, 80, 1–28.
Sader, M. (1969). Rollentheorie [Role theory]. In C. F. Graumann (ed.), *Handbuch der Psychologie*, Vol. VII, *Sozialpsychologie*, Part 1, pp. 204–31. Göttingen: Hogrefe.
Sampson, E. E. (1978). Personality and the location of identity. *Journal of Personality*, 46, 552–68.
Sarbin, T. R. & V. L. Allen (1968). Role theory. In G. Lindzey & E. Aronson (eds.), *The handbook of social psychology*, Vol. I, pp. 488–567. Reading, MA: Addison-Wesley.
SAS Institute Inc. (1982). *SAS User's Guide: Statistics*, 1982 edn. Cary, NC: SAS Institute Inc.
Savin-Williams, R. C. & D. H. Demo (1983). Situational and transsituational determinants of adolescents' self-feelings. *Journal of Personality and Social Psychology*, 44, 824–33.
Scheier, M. F., A. Fenigstein & A. H. Buss (1974). Self-awareness and physical aggression. *Journal of Experimental Social Psychology*, 10, 264–73.
Schlenker, B. R. (1980). *Impression management, the self-concept, social identity, and interpersonal relations*. Monterey, CA: Brooks-Cole.
Schneider, D. J. (1973). Implicit personality theory: a review. *Psychological Bulletin*, 79, 294–309.
Schneider, G. (1986). Psychological identity of and identification with urban neighbourhoods. In D. Frick (ed.), *Quality of urban life: social, psychological, and physical conditions*. Berlin: De Gruyter.
Schwarz, N. (1987). *Stimmung als Information: Stimmungseinflüsse auf die Bewertung des eigenen Lebens* [*Mood as information: mood influences on the evaluation of one's own life*]. Heidelberg: Springer-Verlag.
Seeger, G. (1986). Die Antizipation des Studienabschlusses und deren Wirkung auf das Selbstkonzept [Anticipation of graduation from university and its impact on the self-concept]. Diplomarbeit, Psychologisches Institut der Universität Heidelberg.
Seeger, G. & S. E. Hormuth (1988). Antizipation des Übergangs von der Universität: Ins Arbeitsleben oder in die Arbeitslosigkeit? [Anticipation of the transition from university: into working life or into unemployment?]. In G. Romkopf, W. D. Fröhlich & I. Lindner (eds.), *Forschung und Praxis im Dialog*, Vol. I, pp. 90–3. Bonn: Deutscher Psychologen Verlag.
Serpe, R. T. (1985). Identity salience and commitment: measurement and longitudinal analysis. Doctoral dissertation, Department of Sociology, Indiana University.
(1987). Stability and change in the self: a structural symbolic interactionist explanation. *Social Psychology Quarterly*, 50, 44–55.
Shrauger, J. S. & T. J. Schoeneman (1979). Symbolic interactionist view of the self: through the looking glass darkly. *Psychological Bulletin*, 86, 549–73.

Snyder, M. (1974). Self-monitoring of expressive behavior. *Journal of Personality and Social Psychology*, 30, 526–37.

Snyder, M. & B. H. Campbell (1982). Self-monitoring: the self in action. In J. Suls (ed.), *Psychological perspectives on the self*, Vol. I, pp. 185–207. Hillsdale, NJ: Erlbaum.

Snyder, M. & S. Gangestead (1985). 'To carve nature at its joints': on the existence of discrete classes in personality. *Psychological Review*, 92, 317–49.

Snyder, M. & T. C. Monson (1975). Persons, situations, and the control of social behavior. *Journal of Personality and Social Psychology*, 32, 637–44.

Stewart, A. J., M. Sokol, J. M. Healy, Jr, & N. L. Chester (1986). Longitudinal studies of psychological consequences of life changes in children and adults. *Journal of Personality and Social Psychology*, 50, 143–51.

Stokols, D., S. A. Shumaker & J. Martinez (1983). Residential mobility and personal well-being. *Journal of Environmental Psychology*, 3, 5–19.

Stryker, S. (1968). Identity salience and role performance: the relevance of symbolic interaction theory for family research. *Journal of Marriage and the Family*, 30, 558–64.

(1980). *Symbolic interaction: a social structural version*. Menlo Park, CA: Benjamin/Cummings.

(1984). Identity theory: developments and extensions. International Conference on Self and Identity, Cardiff.

(1987a). Identity theory: developments and extensions. In K. Yardley & T. Honess (eds.), *Self and identity: psychosocial perspectives*, pp. 89–103. Chichester: Wiley.

(1987b). The vitalization of symbolic interactionism. *Social Psychology Quarterly*, 50, 83–94.

Stryker, S. & R. T. Serpe (1982). Commitment, identity salience, and role behavior. In W. Ickes & E. Knowles (eds.), *Personality, roles, and social behavior*, pp. 199–218. New York: Springer-Verlag.

Stryker, S. & A. Statham (1985). Symbolic interaction and role theory. In G. Lindzey & E. Aronson (eds.), *The handbook of social psychology*, Vol. I, 3rd edn. Hillsdale, NJ: Erlbaum.

Swann, W. B., Jr (1982). Reaffirming self-conceptions through social interaction. In S. E. Hormuth (Chair), *Self-originating change and maintenance of the self*, pp. 38–42. Symposium at the Convention of the American Psychological Association, Washington, DC.

(1983). Self-verification: bringing social reality into harmony with the self. In J. Suls & A. G. Greenwald (eds.), *Social psychological perspectives on the self*, Vol. II pp. 33–66. Hillsdale, NJ: Erlbaum.

Tedeschi, J. T. & S. Lindskold (1976). *Social psychology: interdependence, interaction, and influence*. New York: Wiley.

Tesser, A. & J. Campbell (1983). Self-definition and self-evaluation maintenance. In J. Suls & A. G. Greenwald (eds.), *Psychological perspectives on the self*, Vol. II, pp. 1–31. Hillsdale, NJ: Erlbaum.

Tessin, W., T. Knorr, C. Pust, & T. Birlein (1983). *Umsetzung und Umsetzungsfolgen in der Stadtsanierung [Relocation and its consequences in inner-city renewal]*. Balse: Birkhäuser.

References

Thoits, P. A. (1983). Multiple identities and psychological well-being: a reformulation and test of the social isolation hypothesis. *American Sociological Review*, 48, 174–87.

US Bureau of the Census (1984). Current Population Reports, Series P–20, No. 393, *Geographical Mobility: March 1982 to March 1983*. Washington, DC: US Government Printing Office.

Vallacher, R. R. & D. M. Wegner (1985). *A theory of action identification*. Hillsdale, NJ: Erlbaum.

Vernon, P. E. (1963). *Personality assessment: a critical survey*. London: Methuen.

Vinsel, A., B. B. Brown, I. Altman, & C. Foss (1980). Privacy regulation, territorial displays, and effectiveness of personal functioning. *Journal of Personality and Social Psychology*, 39, 1104–15.

Wapner, S. (1981). Transactions of persons-in-environments: some critical transitions. *Journal of Environmental Psychology*, 1, 223–39.

(1987). A holistic, developmental, systems-oriented environmental psychology: some beginnings. In D. Stokols & I. Altman (eds.), *Handbook of environmental psychology*, Vol. II, pp. 1433–65. New York: Wiley.

Wegner, D. M. & T. Guiliano (1980). Arousal-induced attention to self. *Journal of Personality and Social Psychology*, 38, 719–26.

Whitbourne, S. K. (1986). Openness to experience, identity flexibility, and life changes in adults. *Journal of Personality and Social Psychology*, 50, 163–8.

Wicklund, R. A. (1975). Objective self-awareness. In L. Berkowitz (ed.), *Advances in experimental social psychology*, Vol. VIII, pp. 233–75. New York: Academic Press.

(1982). How society uses self-awareness. In J. Suls (ed.), *Psychological perspectives on the self*, Vol. I, pp. 209–30. Hillsdale, NJ: Erlbaum.

Wicklund, R. A. & P. M. Gollwitzer (1982). *Symbolic self-completion*. Hillsdale, NJ: Erlbaum.

Wiechardt, D. (1977). Zur Erfassung des Selbstkonzepts [On the assessment of the self-concept]. *Psychologische Rundschau*, 28, 294–304.

Winchie, D. B. & D. W. Carment (1988). Intention to migrate: a psychological analysis. *Journal of Applied Social Psychology*, 18, 727–36.

Wofsey, E., J. Rierdan & S. Wapner (1979). Planning to move: effects on representing the currently inhabited environment. *Environment and Behavior*, 11, 3–32.

Wohlwill, G. F. & I. Kohn (1973). The environment as experienced by the migrant: an adaptation-level view. *Representative Research in Social Psychology*, 4, 135–64.

Wylie, R. C. (1974). *The self-concept: a review of methodological considerations and measuring instruments*, Vol. I. Lincoln, NB: University of Nebraska Press.

Ziller, R. C. & D. Lewis (1981). Orientations: self, social, and environmental percepts through auto-photography. *Personality and Social Psychology Bulletin*, 7, 338–43.

Ziller, R. C. & D. E. Smith (1977). A phenomenological utilization of photographs. *Journal of Phenomenological Psychology*, 7, 172–85.

Author index

Allen, V. L., 83, 211
Allport, G. W., 48, 203
Altman, I., 3, 48, 110, 117, 203, 213
Amelang, M., 103, 171, 203
Archer, R. L., 2, 34–5, 203, 207
Aronson, E., 32, 203

Backman, C. W., 2, 203
Barker, R. G., 3, 113–15, 203
Baumeister, R. F., 34, 203
Becker, H. S., 2–3, 5, 34, 46, 65, 73–5, 77, 82, 89, 115, 165, 203
Bem, D. J., 32, 34–5, 61–2, 203
Berglas, S., 50, 209
Berscheid, E., 46, 204
Birlein, T., 160, 212
Borkenau, P., 103, 171, 203
Bossong, M., 87–8, 90, 204
Bourestone, N. C., 160, 204
Bower, G. H., 89, 204
Bowman, C., 39, 209
Brandstädter, J., 94, 205
Brett, J. M., 161, 204
Brown, B. B., 110, 213
Brückner, E., 11–12, 19, 169, 198, 204, 207
Brunswik, E., 8–9, 13, 204
Bryson, G., 70, 204
Burke, P. J., 93, 204
Buse, L., 137, 210
Buss, A. H., 38, 40, 92, 104, 205, 211

Callero, P. L., 79, 204
Campbell, B. H., 45–7, 212
Campbell, D. T., 10, 204
Campbell, J., 54, 59–60, 212
Cantor, N., 32–6, 89, 208
Carlston, D., 33, 207
Carment, D. W., 159, 213
Carver, C. S., 38, 40–1, 204, 205
Chester, N. L., 163, 212
Clagett, A. F., 72, 204
Cook, T. D., 10–11, 204, 208
Cooley, C. H., 1–2, 57–8, 70–1, 73, 90, 204

Crowne, D., 104, 204
Csikszentmihalyi, M., 2, 12, 16, 24, 95, 108–11, 113, 133, 137, 204, 209

Darroch, R. K., 107, 204
Demo, D. H., 137, 211
Dermer, M., 46, 204
Diener, E., 43, 205
Duval, S., 5, 32, 37–9, 41–4, 94, 205, 209
Duval, V. H., 42, 205

Earle, W. B., 2, 34, 203
Ebbesen, E. B., 94, 210
Elliott, G. C., 98, 205
Epstein, S., 65, 135, 205
Esser, H., 159, 205

Fabian, A. K., 116, 210
Felson, R. B., 86–7, 205
Fenigstein, A., 38, 40, 92, 104, 205, 211
Festinger, L., 32, 87, 205
Figurski, T., 137, 204
Filipp, S.-H., 94, 104, 166–7, 205
Fischer, M., 160–2, 206
Fischer, U., 160–2, 206
Fishbein, M. J., 35, 62, 205
Fitzgerald, N. M., 10–11, 208
Foss, C., 110, 213
Franz, P., 159, 206
Froming, W. J., 43, 206
Fuhrer, U., 114, 206

Gangestead, S., 48, 206, 212
Gatzweiler, H. P., 159, 206
Gecas, V., 70, 72, 85, 90, 206
Gergen, K. J., 56, 206
Gibbons, F. X., 43, 206
Gilligan, S. G., 89, 204
Goffman, E., 47, 206
Gollwitzer, P. M., 3, 54, 56–8, 60, 74, 81–3, 112, 206, 213
Graumann, C. F., 107, 110, 118, 206
Graziano, E., 46, 204
Greenwald, A. G., 32–3, 207
Guiliano, T., 38, 213

Author index

Hastie, R., 33, 36, 207
Hayden, B., 6, 54, 65–7, 74, 82, 89, 130–1, 207
Healy, J. M., Jr, 163, 212
Heller, T., 17, 160, 207
Hensley, V., 42, 205
Hoelter, J. W., 78, 93, 207
Hoffmann-Nowotny, H.-J., 159, 207
Holtz, R., 39, 209
Hormuth, S. E., 9–13, 15, 19, 31, 34–5, 38–9, 41–2, 99–100, 130, 133, 135, 137, 162, 164, 169, 198, 204, 207–8, 211
Horstmann, K., 158, 208
Houts, A. C., 11, 208

Irle, M., 161, 210

Jackson, S. E., 82, 84, 89, 93, 208
James, W., xv, 1, 4, 48, 70–1, 77, 208
Joas, H., 72, 208
Jones, E. E., 34, 208
Jones, W. L., 160, 162–3, 208

Kaminoff, R., 116, 210
Kaminski, G., 114, 208
Kelly, G. A., 65, 208
Kiesler, C. A., 81, 208
Kihlstrom, J. F., 32–6, 89, 208
Kinch, J. W., 86, 208
Klauer, T., 166–7, 205
Klinger, E., 81, 208
Knorr, T., 160, 212
Koffka, K., 39, 208
Kohn, I., 160, 213
Kruse, L., 3, 114, 208
Kuhn, M. H., 93, 208

Laird, J. D., 35, 50, 62, 205, 209
Lalli, M., 99–100, 208
Larson, R., 12, 133, 209
Layder, D., 72, 209
Lennox, R. D., 132, 209
Levine, J. M., 81, 210
Lévy-Leboyer, C., 114–15, 209
Lewin, K., 48, 57, 113, 209
Lewis, D., 95, 213
Lindskold, S., 56, 212
Lopyan, K. J., 43, 206
Lück, H., 104, 209

McCelland, D., 48, 209
McCuster, A., 100, 104, 209
McGuire, C. V., 36, 209
McGuire, W. J., 36, 93, 209
McPartland, T. S., 93, 208
McPhail, C., 72, 209
Marks, S., 82, 84, 209

Markus, H., 89, 209
Marlowe, D., 104, 204
Martinez, J., 161–2, 212
Mayer, F. S., 39, 209
Mead, G. H., xv, 1–2, 57–8, 70–2, 90, 107, 163, 209
Miller, M., 107, 204
Mischel, W., 94, 210
Modick, H., 103, 210
Monson, T. C., 46, 204, 212
Moreland, R. L., 81, 210
Mullen, B., 39, 210
Mummendey, H. D., 166, 210

Nauck, B., 159, 210
Neely, R., 42, 205
Newman, S. J., 161, 210

Owen, M. S., 161, 210

Padawer-Singer, A., 93, 209
Pawlik, K., 137, 210
Pittmann, T. S., 34, 208
Pratkanis, A. R., 32–3, 207
Prelinger, E., 48–9, 210
Proshansky, H. M., 3, 107, 113, 116–17, 210
Pust, C., 160, 212

Rierdan, J., 96, 125, 159, 213
Ritsert, J., 90, 210
Robinson, J. P., 104, 210
Rochberg-Halton, E., 2, 16, 24, 95, 108–11, 113, 204
Rosch, M., 161, 210
Rose, A. M., 72–3, 210
Rosenberg, M., 56–7, 82, 85–6, 104, 211
Rotter, J. B., 50, 211

Sader, M., 78, 211
Sagawe, H., 19, 203
Sampson, E. E., 46, 49–53, 211
Sarbin, T. R., 83, 211
Savin-Williams, R. C., 137, 211
Scheier, M. F., 38, 40–1, 92, 104, 204, 205, 211
Schlenker, B. R., 3, 34, 211
Schneider, D. J., 65, 211
Schneider, G., 118, 206, 211
Schoeneman, T. J., 1, 54, 86, 211
Schoggen, P., 115, 203
Schwalbo, M. L., 90, 206
Schwarz, N., 56, 94, 211
Seeger, G., 130–1, 211
Sentis, K., 89, 209
Serpe, R. T., 78–81, 211, 212
Shadish, W. R., Jr, 11, 208
Shaver, P. R., 104, 210

Shrauger, J., 1, 54, 86, 211
Shumaker, S.A., 161–2, 212
Smith, D.E., 12, 95, 213
Snyder, M., 32, 45–50, 52, 54, 74, 92, 103, 121, 206, 212
Sokol, M., 163, 212
Srull, T.K., 43, 205
Statham, A., 1, 212
Stewart, A.J., 163–6, 200, 212
Stokols, D., 161–2, 212
Stryker, S., 1, 45, 52, 56, 72–3, 76–8, 80, 82–3, 89, 114–15, 212
Swann, W.B., Jr, 2, 36, 54–6, 60, 212

Tars, S., 160, 204
Taylor, D.A., 48, 203
Tedeschi, J.T., 56, 212
Tesser, A., 54, 59–60, 212
Tessin, W., 160, 212
Thoits, P.A., 80–4, 89, 213
Timaeus, E., 104, 209

Vallacher, R.R., 62–4, 89, 213
Vernon, P.E., 65, 213
Vinsel, A., 110–11, 113, 125, 213

Walker, G.R., 43, 206
Wapner, S., 9, 17, 95–6, 125, 159, 162, 168, 200, 213
Wegner, D.M., 38, 62–4, 89, 213
Whitbourne, S.K., 167–8, 213
Wicklund, R.A., 3, 5, 32, 37–9, 41–4, 54, 56–8, 60, 74, 81–3, 94, 112, 164, 205, 213
Wiechardt, D., 92, 94, 213
Winchie, D.B., 159, 213
Wofsey, E., 96, 125, 129, 159, 213
Wohlwill, G.F., 160, 213
Wolfe, R.N., 132, 209
Wright, R.A., 43, 206
Wylie, R.C., 93, 213

Zeiss, A.R., 94, 210
Ziller, R.C., 12, 95, 213

Subject index

action identification, 62–4, 90
adaptation-level theory, 160–1
appraisal, reflected
   see reflected appraisal
arousal, 38
attention, self-focused, 5, 37–40
attributional ambiguity, 31, 42
attribution, causal, 42–4, 46
'audience segregation', 47
autophotography, 12, 92, 94–8, 105, 118, 138, 140, 152, 155, 181, 193–6, 201

behaviour setting, 113–16

cognitive judgment processes, 56
cognitive structure, 1, 33, 55, 67–8, 82, 89–91
commitment, 3–5, 73–5, 77–85, 89, 199
conformity, 41, 43
'critical multiplism', 11

disclosure
   other-disclosure, 141, 188–90
   self-disclosure, 34–5, 48, 141, 155, 185–6, 189
dissonance
   dissonance reduction, 35
   dissonance theory, 32
drive theory, 38

ecological validity, 6, 8–9, 13, 133, 139, 198
experience sampling method (ESM), 9, 12–14, 133–8, 140–1, 145–52, 155, 164, 178, 180–1, 183–5, 201
externality–internality dimension, 48–51

figure–ground relationship, 5, 36, 39–40, 43, 163–5, 195
focus of attention, 39, 42–3
'front', 47
Future Orientation Scale, 105

Gestalt principles, 39

identity
   constructed identity, 57–8, 68
   identity mastery, 52–3
   identity theory, 3, 72–3, 76–85, 89
   location of identity, 48–53, 124–5, 194
implicative capacity (network), 65–7, 89
implicit personality theory, 65
internality–externality
   see externality–internality dimension

Kelly-grid, 66

localization of identity
   see identity
locus of control, 50, 71
'looking-glass self', 1, 90

migration, 159
mobility, 159–61
mutli-method approach, 6–8, 11–12, 100, 138, 168, 198, 201
multi-study approach, 7, 11, 165, 180, 198, 201

naturalistic design, 8–10, 12

place identity, 113, 116–18, 122
'pragmatic self', 45
'principled self', 46
privacy, 3, 110, 117

quasi-experimental design, 7–13, 125, 138–40, 165, 198

reflected appraisal, 85–90
relocation
   involuntary relocation, 13, 158, 160
roles, 2, 70–8, 83–5, 93, 115
Rosenberg Stability-of-Self Scale, 104

sampling, 8, 12–14, 17–19, 138–40, 170
Sampson IO, 50
satisfaction with self, 31, 98–106, 139–57, 175–9, 190–3
Satisfaction with Self Scale (SSS), 101–6,

218 *Subject index*

    128, 141–56, 171, 176–7, 182, 186–7, 190–3, 199–200
'selective interaction', 47
self
  self-awareness, 5, 32, 36–44, 55, 94, 164–5, 200
  self-completion, 54, 56–60
  self-consciousness, 41, 49, 92, 104–5, 164
  Self-Consciousness Scale, 104
  self-disclosure *see* disclosure
  self-esteem, 6, 31, 60, 68, 90, 92, 98, 200
  Self-Esteem Scale, 104
  self-evaluation maintenance, 54, 59–61
  self-defining goal, 56–9, 82–3
  self-definition, 58–60, 68
  self-focus *see* self-awareness
  self-handicapping, 31
  self-image, 47, 65
  self-importance, 50–2
  self-monitoring, 32, 45–50, 52–4, 92, 103–4, 122, 175–9
  Self-Monitoring Scale, 103, 121, 171, 182
  self-perception, 32, 34–5, 61–3
  self-presentation, 34–5, 57–8
  self-region, 48–9
  self-related cognitions, 2, 35, 40, 65
  self-theme, 64, 89
  self-verification, 36, 54–6, 60–1
social cognition, 32–4
social comparison theory, 87
Social Desirability Scale (SDS), 104–5
social reality, 57, 59
social recognition, 56–7
social structure, 1, 28, 49, 53, 70–9, 82, 85, 87–91, 142–3
standards, 37, 40–4, 165
symbolic interactionism, 33–4, 46, 56–7, 60, 70–3, 76, 85–7, 89–90, 93, 114–15, 162

telephone interviews, 12, 19, 100
telephone survey, 15, 139, 152, 171, 175
transition between environments, 7, 9, 16–17, 31, 95, 124–32, 158–68, 178–96
TST, 93

ZBL, 103